Modern M

Modern Moves

Dancing Race during the Ragtime and Jazz Eras

Danielle Robinson

OXFORD

UNIVERSITY PRESS

OXFORD
UNIVERSITY PRESS

Oxford University Press is a department of the University of
Oxford. It furthers the University's objective of excellence in research,
scholarship, and education by publishing worldwide.

Oxford   New York
Auckland   Cape Town   Dar es Salaam   Hong Kong   Karachi
Kuala Lumpur   Madrid   Melbourne   Mexico City   Nairobi
New Delhi   Shanghai   Taipei   Toronto

With offices in
Argentina   Austria   Brazil   Chile   Czech Republic   France   Greece
Guatemala   Hungary   Italy   Japan   Poland   Portugal   Singapore
South Korea   Switzerland   Thailand   Turkey   Ukraine   Vietnam

Oxford is a registered trademark of Oxford University Press
in the UK and certain other countries.

Published in the United States of America by
Oxford University Press
198 Madison Avenue, New York, NY 10016

Cataloging-in-Publication Data is on file at the Library of Congress.

ISBN 978-0-19-977921-5 (hbk.); 978-0-19-977922-2 (pbk.)

1 3 5 7 9 8 6 4 2
Printed in the United States of America
on acid-free paper

To Jeff

CONTENTS

List of Figures   ix
Preface   xi
Acknowledgments   xv

Introduction: Dancing Race, Modernity, and History   *1*

VIGNETTE: Mr. Vaughn's Dancing Class, the Tenderloin
1. "Let's Go Back Home": The Slow Drag, Black Migration, and the Birth of Black Harlem   *35*

VIGNETTE: Jim's Place, the Tenderloin
2. "A Colorful Nightmare": Immigrant Ragtime Dancing as Participatory Minstrelsy   *59*

VIGNETTE: Danse Chateau, Times Square
3. "The Ugly Duckling": The Refinement of Ragtime Dancing and the Mass Marketing of Modern Social Dance   *83*

VIGNETTE: Grand Lodge of the Fraternal Brotherhood, Harlem
4. "The Eclipse": Ballroom Dancing, Bodily Code-Switching, and the Harlem Renaissance   *103*

VIGNETTE: Fourth Floor of the Dobson Building, Theatre District
5. "Marvelous, New, Dirty Steps": Appropriation, Authenticity, and Opportunity in Broadway Jazz Dance Teaching   *129*

Conclusion: Modern Dancing, Past and Present   *149*

Notes   *155*
Works Cited   *177*
Index   *187*

LIST OF FIGURES

0.1   Ballroom Dance Manual, 1870s   *4*

0.2   Cakewalk Dancers, 1890s   *5*

0.3   Professional Modern Dancers, 1910s   *7*

1.1   Likely Juke Joint Dancers, 1930s   *36*

1.2   Dance Scene from the film *St. Louis Blues*, 1920s   *39*

1.3   *Harlem* Playbill, 1920s   *50*

2.1   Ragtime Lyrics, 1910s   *68*

2.2   Ragtime Sheet Music Cover, 1900s   *71*

2.3   Ragtime Lyrics, 1910s   *72*

3.1   Professional Modern Dancers, 1910s   *85*

3.2   Modern Dancers, 1910s   *85*

3.3   Modern Dance Manual, 1910s   *96*

4.1   Harlem Ballroom Dance Event, 1910s   *106*

4.2   Professional Ballroom Dance Partners, 1930s   *125*

5.1   Blues Dance Instructions, 1920s   *130*

5.2   Broadway Jazz Dance Studio Advertisement, 1920s   *140*

5.3   Jazz Dance Instructions, 1920s   *146*

PREFACE

This book did not begin on a dance floor or in an archive, but in my childhood Sunday school teacher's home outside Nashville, Tennessee. Miss Reba was a wonderful storyteller who loved to talk about her youth, which was spent in the segregated American South of the early twentieth century. During one of our many afternoons together, she told me how, as a child, she spent hours practicing ballroom dancing—partnered only by her family's giant hall mirror. She waited until she was alone to put on records, one after the other.

What struck me was that Miss Reba didn't put on a show for an imaginary audience, as I had done during my early dancing days—choreographing to the *Grease* soundtrack and other popular recordings. Rather, she embraced an imaginary partner: When she closed her eyes, the mirror was transformed into a dashing young man. I left her bright yellow kitchen fascinated, as I had never danced with a partner before, just with a group of girls in my local dance studio. From her description of the magic created between two dancers, I was sure I hadn't felt anything like it before, but I knew I wanted to desperately.

Several years later, even after Alzheimer's disease had fractured her memories, Miss Reba could still remember with clarity her dancing days. In addition to retelling stories of her ballroom dancing afternoons at home, she would sometimes chat about going out dancing with friends as a young woman in downtown Nashville. There was both pride and mock embarrassment in her graveled voice as she described going to clubs where she wasn't supposed to be.

Only on one occasion, though, did she tell me why her family would have objected to those dance clubs. With one hand resting on my knee and one perched on my shoulder, she leaned in and giggled the word "colored" in my ear—even though we were the only ones sitting in her living room at the assisted-care facility. Having grown up in recently desegregated Nashville, I knew that word and what it meant, although I had never before heard it from Miss Reba's lips. For several moments, I sat there with my mouth open trying to imagine this proper octogenarian sneaking around segregated dance clubs. Unfortunately, we were not able to discuss her cross-cultural dance adventures further that day or any other. The window to that particular memory closed shortly thereafter.

Because of her disease, Miss Reba was often mentally living in the 1920s and '30s throughout most of the 1990s. And yet the similarities between her life experiences and mine were striking. She whispered "colored" to me in the same hushed tones that some white folks still used in Nashville during my childhood when talking about any racially charged issue. Her family wouldn't have approved of her going to a social space where African Americans congregated any more than mine would have—be it a dance club, a neighborhood, or even a university. Implicit danger signs cordoned off my world into black and white, just as they did hers.

What surprised me the most, however, was my own reaction to her transgressive dancing. I was absolutely stunned, as I had assumed that nobody in Nashville, the South, or even the U.S. was moving across racial lines that early in the twentieth century, either in terms of social space or social practice—especially not white middle-class girls. If my Nashville world was still segregated (in practice, not law) in the late twentieth century, hers had to be even more so, I had assumed.

Miss Reba's story shattered my understanding of American dance history, which was rooted in my own lived experience of suburban dance studios, as well as my reading of dance history, both of which demarcated dancing into black and white categories. Indeed, the ways in which scholars have typically historicized social dancing in America give the impression that *white* people only did *white* dancing and *black* people only did *black* dancing—at least until the swing era, the twist, or disco, depending on which book you read. Yet, Miss Reba's dance experiences suggest that we have left out an important part of the story.

That day, in her living room, she offered me only a quick glimpse of something that would fascinate me in the years to come: how social dancing has provided a means of cross-cultural exploration, connection, exploitation, contestation, and confusion throughout the twentieth century in North America. Whether dancers are simply trying on another culture's dance moves, going to an "other" dance venue, or actually dancing with people who are culturally different from themselves, social dancing can create a powerful space for body-based articulations of identities. Such physical encounters and expressions of self and other, however, are not always utopian in mission—modeling a world in which all people can interact free from oppression or stereotypes. Hegemonic values are often just as present in cross-cultural dance encounters as in other kinds, if not more so, and rendered all the more powerful as they are manifested in seemingly harmless quotidian practices.

Miss Reba's story reminded me that even when segregation might be the law or social expectation, dancing and dancers did not always obey. North American dancers of all kinds had observed each other's movement practices since colonization, which eventually led to movements being borrowed, taken, or used as creative resources. For example, the cakewalk demonstrates that African and African American slaves sometimes watched their masters' formal balls on plantations, just as ragtime dancing confirms that European American people at times visited "colored" dance spaces. Such cross-cultural dance exploration, long before social integration was fully possible, is a key part of our dance history that is just beginning to be written.

ACKNOWLEDGMENTS

When my mother dropped me off at Miss Becky's Dance Studio at the age of four, neither she nor Miss Becky could imagine where the lessons in ballet, tap, jazz, modern, acrobatics, and clogging might lead. I was there to learn lady-like behavior and self-control as a counterpoint to the sports I loved to play. I thank Miss Becky for fostering over fourteen years of lessons a life-long love of dancing that continues to this day.

It was not until I was at university that I began to think critically about my own dancing. By chance, I attended a lecture on historical images of women in dance at the Blair School of Music, as an undergraduate at Vanderbilt. On that life-changing day, Professor Maureen Needham introduced me to the possibility of researching dance and doing so for a living. At the time, my dancing life consisted of performing an athleticized version of hip hop on the football field and basketball court at halftime while wearing a rhinestone-studded bathing suit and heels. Professor Needham quickly took me under her wing despite this and taught me not only how to engage in rigorous historical research, but also how to think, read, and write academically. I am so grateful for her early mentorship.

My intellectual training was soon thereafter taken up by Susan Manning at Northwestern University. We shared a love of dance history and cultural politics from the beginning. In our short time together, she taught me that scholars had a responsibility to query the dancing we loved most and not to shy away from issues of race, even if we grew up in a white world. Her passion for primary sources and uncovering their secrets rubbed off on me as well. These lessons were continued with Ann Daly at the University of Texas at Austin. Her deep respect for writing and her insistence that academic prose be written accessibly, but elegantly, were tremendous influences. Thanks to her mentorship, I still challenge myself to write for the widest audience possible.

I always tell my graduate students that if their academic training has not completely transformed them, they have not gotten their money's worth. This truism comes from my experiences with a host of faculty members at the University of California, Riverside—inside and outside the dance department. From Susan Foster, I acquired a determination to bolster the new discipline of critical dance studies through a commitment to innovating it from within, with each class I taught, conference presentation I gave, and work I published. Marta Savigliano helped me see and feel the power of white privilege, forever changing my thinking about the lived experience of race and ethnicity. Still to this day, it is Linda Tomko's voice that I hear when I am crafting an argument or engaging with primary sources. I carry her impeccable standards with me and endeavor to impart them to my graduate students.

Of course, my dissertation committee made the strongest imprint on me and my thinking. Although she arrived at Riverside near the end of my doctoral study, Anthea Kraut's encouragement and keen insights were invaluable in the home stretch. Sterling Stuckey generously shared his favorite primary sources and reminded me over and over again that what matters most is the rigor of my research and depth of my knowledge. I learned over the years from Deborah Wong that intellectual ferocity and a big heart could come in the same package. From my first day of doctoral coursework to my dissertation defense to the present day, Sally Ness modeled for me that being a good mentor means letting students follow their own paths while pushing them to the limits of what they can do. Her humility, generosity, grace, and brilliance are an inspiration to all who have had the pleasure of working closely with her.

My graduate school years were filled with many amazing colleagues who changed my thinking, encouraged my progress, and entertained me when the work became too intense. Two, in particular, left a lasting impact. Roxane Fenton taught me to get up off the mat—many, many times—and to find and then trust my inner wisdom. Juliet McMains rekindled my love of ballroom dancing, pushed me to think beyond the conventional, and showed me that *im*patience can also be a great virtue. I have loved every minute of our numerous collaborations over the last two decades—here's to the next twenty years!

At the heart of this research project is my dance reconstruction work. Early on, Cheryl Stafford in Washington, D.C. partnered with me in this endeavor. She shared with me her extensive knowledge of nineteenth-century social dances (which served as a crucial foundation for my early twentieth-century research) with tremendous generosity and was willing to listen patiently to my emerging theories about ragtime dancing and its many iterations. I still miss our mornings dancing together and wish that we lived closer and could have continued our dancing partnership.

In recent years, I have had the good fortune of connecting with scholars working in similar areas who have been willing to share their research with me and/or comment on my own. I still have yet to meet some of them in person. Nonetheless, they deserve my heartfelt thanks. Theresa Buckland, Celia Cain, Susan Cook, Sherril Dodds, Mark Franko, Tera Hunter, Julie Malnig, Kristen McGee, Clare Parfitt-Brown, Kathy Peiss, and Sally Sommer have all been incredibly helpful at key moments along the way when the research needed their unique and valuable insights. Katrina Hazzard, in particular, took the time to talk with me at length about my research on multiple occasions for which I will always be grateful.

At York University, I have been blessed with several generous colleagues and inspiring students. In particular, I would like to thank Barbara Sellers-Young and Sky Fairchild-Waller for helping me carve out precious writing time when I needed it most. For their exquisite research and proofreading skills, I would like to express my profound gratitude to Jennifer Taylor, Samantha Mehra, and especially Boké Saisi.

Archival work is mainly a solitary task, of course. Nonetheless, it is made so much more productive and pleasurable by archivists, librarians, and copy room staff who go out of their way to assist researchers. For their investments in the success of this project, I sincerely thank the staff members at the Institute of Jazz Studies at Rutgers University, the New York Historical Society, the New York City Municipal Archives, the New York Public Library Manuscripts, Archives, and Rare Books Division, the Schomburg Center for Research in Black Culture, the New York Public Library for the Performing Arts, the NYU Tamiment Library and Robert F. Wagner Labor Archives, the Smithsonian Institution Archive, the New York Public Library for Science, Industry, and Business, and the Smithsonian National Museum of American History. Now that the trend is toward online engagements with primary source materials, I fear the next generation of scholars will miss out on the valuable contributions that archival staff can make to projects while they are still in development.

As you just read in the preface, Miss Reba—my first Sunday school teacher and surrogate grandmother—provided the spark for this project through her storytelling. This was further kindled by my husband's great-aunt Lillian who told me stories of her immigration to New York as a young Jewish refugee and the dancing that filled her evenings. The stories of these two spirited, independent women propelled my research and writing early on.

I am lucky enough to have two families now—one I inherited with my husband and the other I was born with. Without the timely, generous, and unquestioning support of these two groups of people as I pursued the unlikely career of a dance scholar, this book would never have come to fruition. Thank you so much for never asking why in the world someone would want to pursue a Ph.D. in dance, much less write about social dancing.

It gives me tremendous pleasure finally to be able to thank my husband, ethnomusicologist Jeff Packman, for his contributions to this project, which have been manifold and longstanding. For talking through my first insights as they emerged from the archive, cheering me on as I tried to corral them into scholarly prose, editing the first drafts with both compassion and brutality, never letting me give up on this book when teaching and service filled days and nights, and for not once begrudging the time away from him required for the manuscript's completion—I will always be grateful. Normally there are not many benefits to marrying within academia, especially when looking for work. In Jeff, though, I was fortunate to have found a rare colleague and collaborator who is generous, supportive, brilliant, hardworking, and understanding. I dedicate this book to him as a small recognition of his huge influence on this book and my career.

Special thanks to *Dance Research Journal*, *Dance Chronicle*, and *Dance Research* for giving me permission to use portions of the following previously published articles:

"'Oh, You Black Bottom!' Appropriation, Authenticity, and Opportunity in the Jazz Dance Teaching of 1920s New York," by Danielle Robinson, *Dance Research Journal*, Volume 38, Issue 1/2 (2006). Copyright © 2006 Reprinted with permission of Cambridge University Press.

"Performing American: Ragtime Dancing as Embodied Minstrelsy," by Danielle Robinson, *Dance Chronicle*. Volume 32, Issue 1 (2009). Copyright © 2009 Reprinted with permission of Taylor and Francis.

"Ugly Duckling: The Refinement of Ragtime Dancing and the Mass Marketing of Modern Social Dance," by Danielle Robinson, *Dance Research*, Volume 28, Issue 2 (2010). Copyright © 2010 Reprinted with permission of Edinburgh University Press.

Modern Moves

Introduction

Dancing Race, Modernity, and History

Growing up in the recently desegregated South and dancing in a sub-urban dance studio, I came to see dance as racially marked at an early age: All of my experiences led me to accept unquestioningly that ballet was white, tap was black, modern was white, and jazz was (mostly) black. Being primarily of European descent myself, and certainly being taught to regard myself as white, I felt entitled to learn and perform all these dances. Like most middle-class American girls, appropriation was part of what I did for fun every afternoon after school, an activity to which I did not give a second thought for many years. It was not until I happened to hear a research presentation by a dance scholar at Vanderbilt University—where I happily performed as part of the Danceline during halftime at football and basketball games—that I caught a glimpse of the politics behind my cross-cultural dancing, which by that point had come to also include Latin ballroom dances and even hip hop. Eventually, I came to ask a tangled web of questions: Why could I adopt any dance I liked, while African Americans were so often expected to dance "black"? What did dancing "black" even mean? How was that meaning entangled with stereotypes? Had dancing always been racialized in America? When did Americans begin crossing racial boundaries through their dancing? In the following pages, I try to answer some of these questions, at least in part as a way of understanding the historical roots of the interconnected dancing and race thinking I was taught as a child and many children continue to be taught today.

This book aspires to be a desegregated history of modern American social dancing of the early twentieth century that looks critically at the appropriation of expressive culture without reducing it simply to stealing, although sometimes this was certainly what it was. It focuses instead on the kinds of cultural work accomplished by dancers drawing inspiration from one another's moves. It explores: What ideas relating to self and other were constructed through cross-cultural dancing? What stereotypes were mobilized? What social aspirations and desires were expressed? What professions were enabled?

Nonetheless, this is not a study of black *or* white dancing, though they were and often are imagined as distinct categories, but of *race relations* embodied in dancing. Most people, including scholars, would consider the dancing discussed here—blues and jazz dancing especially—to be black or African American in nature. However, these practices can all be productively understood as hybrid in origin and practice—which of course doesn't make them any less racially marked or politically complex, as is made clear in the following chapters. I do not trace dance lineages or racially organize dance steps. Instead, I pursue how these dance forms can help us understand the interrelationships between racial thinking and social practices of the early twentieth century.

And yet, to focus on race exclusively would leave out at least half of the story. Understandings of race then were as deeply entangled with notions of class as they are today. Among those who self-identified as white (or aspired to this marker of social status), dancing movement understood as black could be a statement of modernity, American citizenship, or civilization, more so than of admiration or affiliation with African Americans. In a similar fashion, African Americans performing dance movements borrowed from European dance traditions might proclaim their education, cosmopolitanism, urbanity, or elite status. By dancing cross-culturally in these ways, dancers certainly enjoyed a night out on the town—these dances were highly entertaining to do. At the same time, dancers could seize the opportunity to work toward their own sense of empowerment through the implicit performance of their social aspirations. For these reasons, this study addresses the nexus between class and race concerns, as they were articulated in social dancing.[1]

The partner dancing of the early twentieth century also helped empower those who made social dance teaching and performing a new profession and built a new dance industry. Over time, these dance professionals of many racial and ethnic backgrounds transformed community dancing into dance products that could be more easily sold and consumed on a mass scale. Their authority as professionals rested on their ability to convince

consumers that they possessed and controlled highly valuable dance knowledge and that social dancers, left to their own devices, would embarrass
themselves by inadvertently appearing less moral, fashionable, refined,
and modern than they would prefer. By constructing dance products in this
way, these professionals relied on implicit race and class-based marketing
strategies that appealed to consumers seeking to achieve or maintain their
own social dominance.

This era's social dance professionals often called their "refined" dancing
modern, to imply newness, sophistication, and fashionability. In retrospect,
though, all of the social dance practices discussed in this book—not just
those described by practitioners as refined—could be considered modern,
owing to their entanglements with both rapid industrial development
and essentialist racial thinking, as will be explained later in this chapter.
Although modern dance is a term that has been frequently applied to
Western concert dance, from the 1900s to the 1950s, the term is used in
this book in reference to social dancing. In so doing, I hope to demonstrate
the inextricability of social dance from social context.

INTERTWINED HYBRID DANCE HISTORIES

Modern Moves focuses on a range of social dancing practices happening during the early twentieth century in New York City—an important crucible
for new dance forms, perhaps the most important in North America at this
time—including blues, ragtime, modern, ballroom, and jazz dance forms,
among others. Such terms, however, were not used exclusively or even
clearly during this time period. Dancing that happened to blues music could
be called ragging, good-time dancing, or even shouting. What I call ragtime
dancing, for the sake of simplicity, has also been called new dancing, modern
dancing, and animal dancing. And modern dancing—as just mentioned—
was a term typically used by 1910s ballroom dance professionals to market
their "refined" dance teaching and performing. This was a time of flux and
flow in social dancing, and participants' terminology choices struggled to
keep up and, as a result, never crystallized into a fixed vocabulary.

Most of the dancing I discuss here shared a pair of influences: nineteenth-century African American and European American dancing.[2] (See
Fig. 0.1) Although all of the modern dance forms looked quite different
from one another, each was the result of an integration of dance traditions
that happened sometimes in Southern and Mid-Western dance spaces and
other times in Manhattan itself. The results of these cross-cultural combinations, wherever they happened, were far more than just a few fleeting

THE POSITION IN QUADRILLE.

Figure 0.1 Ballroom Dance Manual, 1870s. William B. De Garmo, *The Dance of Society: a critical analysis of all the standard quadrilles, round dances, 102 figures of le cotillon ("the German"), &c., including dissertations upon time and its accentuation, carriage, style, and other relative matter* (New York: Wm. A. Pond & Co., 1875). Courtesy of an American Ballroom Companion: Dance Instruction Manuals, ca. 1490–1920, Library of Congress, Music Division (public domain).

dance trends; the hybrid dancing of this period laid the foundation for the entire twentieth century's social dancing practices in North America and Europe.

It is likely that the cakewalk was the first African-influenced dance to cross over into mainstream European American dance practices, albeit in a much altered form. (See Fig. 0.2) While there were many ways to cakewalk during the nineteenth century, the dance usually involved an ostentatiously dressed male-female pair prancing and strutting forward and backward together while they both faced forward and held inside hands. Sometimes props such as fans and canes were used to add a comic element as well. This

Figure 0.2 Cakewalk Dancers, 1890s. William H. Krell, *Shake Yo' Dusters or Piccaninny Rag* (New York and Chicago: S. Brainard's Sons Co., 1897). Digital image from the Duke University Historic American Sheet Music Collection. Courtesy of the Rare Book, Manuscipt and Special Collections Library (public domain).

dance began on plantations in slave parodies of the grand marches of nine-teenth-century European American ballroom dancing.[3] Later it appeared on minstrel stages, as a parody of the original slave parody, performed by black or white dancers in blackface. By the 1890s, a brief "cakewalk craze" to early ragtime music ensued that involved comedic public competitions and theatrical representations by such professional dance couples as Charles Johnson and Dora Dean, as well as Aida Overton Walker and George Walker. While this dance did cross over into the European American social practices of urban centers, it was not widely embraced across America or across class groups, except within African American communities where it remained a vital part of social practice during the nineteenth century. It did become quite a fad during the 1890s, though, in elite ballrooms, and involved New York's most prominent families—as well as the royal family in England—who sought cakewalk lessons from African American star performers.

The next hybrid dances to cross over from African American to European American dance spaces were the animal dances (turkey trot, bunny hug, grizzly bear, and so forth) of the early 1900s, which were also called tough, new, and half-time dances. These dances, as enjoyed by European immi-grant youth, are the focus of chapter two. Before they were adapted into modern social dances by ballroom dance teachers, these ragtime couple dances often included animal imitations and were seen by many as silly or cute. A turkey trot might involve two dancers circling each other and flap-ping their arms, whereas a bunny hug could have dancers' arms wrapped around each others' necks or the couple hopping around the floor together. Many of these dances, in their earliest manifestations, were secular African American plantation and jook house dances.[4] They likely came to New York with early waves of black migrants from the South and were seen by European Americans in dance spaces in Manhattan. They also came via cir-cuits of black musical theatre performers who traveled into and out of the city frequently. Interestingly, the animal dances did not have star perform-ers (black or white) publically representing them through commercial ven-tures, like the earlier cakewalk and later jazz dances; instead, they remained primarily in dance halls where endless variations and new versions could be explored by community participants.

The animal dances eventually became the focus of an emerging ball-room dance industry, which catered to the white middle classes. During the 1910s, European American dance professionals established their busi-nesses and their authority as teachers and performers by transforming, or what they called "refining," the playful and jaunty ragtime dances into more glamorous modern dances (one-step, foxtrot, and others)—the topic of chapter three. The transformed practices kept some of the rhythmic play and jubilance of the animal dances. Mainly, though, they involved walking gracefully and upright with a partner in very simple spatial patterns. The modern dances were among the first social dances to be successfully mass marketed across North America and eventually Europe.[5] (See Fig. 0.3) They were publicly represented by white celebrity dance couples like Vernon and Irene Castle and Maurice Mouvet and Joan Sawyer. We still dance one

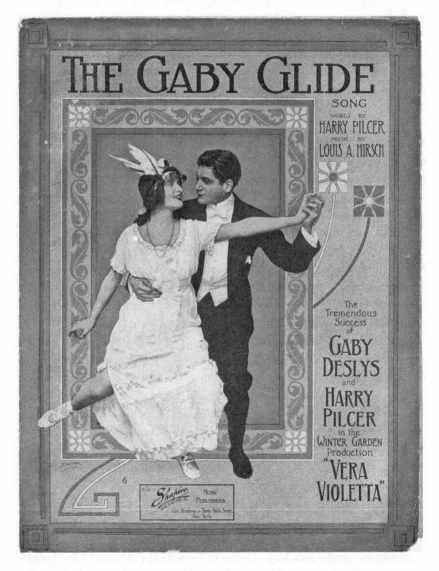

Figure 0.3 Professional Modern Dancers, 1910s. Louis A. Hirsch, *The Gaby Glide* (New York: Shapiro, 1911). Digital image from the University of Colorado Digital Sheet Music Collection. Courtesy of the American Music Research Center at the University of Colorado (public domain).

of these dances today as part of more traditional ballroom dancing practices—the foxtrot—but the widespread popularity of the modern dances
waned with the advent of jazz dancing in the early 1920s.

At the same time as these social dances were moving from black communities into white ones—and thereby helping to define mainstream American
social dance practices of the twentieth century—dance practices popular
among African Americans were also being deeply influenced by European
American dancing styles. It is important to remember that appropriation
went in both directions during this period, although with very different political implications. During the late nineteenth century, social dancing in black
communities became generally less group- and more couple-oriented.[6] This
eventually gave birth to blues dancing and, more specifically, the slow drag,
which is discussed in chapter one.[7] This dance brought couples into a very
tight embrace and sent them languidly walking around the dance floor in no
fixed pattern, while also occasionally pausing to pivot, sway, and undulate
in one place. This social dance was a practice that encouraged participants
to focus on enjoying their partner and the music. As Harlem Renaissance
writer Zora Neale Hurston said, "The Negro social dance is slow and sensu-
ous. The idea in the Jook is to gain sensation, and not so much exercise.
So that just enough foot movement was added to keep the dancers on the
floor."[8] As with the animal dances, blues dancing did not become successfully popularized for the general public through star performers or teachers.
It remained primarily a social practice in black communities throughout the
South and later the North—both urban and rural—as a result of migration
during the first several decades of the twentieth century.

In addition, traditional European American ballroom dancing—albeit
with some modifications—became a cornerstone of black elite entertainment practices throughout the early twentieth century, as discussed in chapter four.[9] Given its associations with civilization, dominance, classiness,
and morality, it was deployed as part of Harlem's "uplift" efforts beginning
in the 1920s. Harlemites drew upon nineteenth-century ballroom dancing
in particular—not usually the more recent modern social dances that were
based on the animal dances. As a result, black elite dancing favored revolv-
ing couples, elegant arcs, simple rhythms, and clear lines. In this context,
couples rarely engaged in soloing, if at all. Such dancing created an image of
order, harmony, and unity.[10] An emerging dance industry coalesced around
these ballroom dance practices that included a network of studios, performance spaces, and dance halls. Owing to these changes, eventually, African
American dancers were able to establish dance as a viable profession for
themselves through teaching and performing European-derived ballroom
dances—at a time when very few professions were open to people of color.

During the Harlem Renaissance, approximately 1925 to 1935, the rest of Harlem and much of Manhattan, and indeed America, embraced jazz dancing. Building on the plantation ring shout, as well as hybrid blues and ragtime partner dancing, 1920s jazz social dancing comprised a way of moving, speaking, and dressing, as well as a partner dance and style of stage performance.[11] Generally speaking, jazz dancing was fast and energetic, with limbs asserting themselves outwardly into space. Hips and shoulders shook, punched, and circled, while angular body shapes prevailed. If danced by a couple, partners may or may not have remained in contact at all while dancing together. A few specific dances gained national popularity, like the Charleston, shimmy, and black bottom—all of which were initially represented to the general public by white Broadway starlets, many of whom were taught by African American dancers behind the scenes in jazz dance studios. These commercial dance spaces sprung up in the Manhattan theatre district to sell "authentic black dancing," as discussed in chapter five. Over the course of the 1920s, black musicals and their dancing and singing stars eventually were able to gain name recognition outside of black communities and a degree of financial success. The hard-won accomplishments of all these dance professionals eventually formed the foundations for the jazz studio system, a precursor to the suburban dance studios so popular today and the black entertainment industry that continues to thrive.

IMMIGRATION AND MIGRATION

My archival journeys in Manhattan took me the length of the island from Harlem's Schomburg Center for Research in Black Culture all the way down to the city's Municipal Archives near the World Trade Center—back when there was a World Trade Center. Despite this archival reach, I discovered relatively quickly that—with the exception of Harlem—my primary research focus actually encompassed a relatively tiny area. Midtown to Chelsea turned out to be largely the scope of my project—a region that has been made over, and made over again, many times since the dancers I am interested in lived, worked, and/or entertained themselves there.

This small region, known as the Tenderloin for part of its life, was home for most of Manhattan's African American residents prior to the construction of Penn Station and the rise of Harlem as a black metropolis. It was also an entertainment district that included dozens of dance spaces—from basement rathskellers to chic rooftop gardens that welcomed diverse crowds but specialized in black-influenced music and dances.

Interestingly, it was also home to Manhattan's retail centers, where thousands of "native-born" working girls and boys labored in shops along Fifth Avenue. Near the heart of this neighborhood was the garment district, where dozens of factories occupied the time of immigrant youths, who mainly lived across town on the Lower East Side. Bisecting all this was Broadway—where these young men and women could find a horse-drawn streetcar and eventually a subway ride on their way home or when going out dancing. This street, in turn, leads to the city's famous theatre district in which new dance creations could be popularized for the general public.

When I walked around the west midtown region during my year in Manhattan's archives, I was surprised to find that business and entertainment were still the focus of the neighborhood. And yet, armed with a list of addresses of former dance clubs and schools, I discovered that almost nothing remains to testify to the exciting dance history of the area. Instead, as I walked, I was dwarfed by massive hotels, museums, theatres, and European fashion houses. The scale of life had changed dramatically in a hundred years.

Meandering the streets of the Tenderloin, I spent time imagining how the dancers I researched might have encountered each other in their daily lives. Did a migrant woman work as a maíd in the house of a ballroom industry star? Might an immigrant girl have ridden a streetcar with a ragtime drummer? Would a Harlem socialite buy a pair of gloves from a midtown shop girl? Manhattan was the same geographic size then as it is now, but with a smaller population. Nonetheless, people could not and did not live in isolation; even though racially and ethnically segregated neighborhoods were the norm, work and play sent people far from disparate spaces and integrated their lives at various moments throughout the day.

Entertainment spaces within the Tenderloin in particular served a cross-pollinating function—to greater and lesser degrees depending on the venue and time of night. Amateur investigative reports written during the first decades of the twentieth century tell us that even in restricted white clubs, African American wait staff and entertainers were common. In black dance venues, anywhere from a curious few to a majority of patrons could be European American on any given evening. In this way, social dancing inspired a cross-cultural sharing of public space that was less possible in other contexts. Indeed, during the early twentieth century, all of Manhattan's citizens were living and working in closer proximity than before to people who often looked and sounded different from themselves. It was a time of curiosity, and also a time of bigotry, as people negotiated their own identities in the face of difference.

New York City was the site of a collision between two major demographic shifts in the early twentieth century: Massive waves of European immigration met with flows of African American migration from the Southern U.S.[12] While the number of European arrivals was far higher, the dramatic influx of people from both groups was felt intensely by "native" New Yorkers. Prior to this period, much smaller numbers of African Americans had come to Manhattan, but the city's black community remained relatively small and, thus, seemed less threatening to white residents. With regard to European immigration, before this time, around 90 percent of the city's immigrants hailed from Northern and Western Europe, the same demographic that had settled America in the first place. The new immigrants, however, came largely from Southern and Eastern Europe instead and were darker in skin and hair color. And so, with these early twentieth-century increases in migrant and immigrant populations, New York City's complexion was transforming—to the surprise and dismay of many long-time residents.

During the first two decades of the twentieth century, those born outside the United States and their American-born children increasingly dominated New York City's citizenry. Census reports suggest that the all-time zenith of immigration into New York City occurred between 1900 and 1915—the *exact* period of ragtime's height of popularity.[13] In fact, in the first decade of the twentieth century, New York's "foreign-born white" population, to use census terminology, nearly doubled. If individuals with at least one foreign-born parent are included, the percentage of "alien" New Yorkers rises to nearly 70 percent, a huge majority of the city's population.

More importantly, these immigrant men and women did not blend seamlessly into the social fabric of Manhattan. The vast majority of the new arrivals came from Southern Italy and the former Russian Empire, in particular Russia, Poland, and Lithuania.[14] According to historian John Higham, these immigrants seemed to differ most significantly from the native-born in terms of education, financial resources, and religion.[15] Rather than easily assimilating into Manhattan society, these foreigners (or aliens as they were called in census documents) tended to live in ethnic enclaves where they could more easily maintain distinct languages and customs.[16] The Lower East Side—on the other side of Broadway and further south than the Tenderloin—was the primary destination for these immigrants, becoming a crowded, teeming ghetto in just a few years' time.

At the same time that Eastern and Southern European immigration was overwhelming New Yorkers, Manhattan's African American population almost tripled as a result of the migrations from the South that began at the end of the nineteenth century and escalated in the 1910s, the *same* period when blues dancing was beginning. The waves of black migrants of the early twentieth century were far larger and more dramatic than any New York had experienced before. The city's African American population almost quadrupled between 1910 and 1930. More than one hundred thousand Southern migrants arrived between 1920 and 1930 alone. Unlike earlier waves of black migrants from urban settings along the Atlantic seaboard, these later arrivals were not necessarily well-educated or accustomed to city life; furthermore, they did not possess skills that transferred well to the available jobs in New York City. And so, after relocating, they did almost exclusively menial and manual labor, if they were able to find work at all.

As a means of self-protection, the majority of New York City's black population (native New Yorkers and new migrants alike) moved from downtown to uptown during the early twentieth century, in the hope that isolation would yield greater safety. African Americans had initially settled on the west side of Manhattan during the nineteenth century, in the Tenderloin and San Juan Hill areas (which today are just above Chelsea and below Central Park). According to musician, diplomat, and writer James Weldon Johnson, however, some began moving to Harlem as early as 1900.[17] The progression uptown was slow at first. It wasn't until the 1920s that Harlem was considered home to most of Manhattan's black residents. By 1924, this city within a city spanned from 126th to 145th Streets and from 8th to Park Avenues.

INDUSTRIAL DEVELOPMENTS

The confluence of large-scale immigration and migration created the conditions of possibility for new dance forms like blues, ragtime, modern, and jazz. In turn, these practices established the foundation for the American ballroom dance industry—an industry that continues to thrive today and has recently expanded into prime time television through such shows as *Dancing with the Stars*. This now global industry was founded during the early twentieth century and retains many connections to its original iteration. Questions relating to appropriation and authenticity resonate today just as strongly as when the industry was founded. For this reason, it is important to examine American ballroom's beginnings, given its continuing legacies and their political implications.[18]

Prior to the twentieth century, there were certainly professional social dance teachers, but they did not operate as an industry in any formal sense. In America, during the nineteenth century, the few dance teachers who sustained careers ran their businesses independently and on a very local scale. The most successful teachers may have owned a school—where they taught classes and held public receptions and balls—and independently published manuals and sheet music for their students and community. These teachers were often Western European immigrant men from working-class backgrounds. Female dance teachers of this period tended to teach part-time out of their homes, to the great frustration of the male teachers who regarded them as "illegitimate" instructors.[19]

Although dance teachers of this period were clearly selling dance knowledge, I do not consider their collective labors to be a formal dance industry. Industry is typically defined as "a distinct group of productive or profit-making enterprises"[20]; in common usage, however, the term refers to a set of interrelated businesses. At the end of the nineteenth century, social dance teachers did not typically work together or with related industries such as theatre or publishing. They performed rarely; their publishing efforts were usually intermittent and aimed at a local market. Thus, their labors were more isolated than interconnected. Furthermore, social dance teachers of this period did not share a common product; they simply sold dancing—not round dancing, couples dancing, or Victorian dancing. In other words, they had not yet branded their product, which is crucial for industrial development.

It was during the 1910s that the labors of American social dance teachers became more interconnected, diversified, and national in scope. They partnered with local businesses to expand their teaching practices into public entertainment spaces, such as restaurants, hotels, and cafés. Besides teaching, 1910s dance professionals published widely in magazines, as well as books. They performed in musicals and vaudeville shows that toured nationally. The most successful of these professionals endorsed a wide array of commercial products from shoes to corsets to phonographs. Importantly, by the 1910s, women taught dance publicly, albeit usually in conjunction with a male partner. This development may be related to shifting gender roles that enabled women's increased presence in public spaces during the first decades of the twentieth century. With these changes, modern social dance professionals eventually came to constitute an industry—one that sold modern social dances through modern industrial practices.[21]

Cross-cultural borrowing was at the heart of this industry; it was a major source of innovation in social dancing. This period established the practice among European Americans of borrowing, stealing, and/or being influenced by dance forms thought to be black. In this way, early twentieth-century dancing laid the groundwork for swing, rock and roll, disco, and hip hop's cross-cultural moves; it helped normalize dancing "otherness" in American culture. Moreover, this trend was reinforced by theatre dance artists like Ruth St. Denis and Maude Allan who embodied exotic dances on stages across America. Prior to the twentieth century, African American dancers and dancing had certainly informed dance trends on stages, especially minstrel stages, but not European American community movement practices. Thus, dance activities of the early 1900s established a pattern that has defined American social dancing for at least the twentieth century, and perhaps beyond.

DANCE HISTORIES AND HISTORICAL ABSENCES

I began my archival work on these social dances over ten years ago by chasing a moving target. I had heard rumors of an exciting multimedia museum exhibition on African American dance that was touring the United States, called *When the Spirit Moves*. It was developed by the National Afro-American Museum and Cultural Center in consultation with a range of scholars and educators. Thankfully, our paths eventually intersected in Washington, D.C., where I was doing archival research and dancing with noted dance reconstructor and performer, Cheryl Stafford. At the first opportunity, I walked across the National Mall and into the exhibit hall with nervous anticipation of what I might discover; several hours later, I walked out disappointed, but also with a new motivation for my research—not because the exhibit was bad, on the contrary it was extraordinary, but because it barely addressed my particular interests.

During my first visit to *When the Spirit Moves*, I restrained my enthusiasm and proceeded carefully, sketching the layout and taking notes on the information provided on every plaque. Although I was interested in everything there, the early twentieth century was my chief concern. After winding my way past jazz-inspired paintings, an interactive video dance lesson, a reproduction of a jook house, and even a child's minstrelsy kit, eventually I found cakewalk sheet music covers—and I knew I was almost there. I eagerly looked to my right, expecting to find photographs or artist's renderings of ragtime, blues, or modern dancing, but I only encountered illustrations of the Charleston and black bottom—1920s jazz dances. At least twenty years and dozens of dances separate cakewalking and jazz, and yet I found nothing in between them. I circled the exhibit again, wondering if I had somehow overlooked images elsewhere. Empty handed, I returned to the cakewalk and Charleston, looking left and then right, eventually slowly shaking my head in frustration that this huge, important exhibit could have omitted such an exciting era of social dance history.

Scant attention to ragtime, modern, and blues social dancing in accounts of African American dance history—or any dance history—is not unusual, I now know. In fact, these dance forms have received fleeting scholarly treatment over the years, despite animating dance floors across America during the early decades of the twentieth century. A few dance scholars have, however, discussed some of this dancing. In 1986, Kathy Peiss argued in one chapter of her *Cheap Amusements* that European American ragtime dancing (by turn-of-the-century Manhattan's young working women) was a means of announcing a desire to be more American, modern, and mature. In the 1990s, dance scholar Julie Malnig and musicologist Susan Cook in their individual articles both suggested that European American middle-class modern dancing was entangled in period class politics and that it empowered women, in particular, personally and professionally.[22] During this same period, historian Tera Hunter and dance sociologist Katrina Hazzard indicated in chapters of their books that blues dancing was crucial to black identity formation processes post-Civil War. Finally, in the twenty-first century, Nadine George-Graves's recent chapter on ragtime dancing demonstrates how it was connected with period discourses of animality and primitivism.

Building on all this valuable work, *Modern Moves* considers blues, ragtime, modern, ballroom, and jazz dancing together in a cross-cultural way in order to better understand the relationships not only between dances, but also between peoples and cultures. Dance is not just a part of culture, but intrinsic to it. If, following anthropologist Clifford Geertz, one views culture as "webs of significance" in which people live and which people make, then dance, as a practice that is intensely meaningful, is implicated in bringing culture into being, as I discuss further in the next section.[23] In the particular cultural context of early twentieth century Manhattan, social dancing practices and discourses worked together to reify racial differences. Racialized thinking, at the time, which viewed black and white as absolutes, was certainly not new. Nonetheless, dancing helped cement these ideas into public consciousness.

Although seemingly far removed from the present, early twentieth century social dancing still influences our thinking about dance and race today. For example, competitive ballroom dancing is still divided into two racially discrete categories—standard and Latin.[24] Standard dances include all the "smooth" dances, which are almost exclusively European-derived. Arguably, one seeming exception here is the tango, but the version drawn upon is the 1910s Parisian adaptation of practices from Argentina. The only other possible exception would be the foxtrot, which has hidden African diasporic roots according to some origin stories, as discussed in the next chapter. The Latin dance category, not surprisingly, is comprised primarily of dances from Latin America. It also includes swing (sometimes known as jive), which is typically thought of as an African American dance. So we find, in the twenty-first century, dance categories reflecting particular notions of white and not white. Such categorizations echo the race-based thinking of early ballroom dance professionals, who began dancing during the racially charged first decades of the twentieth century when immigration and migration were rapidly changing the complexion of American cities and dance became a means of mapping racial boundaries and identities.

By looking at several of this period's social dance practices together, this book highlights how different communities have at times used dancing they perceived to be black or white to transform their lives; how cross-cultural dancing can play a role in both European American and African American identity-formation processes; and how dance as employed by people of different racial backgrounds can be part of efforts toward and expressions of social mobility. Indeed, *Modern Moves* examines cross-cultural dancing's potential to assist assimilation efforts by migrant and immigrant peoples, and finally, it uncovers social dancing's crucial role in the launching of professional dance careers and industries. In so doing, it emphasizes the power of social dancing in the lives of many people and their communities as well as its potential to impact our racial thinking, both now and in the future.

DANCE, CULTURE, HISTORY, IDENTITY

I discovered what would become another primary research interest of mine—the embodiment of identity through dance—while watching the 1937 film *The Bride Wore Red*. In this film, Joan Crawford plays a cabaret singer who masquerades as a socialite to win the heart of a wealthy man. At a crucial moment in the film, as she and her blue-blooded love interest whirl, sway, and slide around the dance floor together, he whispers to her, "You don't dance like a debutante." His words are not an accusation, but rather a titillating observation that suggests he is excited to have found a proper girl with some sexual knowledge, or at least, interest. Fearful that her moving body has betrayed her true background, she carefully asks him, "How *do* debutantes dance?" To this he replies simply, "with stiff knees"—a powerful image that evokes ballet, as well as legs clamped shut in sexual refusal and the upright dancing of 1910s elite ballrooms. By this comment, he also differentiates debutantes, and the upper classes in general, from the knee-bending and hip-rocking associated with African-influenced dance forms of the twentieth century.

In a telling moment, this scene highlighted for me how subtly dance can communicate who we are and who we want to be, to others and to ourselves. Without our awareness or permission sometimes, our movement speaks of our gender, nationality, race, class, age, religion, sexuality, etc., and of our aspirations in these regards. This is not to suggest that "movement never lies,"[25] but that it is constantly communicating kinesthetic markers of identity that we have learned, deliberately or not. It is this bodily communication that interests me as a dance researcher. I want to explore: How are ideas about culture and politics communicated through bodies in motion? Alternatively, what can dancing tell us about human experience and social relations?

It is perhaps easier to answer these types of questions when doing contemporary, rather than historical, research. Being able to talk with participants, see their movement live, and embody it with them is an ideal situation, of course. Watching video recordings in lieu of live interaction is an excellent research tool as well. In the absence of all these options, historical dance researchers are left with archival evidence, our own bodies, and our imaginations. With such tools, one can indeed recover many aspects of bodily movement, but not necessarily its meanings, roles, uses, and importance. This is where historical contexts become crucial as well as critical tools—if the focus is on dance as cultural experience.

In order to pursue my research questions that relate to the embodiment of culture, identity, history, and politics, I crafted a hybrid methodology, much like the dances at the center of my study, that bridges different worlds: dance reconstruction, dance ethnography, and dance cultural studies. The latter two fields emerged within dance studies in the last few decades and have cross-pollinated in exciting ways, such that both often draw upon ethnographic methods and emphasize cultural politics. They are rarely combined with dance reconstruction, however, as this area of inquiry has remained quite performance-focused since its beginnings in the 1970s.[26]

My historical research does not involve ethnographic field methods per se, but rather a deep engagement with ethnographic issues as modeled by scholars like dance anthropologists Sally Ness and Cynthia Novack. Although trained primarily as a historian, my interest is in social practice, human experience, and, more broadly, culture; my methods emphasize physical experience and respect for cultural difference. In particular, I view the dancing body as being dense with meaning and playing a key role in social relations as a conveyor and purveyor of historically situated ideologies, identities, and symbols. An ethnographic approach to dance history resituates dancing as social practice, instead of as an art object or text, and pushes researchers to ask who dances, why do they dance, and especially what are the effects of their dancing on their own lives and those of others?

Dance is inextricably linked to culture in my mind, even if located in the past. Novack argued in her 1990 study of contact improvisation, *Sharing the Dance*, that dancing is both an aesthetic *and* social event. It references ideas implicitly and explicitly that relate to life on and off the dance floor. Dance has the power to propagate cultural and countercultural norms and values, and in this way, is affected by and affects social life.[27] Moreover, Ness tells us in *Body, Movement, and Culture* that a body's movement can be a symbol for the surrounding social world's values and beliefs. She writes, in her study of a Philippine community's movement practices:

> The *sinulog* choreography, as I came to understand it, was an expression of this urban world, a "pressing out" or a symbolic abstraction of that world's dynamics: its climactic conditions, its patterning of time, space, and people, and its contemporary religious, socioeconomic, and socio-political situation.[28]

As a symbolic abstraction of social dynamics, dance has tremendous power. It represents social life and thus offers participants a means of expressing their own views on its hierarchies, roles, and stereotypes (for example) through their bodies.

Both Novack and Ness did ethnographic research in the present. Yet ethnography, and the embodied research that it facilitates, need not be limited to contemporary subjects of study. As a methodology, it can be adapted to historical inquiry, allowing those invested in social practice and bodily engagement to research in the past. Ethnomusicologist Philip V. Bohlman's model for "ethnography of the past" offers a means of merging archival research and experience-focused ethnography.[29] This author's approach differs from conventional historical research in its imaginative and embodied explorations of everyday life through physical experiences in historical spaces and with historical texts and objects. Bohlman's model enables the body and imagination of the researcher to bridge gaps between surviving source materials toward an understanding of collective experiences. As historian Hayden White (2009) has demonstrated, historians are always bridging gaps between their sources and drawing upon their imagination; the difference here is that Bohlman encourages us to self-consciously use our bodies to do so.

The vignettes that open each of the following chapters are in many ways a means of manifesting my ethnographic impulses as well as drawing upon Bohlman's license to rely on my own bodily knowledge and creativity. They provide dynamic scenes of people dancing within very specific social contexts that are based upon my own bodily investigations of a wide variety of period source materials. More than just evidence of my reconstruction work, they aim to breathe life into textual analyses and avoid the codifying impulses that might otherwise turn "dancing" into "the dance."[30]

Each vignette introduces the reader to a cluster of characters that I have devised, in some cases from real archival examples. As the book unfolds, some of these characters return in different roles. These crossover characters—Lillian, Leroy, Charlie, and James—are meant to demonstrate how disparate social spaces in Manhattan were actually interconnected and how developments in one period laid the groundwork for later changes. I hope that by putting a human face on the social dancing of this period, readers will connect more emotionally and physically to the dancing.[31]

To this ethnographically informed historical research, I bring an intense focus on cultural politics, which owes much to the influence of cultural studies within American dance history research by authors such as Jane Desmond, Ann Daly, Susan Manning, and Amy Koritz. Dance cultural studies' primary focus, since its inception during the 1980s, has been the establishment of dance research within the humanities. Western concert dance has been the main focus of most dance writers within cultural studies, and ballet, modern, and postmodern dance have been the favored topics within that area.[32] This emphasis distinguishes dance cultural studies from cultural studies because the latter, especially in its British iteration, has focused on popular culture topics more so than "artistic" products. Even those few dance scholars who have researched social dancing, such as Julie Malnig and Susan Cook, have tended to frame it as a professional rather than social practice. This might be attributed to the greater availability of published sources for professional practices and to the suitability of professional dancers to the choreographer/choreography authorial model that has been well established within Western concert dance and research on it.

Dance research's embrace of Western concert dance and its authorial model has affected the methodological approaches taken by dance cultural studies researchers. Such scholars have demonstrated a propensity toward approaching dance as representation rather than as experience—as an audience member would view a dance concert, for example, which makes sense given the number of dance critics who become scholars. For them, in their writing, dance is often something watched rather than done. They *read* the filmic, graphic, and textual remnants of choreography in the form of reviews, photographs, videos, autobiographical writing, and interviews, as literature scholars might read a novel or poem—for their potential meanings within relevant social contexts as they relate to cultural politics. Jane Desmond herself agrees with this assessment, writing that "critical work on 'the body' is focused more on representations of the body and/or its discursive policing than with its actions/movements as a 'text' them-selves."[33] What can often be lost in this approach is a sense of human expe-rience as well as sensation; as a result, vibrant and dynamic social practices can be rendered more fixed than they were in actuality.

To mitigate these tendencies, in this project, I adopt dance reconstruc-tion's close examination of movement and reliance on embodiment as a research tool—as one of the few methods indigenous to dance research—but also adapt it to my project's emphasis on culture and politics. In her entry on reconstruction in the *International Dance Encyclopedia* (2003), Linda Tomko discusses how the goal of traditional dance reconstructors has been the re-animation of historical artifacts—in other words, to accu-rately and precisely demonstrate dances of the past in a manner that illus-trates how they are believed to have been performed in their historical moment based on scrutiny of primary source evidence.[34] Methodologically speaking, this type of dance reconstruction requires that representative choreographies and steps be derived from primary source materials by a process of exclusion. Some primary source materials (and the dance experi-ences they depict) are highlighted, while others are not, in order to arrive at a definitive version of a given dance.

In order to adapt dance reconstruction's methods to a project that is invested in both diversity and specificity of practice, I had to develop a fundamentally different way of embodying my primary source materials, one that endeavored to preserve difference. Rather than seeking out and privileging the most "correct" evidence in order to create a representative performance, I instead embraced all evidence of a social dance that could be found—each one a bodily trace of a different perspective. For example, dance manuals usually spoke of the intentions of dance teachers and their elite customers, whereas investigative reports of so-called low dance halls represented working-class practitioners and the middle-class investigators obsessed with finding moral degeneracy. The dancing described in these sources, from my perspective, was all enlightening and useful—one was not more correct than the other.

Considered together, evidence from a wide range of sources enabled me to work toward building a movement repertoire that tracks a spec-trum of dancing—from the most rigid, codified versions that were sold to upper-class customers interested in "safe" modern dancing to the most cakewalk-like, raucous working-class versions of ragtime that animated Tenderloin dance clubs.[35] In this way, I aimed to learn movement much like a social dancer of the period—developing, drawing on, and varying an arsenal of moves while dancing.

Here I draw upon the ideas of performance studies scholar Diana Taylor, who has argued that an "archival" model for historical research that relies on texts and documents alone can be resistant to change and gives the illusion of fixity and fact. [36] A "repertoire" model, on the other hand, works with—not against—ephemerality and embodiment. It enacts and activates embodied memory in a way that allows for individual agency and embraces change. Within a repertoire model, even if their relevance and meaning are relatively stable, the forms themselves are constantly shifting given their bodily medium.

A repertoire approach to reconstruction allows the dancing to constantly vary and transform, with each new piece of evidence located and each new perspective discovered. Rather than creating a chaotic mass of information, this flexible approach generated over time a series of fluid improvisational structures, within which I danced and came to know the dancing. These variable structures are the culmination of my reconstruction work, not an archive of steps or beautiful choreographies. I don't expect or want the dancing to become fixed in my mind or in anyone else's. Fluidity and individuality were at the heart of social dancing during the early twentieth century and that should continue to be the case in early *twenty-first century* dance research on it.

Besides saying yes to all period sources, as part of my reconstruction practices, I also took the liberty to read against and beyond the "truths" of each dance manual and article.[37] In other words, while accepting all sources as valid, I rarely read them in the way the author might have wished. For example, when an author told the reader how *not* to dance, I paid close attention, as the writing offered me a window into a community of practice that did not adhere to the same values as the author. So, rather than viewing the dancing they described as incorrect or bad, I saw it potentially as more moves to add to my repertoire. My logic was this: Why would a dance writer tell someone *not* to move a certain way, unless that was exactly what some dancers were doing?

To reiterate, what was important to me in my body-based archival research was not to get it exactly right, as in a historically accurate performance, but to get the theory within the practice right instead—to me, this was crucial. In many ways, Mark Franko's groundbreaking reconstruction work paved the way for this particular approach.[38] In his research on Baroque court dance, he focused on reproducing stylistic *effects* such as stasis, chaos, or interruption. His work culminated in performances that aimed to construct, or rather reinvent, the impact of baroque dance on its period audiences. For Franko, it was the *significance* of the movement that mattered most.

In the case of ragtime, based on my bodily engagement with primary source materials, the theory at work was an overall aesthetic of rupture, which fits with its early modernist positioning. Some boundary somewhere was always being crossed. Even though a rather intimate version of a closed dance position was deployed as ragtime dancers traversed the floor, my evidence suggested that they frequently broke apart to solo. As they soloed, they often divided their torsos into discrete parts, such as shoulders, waist, and hips. In addition, the use of accented movement, even among the most staid dancers, frequently departed from ragtime music's steadily rocking bass line. Finally, angular bodylines proliferated as limbs would suddenly jab into space—elbows and knees protruding. It was this constant setting of boundaries and then breaking them that I most wanted to experience in my reconstruction work.

The long-term impact of my nontraditional reconstruction choices on the larger research project was profound. It helped me shift my focus from the *dance* to the *dancers* and their experiences—not as star performers, but as community members and culture-bearers. I was interested in which groups of people were dancing and how they were moving differently from one another. This, in turn, led to questions relating to meaning: Why were people moving differently to the same music, and what did the dancing signify within each specific community? In short, the project became more ethnographic just by considering *who* was dancing.

TACTICAL MOVES

While I am certainly invested in what the dancing looked and felt like, what I am most interested in are the ways in which people made use of these dances and their meanings, and made meanings through their dancing. In this way, cultural theorist Michel de Certeau's conceptualization of "tactics" has been central to my theoretical framework. In his 1984 book *The Practice of Everyday Life*, de Certeau advocates for the study of processes that determine socioeconomic order alongside the ways people transform and manipulate such processes, what he calls "making do." He describes such tactical maneuvers as conforming "only in order to evade."[39] In fact, he sees everyday life as a process of "poaching" on the territory of others, recombining the rules and products that already exist in culture in a way that is influenced, but never wholly determined, by those rules and products. Here de Certeau models an approach to research that represents people who are marginalized by dominant power structures as agents who quietly pursue their own empowerment through quotidian choice-making.

Social dancing operates in a similar fashion. There are certainly genres, steps, norms, social expectations, and understood rules, but there are also opportunities for choice-making, playful rule-breaking, and appropriations. When reading a period dance manual or magazine, it seems as though discrete dances and steps simply exist, and that everyone does them the same way. In everyday practice, however, social dancers conform tactically depending on the environs where they dance, among other factors; they recombine, adapt, and transform dance moves every moment they are on the dance floor. Through my reconstruction activities, I am searching for the structures within which dancers made their movement choices and the creative possibilities they might have generated.

Through tactical choices, social dancers craft and perform their movement, as well as their own self-understanding, both descriptive and/or aspirational. To borrow from cultural theorist Michel Foucault's "Technologies of the Self," dancers "transform themselves in order to attain a certain state of happiness, purity, wisdom, perfection, or immortality."[40] I would add to his statement "a sense of belonging," because my research suggests that dancers seek happiness, etc., often by articulating, negotiating, and legitimizing who they are and/or who they want to be, or what Foucault calls their "truth." They do this through discursive engagement, by embodying ideas and identity markers embedded within movement that design and perform the self.

Such performances of self can be an important means of seeking social mobility by establishing an elevated social status or increasing distance from an undesirable identity. Moreover, dance—when thought of as a kind of cultural product—is well-positioned to offer participants a means of demonstrating their "distinction," to borrow sociologist Pierre Bourdieu's terminology for what sets people apart from one another through a simultaneous differentiation and elevation. He writes:

> If, among all these fields of possibles, none is more obviously predisposed to express social differences than the world of luxury goods, and, more particularly, cultural goods, this is because the relationship of distinction is objectively inscribed within it, and is reactivated, intentionally or not, in each act of consumption, through the instruments of economic and cultural appropriation which it requires.[41]

Social dancing, like the more conventional material goods and knowledge about them that Bourdieu discusses, has the power to establish fields of distinction. Through dancing or even just watching it, participants can tactically establish a new truth of self by aligning themselves with specific, empowered aesthetic values. Certain kinds of social dancing can therefore be creative and powerful forms of embodied "cultural capital," to borrow another concept of Bourdieu's, a knowledge asset that provides a means of elevating one's social status. In this capacity, social dancing impacts one's "way of thinking" and provides a crucial "means of communication" and "self-presentation".[42]

Dancing one's sense of self and/or social status is an inherently and intensely political move that connects with multiple vectors of identity—class, race, gender, and religion, among others. Yet these areas of identification rarely operate independently. Cultural theorist Stuart Hall reminds us that race and class, in particular, can be "articulated" through one another. More specifically, he argues that it is through the appropriation of racially marked cultural forms that social classes frequently attempt to elevate their position. He explains: "race is thus, also, the modality in which class is 'lived,' the medium through which class relations are experienced, the form in which it is appropriated and 'fought through.' "[43] This plays out in modern forms of social dancing when performances of self, designed to empower the mover, use the discourse of class but embodied markers of race. For example, socioeconomic status is demonstrated through mastery of black or white movement, depending on the background of the dancers: African American dancers have used European-derived dance forms, and European Americans have practiced African-influenced dancing to advance their own social mobility projects. In these ways, movers can creatively improvise a new truth of and for themselves. Through social dancing movers can distinguish their "self" from others through temporary embodiments of otherness—all while enjoying a Saturday night with friends. Pleasure is not at all divorced from the cultural politics embedded in leisure pursuits.

CONSTRUCTING AND DECONSTRUCTING TERMINOLOGY

Even as I aim to tell a desegregated history of modern American social dancing, I must use concepts derived from the early twentieth century's highly polarized racial climate. In short, I sometimes write in black and white terms about hybrid realities—using linguistic essentialism in order to better represent and analyze the binary thinking of the period.[44] To this end, throughout this text, I often use the terms black and white, and blackness and whiteness, to refer to dancing and people who were at the time described as Negro and Caucasian as a result of period views on race. I choose to use the terms black and white not because they were always used during the early twentieth century—although they were at times—but because they communicate a perceived distinction between races that was endemic during this period. European or African, Caucasian or Negroid, as well as a host of less polite monikers, were more commonly used during the opening decades of the twentieth century. I prefer to use black and white because these provide the same effect for contemporary audiences without the confusion and offense of more historically accurate terminology. That said, at times in the following chapters, I do, at times, reference unpleasant racial, racialist, and racist terms when discussing period discourses and/or concepts. For example, the term "Niggerati" was deployed frequently by younger Harlem Renaissance artists as an ironic combination of the pejorative "nigger" and elitist "literati". Through this provocative word choice, they inspired an important discussion of class politics within the movement. I use their term (and others like it) throughout this book, albeit as sparingly as possible, for the sake of historical accuracy, not to offend or in any way normalize problematic language.

In this way, my approach reflects the position taken by many dance scholars influenced by post-structuralist theories.[45] Most notably, Susan Manning argued in her 2004 *Modern Dance, Negro Dance* that "[b]lackness and whiteness became perpetual constructs on stage, ways for linking physical bodies and theatrical meaning, ways of reading bodies in motion."[46] To say that race is socially constructed, however, is not to suggest that perceptions and lived realities of race do not greatly affect individual lives and social conditions—and in this project, social dancing.[47] I feel strongly that it is possible—indeed, important—to talk about race as a social construct without dismissing it as fantasy, abandoning it as a vector of analysis, or ignoring the problem of racism.[48] It is also possible to acknowledge the constructed nature of race, while honoring the material impact of it on lived experience and the ways in which strategic essentialism might have been a vital means of empowerment at particular times and in specific places. Race is undeniably a powerful force in America that has been used to control, subordinate, and elevate—and looking at race as a social construct better positions us to perceive its changing roles within society and its entanglements with power.

As mentioned earlier, beyond black and white, I consider all the dances discussed here to be "modern," as did many people during the opening decades of the twentieth century, before the term commonly was used in reference to concert dance practices. However, I use "modern" for very different reasons: Like Western modernity itself, this period of social dancing was dependent on the cultural production and labor of black people—even as they were excluded from many of its rewards—and tied to the growth of industry and globalized capitalism.

Modern social dance and Western modernity share roots in slavery and its legacies, including industrialization. Sociologist Paul Gilroy has argued that the modern world was economically possible because of the Atlantic slave trade and was philosophically grounded in race-based distinctions, hierarchies, and oppression. Gilroy views slavery and the master/slave relationship as a defining feature of Western modernity, as it "catalyzed the distinctive regimes of truth, the world of discourse ... call[ed] 'raciology.'"[49] This term, raciology, signifies a racialized and, at times, racist logic. Following Gilroy, I can see that race was similarly an organizing principle of modern social dance, as will be made evident in the following chapters. Indeed, through attempts to embody, eradicate, and market conceptualizations of blackness and whiteness through dancing, participants were investing in a modern and moving raciology.

The industrial growth that facilitated modernity's capitalist expansion was likewise rooted in race-based ideologies and racist realities given its initial reliance on the slave trade in particular and colonization in general, according to sociologist Howard Winant. He takes Gilroy's arguments even further through his linkages to race, empire, and capitalism.

> Race has been a constitutive element, an organizational principle, a praxis and structure that has constructed and reconstructed world society since the emergence of modernity, the enormous historical shift represented by the rise of Europe, the founding of modern nation-states and empires, the conquista, the onset of African enslavement, and the subjugation of much of Asia.[50]

Race and industry in many ways partnered with one another throughout modernization processes. This was certainly true with modern social dancing as well.

In fact, the modern American ballroom dance industry did not emerge until social dancing engaged with black dancing sources and whiteness became a primary, although implicit, marketing feature. For these reasons, I call the social dances of the early twentieth century *modern* and in so doing hope to underscore their embodiment of this period's racial logic and industrial growth in dance. This does not mean that participants were racists, only that their dancing was intimately connected with period notions of race. Owning up to the *raciology* at the heart of our embodied practices is a crucial step towards understanding race relations in America as well as dance's role in society more broadly.

BOOK STRUCTURE

Modern Moves examines the movement of American social dances between black and white cultural groups and immigrant and migrant communities during the early twentieth century. Partially inspired by E. L. Doctorow's famous novel *Ragtime*, the book focuses on each community separately to facilitate a more in-depth consideration.[51] It is structured by five overlapping case studies culled from disparate and yet related dance scenes of Manhattan, a black Atlantic capital into which diverse people and dances flowed and intermingled and out of which new dances were marketed globally. The chapters focus on the partner dancing of African American migrants; the ragtime dancing of European immigrant youth; the marketing of ragtime dancing as "refined" modern dance by European American dance professionals; the European ballroom dancing of African American elites; and the selling of jazz dancing to white Broadway stars through a nascent studio system begun by African American dance teachers. Together, these case studies offer snapshots of social dancing's important role in social, cultural, and political relationships at this time in the United States as well as the interrelationships between urban cultural groups.

In the following chapter, I draw upon Harlem Renaissance literature, Marshall and Jean Stearns's jazz research interviews, and 1940s Works Progress Administration (WPA) reports to examine the social dancing that was practiced among working-class African Americans in New York City around the time of large-scale migrations from the Southern U.S. As people and dances transitioned from the rural South to cities in the North, hybrid practices emerged. Using the slow drag—a dance that actually defies labels such as ragtime, blues, or jazz—as a focal point, chapter one analyzes what happened when group-based African-derived dance movements became reframed within European couple formations. African American migrants utilized the social practice of dancing as a means of reconstructing home and a sense of self in new and rapidly changing environs.

Chapter two considers ragtime dancing among European immigrant youth within the contexts of American minstrelsy, African American migration, and European immigration. Based on period sheet music and investigative reports by the Committee of Fourteen (a Manhattan-based, middle-class community watchdog organization that was active from 1900 to 1930 and concerned with social vice), I argue that ragtime dancing of the early twentieth century can be understood as a form of participatory minstrelsy, a social practice transformed from theatrical practice. This form of dancing allowed movers to borrow markers of blackness in a way that built upon "coon singing" and prefigured the covering of black music by white artists in the wake of race records.[52] Read through the minstrelsy scholarship in dance, theatre, literature, and film—especially that by social historian Eric Lott—while dancing "black" to ragtime music, European immigrant youth found a means of assimilation as Americans.[53]

The focus of chapter three is the transformation of ragtime dancing into modern dance by social dance professionals, some of whom were immigrants or the children of immigrants. Dance teachers, writers, and performers collectively created new products (i.e., dances) that could be more easily mass-produced and marketed through processes that replicated many of the cutting-edge mass-production techniques of the time, such as those developed by Frederick Taylor.[54] Period social dance professionals called their transformation of ragtime "refinement;" the changes they made to the dances, however, not only made them more marketable, they also shifted their racial associations from black to white. This illustrates how the mass production and marketing of modern social dance was deeply entangled with powerful period racial discourses.

Chapter four examines the social practice of nineteenth-century European American ballroom dancing among early twentieth-century elite African Americans through Harlem WPA reports and articles in a local society magazine relating to dance teaching in Manhattan's upwardly mobile black communities. This dancing did not simply express a desire to be white or to create a distance from blackness. Rather, understood through the scholarship of historians Kevin Gaines and Alessandra Lorini on the black elites of this period, such dancing provided opportunities for dancers to construct an elite identity that was uniquely African American—both African-derived and American in perspective.[55] Dancers traded on the white racial signification of the dances to claim an elevated class status within black communities while also inserting moments of African American movement to make the dancing their own. In this way, social dancing enabled new black elites to firm up their social position and add their voice to debates on the nature of the "New Negro."

In my closing chapter, analyses of period dance magazines and the Stearns's research interviews help me reconstruct the lives and labors of the earliest black jazz dance teachers. These teachers were among the first African Americans to be able to make a living "selling" black dances to white Americans, a task that had been virtually impossible during the ragtime era. While carving out an important new profession and privately countering pervasive black stereotypes, these teachers also formalized an appropriative relationship between black and white dancers in Manhattan that was rooted in essentialist notions relating to black and white racial differences that were the bedrock of the 1920s Jazz Age.

These five dance scenes tell a story of intertwined empowerment efforts among diverse groups of people, all navigating intense social change. Some reached forward toward modernity and others reached back nostalgically, but all created powerful feelings of sameness and belonging at a time when difference was not just inconvenient, it was dangerous. For early twentieth century Manhattanites, assimilation was a means of survival, not a luxury, and dancing was one of the many ways they chose to achieve it. From the twenty-first century, we can look back and see the essentialisms that they mobilized as part of their efforts as well as the hegemonic forces they at times supported through their tactics. Looking at their practices together, however, we can also appreciate the innovative ways they contributed to what it meant to be modern in America, and indeed, American.

Taken together, I hope that these five case studies tell a history of modern American social dancing that includes those of us for whom cross-cultural dance exploration has been a crucial part of our social practice and human experience. The story of our social dancing as deeply rooted in cross-cultural encounters, however, does not proclaim the resolution of racial strife or the discovery of a utopian social space. Rather, it illuminates how dancing can be deeply implicated in cultural politics.

Furthermore, *Modern Moves* demonstrates how hybridized American social dancing has been for decades, despite historical and contemporary discourses that have segregated our dance worlds. To echo dance scholar Susan Manning's thoughts with regard to American concert dance, there are many new histories to be written once we stop seeing dancing strictly in black and white.[56] Although this study does focus on racially and/or ethnically separate dance communities, the dancing it brings to life is decidedly hybrid—moving between, back and forth, and among these diverse groups of people during the first decades of the twentieth century in Manhattan.

Mr. Vaughn's Dancing Class, the Tenderloin

Midnight, Thursday, September 1908

A large meeting hall perched over a packed basement bar. Neighbors and strangers huddle and mingle on the sidewalk outside and along the dark staircase, which leads to the pulsating room upstairs. In the corner of the hall, a piano and player vibrate and sway, sending the hundreds of men and women present into motion. Sounds of laughter, singing, and shouting radiate. Stylishly dressed men and women ring the dance space, chatting and taking brief respites from the dancing. Longstanding and newly found couples lurk in the darkest corners.

Josie and Charlie heavily tread their way up dusty stairs toward the pounding beat above. After a week of cleaning on her knees and cooking on her feet, Josie is ready to shake it off with friends. Charlie is even more spent than she is, which is hard to imagine, but he has to lug crates all day at the docks. The work is hard in New York, but pays better than it did in Charleston, for sure.

As usual, they are met by slaps on the back and shouts across the room: "Hey Josie!" . . . "There's Charlie!" . . . A dapper young man named James slides over to collect a 10¢ admission charge; he is a new protégé of Mr. Vaughn, who is nowhere in sight. At some point before the sun comes up, though, the dancing master will make an appearance in the same suit he always wears, complete with a carnation on his lapel. Never seen him give a lesson; never seen him dance, in fact.

Charlie's ears tell him that Leroy is at the keys. That man could rag anything and everything—from waltzes to cotillions—but "good-time" music was his calling. The circular crowd echoes his rhythms and frames whoever wants to *enter the vibrant space created by the music. The ring is crammed with pairs of dancers, and yet there always seems to be room for another couple. Scanning the space, Charlie sees new-fangled moves and old favorites merge and collide across time and space. Jaunty turkey trots in the middle of a rowdy schottische; cake-walking comics in every corner. All right alongside sleek new moves he had never seen. For every move there is a sound, and for every sound, a movement, as sonic and physical energy fuel one another.*

Josie looks on from the doorway, but Leroy spies her through a break in the crowd. She pretends not to see him—so he hollers for Josie: "grab that dance partner of yours and get in here." The circle immediately opens and pulls her and then Charlie in. He grabs her tight around the waist as he leads her into a galloping and swooping two step around the room, weariness melting away with just a few bars of the ragged music. His feet urge hers into bouncing pitter-patters, right then left, around the room. After a round or two, Josie nudges Charlie away while giving him a playful smile. He immediately releases her, waiting to see what she has planned. She starts with a pose—hands perched on her hips and legs akimbo under a slightly raised skirt.

Then her body reaches back homeward and she finds steps she saw her mother and aunts do at prayer meetings and Lucille's jook house. The movements—shuffling, reaching, shaking, and stomping—no longer seem to have specific names, just firm imprints of place and time. Charlie, on the other hand, does the cross-over turns he saw someone do last week at another "dance class." But he ends with a really old dance he had seen his grandfather do—a buzzard lope—with arms stretched wide and a languorous, undulating torso. "Give it to her, Daddy," James calls out cheekily from the sidelines.

Charlie reaches out for Josie, to return to their syncopated galloping around the floor, but Leroy suddenly slows everything down. No one could keep up that pace for long. Charlie wraps his arms around Josie, to catch his breath and reconnect. She wraps hers right around him too. For a moment they just wait, while swaying softly to the music, as Leroy finds his way toward a melody. This time it is a drag, one they had heard back in Charleston, but not much in New York since arriving. Without noticing, both start lifting their feet and inching across the space—hip to hip, thigh to thigh, cheek to cheek, until Josie decides to rest her head on his shoulder. Charlie leads them in a few strides to a quiet corner where they can have a little more room to move. Gently, he nudges them apart—still swaying in tandem. He keeps Josie's hand as she begins to swivel and kick softly, matching the accents of the music. Charlie mimics her smooth, dreamy movements and adds to them a percussive "Ah" with every kick she makes.

Then he reels Josie back in. This time they walk together, through the other couples who are pausing to enjoy the music. With each step, he adds a little more hip, and she adds a little more shoulder. It is like they are part of the band—soloing and accenting over Leroy's languid blues melodies, their bodies hearing, feeling, and responding in one continuous action. That is until the music cruelly stops and Leroy suddenly stands up: break time. Without skipping a beat, Josie and Charlie grab hands and sprint for the stairs, trying to get a head start on the crowd. Drinks are in the basement.

CHAPTER 1

⌒◟⌒

"Let's Go Back Home"

The Slow Drag, Black Migration, and the Birth of Black Harlem

The Civil War's transformations in labor ushered in widespread altera-
tions to African American dancing practices at the end of the nineteenth century. Most significantly, they eventually brought African
American group dancing movements into the closed couple hold, derived
from European American ballroom dancing traditions. Over time, a new
approach to dancing emerged, accompanied by blues music, that transformed sensual group dancing (from the plantation era) into sexualized
couple dancing in African American communities across the United States.
In this chapter, I focus on the slow drag, a key dance of this new era of
African American social dancing, as a touchstone for understanding the
black migration experience in early twentieth-century New York.

The slow drag, a partner dance that was transported to New York City by
hundreds of thousands of Southern black migrants during the first decades
of the twentieth century, represented home for these displaced men and
women—more specifically, it represented the rural homes they left behind
to carve out better, safer lives. (See Fig. 1.1) In addition, this dance's improvisational structure enabled migrants to construct a new sense of home for
themselves in Manhattan, built from a combination of embodied memories
and new urban dance movements. Together these memories and movements helped create a "home" for migrants that inspired feelings of belonging in their new environs, and thus a much needed sense of community and
identity. In this way, the slow drag was a tool deployed by new arrivals in

Figure 1.1 Likely Juke Joint Dancers, 1930s. (https://musiqology.wordpress.com/tag/dr-guys-musiqology/) (public domain).

their fight to survive under challenging new conditions, in addition to also being a powerful source of physical pleasure, recreation, and escape.

During the 1920s and 1930s, a small group of younger artists within the Harlem Renaissance (the ironically self-identified "Niggerati", mentioned in the introduction), who were united in their rejection of black elitism, saw in the slow drag a symbol of "authentic" blackness that could represent "low" Harlem to the world. They believed that the essence of what was uniquely African American resided in folk practices, which should be the basis of black artistic expression as well as modern black identity formation.[1] As a folk practice, the slow drag was publicly celebrated by these artists for its embodiment of "real" black experience, in their plays, books, and art.[2] Black migrants, Southern culture, and folklore were to be embraced and mined—not ignored, which they felt was happening among the older generation of Harlem Renaissance leaders at the time. The younger artists feared that post-migration urban life was quickly diluting and standardizing black culture.[3] To combat processes of assimilation, they used dances like the slow drag to assert a black distinctiveness within American culture.[4]

Thus, for many within Manhattan's black communities, dance was a means of empowerment, but for very different reasons. The new migrants were seeking amusement and comfort, whereas the younger generation of Harlem Renaissance leaders pursued recognition of and respect for black culture and the black working classes more specifically. They were fighting together, yet separately, for belonging and citizenship in white-dominated America, which required complex negotiations of longstanding black stereotypes and emerging constructions of black identity. For both groups, dancing was a crucial means of pursuing their goals.

And yet, during this same period when dancing was a central part of empowerment efforts by many African Americans, black dancing practices became the basis of popular commercial products of the ballroom dance industry, as was discussed in the introduction and will be again addressed in later chapters. For example, raucous ragtime era dances that began in African American communities were simplified and stripped of many of their distinguishing elements in order to render them "safe" for white consumption. The slow drag, however, escaped such treatment—or at least, a dance called the slow drag never attained mass popularity among European Americans during this time. It remained in black communities, creating a bridge from rural to urban, South to North, and past to present. That said, as I will discuss, the slow drag might have influenced—depending on whose origin story one gives credence to—the creation of the foxtrot, the most popular dance of this era that continues to be practiced today around the world.

To illustrate these arguments, this chapter begins with an analytical description of the slow drag and a discussion of its hybridity. [5] Afterward, it explores this dance's role in black migrant resettlement experiences and how a subgroup of young artists associated with the Harlem Renaissance responded to the dance through their creative work. The conclusion addresses the slow drag's potential relationship with the American ballroom dance industry of the period.

HYBRID DANCING

The slow drag was a partner dance that was border-crossing and blurring on many levels—genre, geography, and race, in particular. It emerged in the Southern U.S. among working-class African Americans during the late nineteenth century, parallel to the rise of jook houses and honky-tonks, and was brought into northeastern cities as black migration increased exponentially in the twentieth century.[6] It could not be confined to just one genre of music as it might accompany blues, ragtime, jazz, and "lowdown" music of all kinds. Importantly, the slow drag merged African American and European American dancing into one dance form, much like the cakewalk did on stages at the end of the nineteenth century. The resulting hybrid dance animated black communities and propelled ongoing efforts toward greater respect and rights during the early twentieth century.

The slow drag went by many names over the several decades of its popularity, including lowdown dancing, blues dancing, walking, and grinding. Among African Americans, though, it was usually called a slow drag or slow grind. As might be assumed, one quality that distinguished it from other dancing of the period was its slowness.[7] It was the dancing that accompanied African American popular music when the tempo dropped. There was not really a basic step per se; dancers might traverse the floor with dragging steps or they might pivot and sway in one place. What was consistent though was that the dance bonded the dancing couple in intense ways.

It was an exceedingly accessible dance. Dancers walked, slid, dragged, stamped, and paused—all pretty easy movements to do. What made it exhilarating was how dancers sequenced these options in response to the music and their partners' movement choices. Harlem Renaissance author Langston Hughes once described a slow-dragging couple as follows: "A tall brown boy in a light tan suit walked his partner straight down the whole length of the floor and, when he reached the corner, turned leisurely in one spot ... then they recrossed the width of the room, turned slowly, repeating themselves, and began again. ...."[8] Here we can see how simple walking could be combined with turning to create a dynamic experience for the movers.

In addition, period observers frequently commented that the dancers seemed to be barely moving.[9] This is certainly shown to be the case in the blues singer Bessie Smith's short film *St. Louis Blues* (1929) in which dancers wrapped their arms around one another tightly and rocked in one place on the dance floor. (See Fig. 1.2) This dancing sequence looks more like a syncopated hug than anything else. Through these two examples, it is clear that the slow drag could involve both dramatic traversals and/or stationary undulations—thus it could vary greatly in terms of its use of space.

The slow drag was a dance that closely bonded one person to another, rather than individuals to the larger group—which was a dramatic shift from the collective dancing that had figured prominently in Southern social life.[10] Harlem Renaissance writer Claude McKay described one dancing couple as "an exercise of rhythmical exactness for two. There was no motion she made that he did not imitate ... smacking palm against palm, working knee between knee, grinning with real joy. They shimmied breast to breast, bent themselves far back and shimmied again. ... They were right there together neither going beyond the other."[11] Here McKay demonstrates how connected dancers could become through their shared interpretations of the music.

As an extension of this bonding, dancers also separated from one another while slow dragging, thus creating important moments of shared movement innovation. These solo sections could last a few counts or several bars. Each couple would decide in the moment if they were going to solo in tandem or independently. In all cases, though, their soloing provided a

Figure 1.2 Dance Scene from the film *St. Louis Blues*, 1920s. Bessie Smith, film stills: *St. Louis Blues*, directed by Dudley Murphy (New York: RCA Phototone, 1929) (public domain).

type of variation from the slow drag's walking. It was here that individual and couple-based creativity were allowed to flourish. Hughes describes: "a long, tall, gangling gal stepped back from her partner, adjusted her hips, and did a few easy, gliding steps all her own before her man grabbed her again."[12] His writing helps us picture how new dance steps were created and dispersed through the slow drag's fairly open improvisational structure.

During these shared solos, dancers drew from their personal dance repertoires that were strongly influenced by where they had lived. Older and newer African American dance forms from specific places were merged and combined in exciting ways. Arm gestures could be reminiscent of jook house dances like the turkey trot, while leg actions could reference old plantation dances like the cakewalk—right alongside a new style of heel stomp invented that evening. This was described by another Harlem Renaissance writer, Wallace Thurman in his essay on dance in Harlem: "Negro cabarets in northern centers were a sort of clearing house where the Negroes from southern plantations and Mississippi levee camps merge their unsophisticated, semi-primitive dance music and dance tunes with the current northern output." Dancers would also "attempt to contribute something new to the evening's fun, some tricky foot shuffle or rhythmic body movement which had long been in vogue in their part of the country but which was as yet unknown in their new environment."[13] In this way, geographic spaces were traversed creatively, while time constraints were unheeded in these solo-dancing moments. Dancers unknown to each other could see from each others' dancing how much they had in common, or not, in terms of background. Through such cycling and recycling of movement, dancers placed themselves firmly within a shared African American movement tradition and, by extension, an African diasporic culture.[14]

The slow drag was one of the first closed couple dances in America with strong African American influences. According to music scholars John Szwed and Morton Marks, prior to this dance's emergence, slaves and former slaves enjoyed contra dances, square dances, cotillions, quadrilles, and occasionally even the waltz—all of which were considered to be European or European American dances. (See Fig. 0.1, introduction) Szwed and Marks are careful to point out, though, that all these dance forms were used flexibly, with African-derived dance steps inserted, like juba and buck dancing.[15] Similarly, later in the nineteenth and early twentieth centuries, two steps and schottisches were adapted by African Americans. What is unique about the slow drag, however, is that it is not a European, African, or American dance with a few nontraditional steps inserted; it is a new dance that used a European dance couple formation with African-derived movements as will be discussed shortly.

Despite being unique in structure, the slow drag shared a somewhat porous boundary with several dance forms, in particular the cakewalk and country/square dances practiced within black communities. As discussed in the introduction, the cakewalk was a nineteenth-century dance that originated in slave parodies of the grand marches of European American ballrooms. (See Fig. 0.2, introduction) Cakewalkers deployed angular limbs, playful facial expressions, rhythmic footwork, strutting, and the frequent use of props. Interestingly, this style of dancing appears at times in descriptions of the slow drag. In Scott Joplin's *Treemonisha* (1910), a song called "A Real Slow Drag" closes his self-described "ragtime opera." The extant score includes dance instructions, which Joplin wrote himself (according to biographer James Haskins), that describe many movements that are much more like a cakewalk than a slow drag.[16] Dancers are told to salute their partners, march, hop, skip, and prance. This example suggests that period participants might not have recognized firm distinctions between the slow drag and the cakewalk—or perhaps that Joplin didn't expect his audiences to do so.

Another dance form that shared blurred boundaries with the slow drag was its predecessor country or square dancing (also known as barn dancing).[17] Willie Thomas, a blues musician who was interviewed for the book project *Conversations with the Blues*, felt that the main difference between blues dances like the slow drag and square dances was the tempo.[18] He noted that slower music meant more time for enjoying the spaces between the beats with torso undulations and sliding feet, whereas faster tunes kept dancers focused externally on where they were headed and where the other dancers were. Another blues musician interviewed in the same book, Eddie Boyd, claims that the slow drag was created simply as a result of musicians slowing the tempo down at country dances when participants got tired. These comments indicate that dance genre divides were not terribly important in such contexts, at least not to musicians.

In addition, the slow drag crossed many music genre boundaries. Ragtime, blues, and early jazz could all accompany this kind of couple dancing, as long as the tempo was slow. Nonetheless, music researcher Paul Oliver has asserted that the slow drag is most typically associated with the blues. "With the popularization of the blues, as both song form and dance, slow dragging became increasingly evident at black dances. The beat of the blues, and its frequent use of medium and slow tempos were ideally matched by the shuffle, rock, and drag dances."[19] And yet, the first sheet music to mention the existence of the slow drag, the *Sunflower Slow Drag,* was published by *ragtime* composers Scott Joplin and Scott Hayden in 1901. As might be expected, the tune itself sounds like ragtime, not blues. Furthermore, close readings of Harlem Renaissance writing by a variety of younger authors show that social dancing to jazz music of the 1920s often matches the movements associated with the slow drag.[20]

Besides operating within and between other dance and music practices, the slow drag offered practitioners a link between rural and urban, as well as Northern and Southern spaces. As mentioned, this dance was created in the Southern states during the latter decades of the nineteenth century. It was a working-class practice that developed in rural jook houses and honky-tonks of the semi-urban South.[21] During the first two decades of the twentieth century, it was brought to the North's urban centers in the embodied repertoires of black migrants seeking a better life than was possible in the post-Civil War Southern U.S. Within the context of migration from known to unknown, one of the few things that migrants could easily bring with them was their dancing, which provided an important bridge across geographic differences for this transitioning generation.

Yet the most significant way that the slow drag crossed borders was its combination of dance traditions from two culture groups, European American and African American. Thurman himself called the social dancing of this period "miscegenated prodigies with the Negro characteristics tending to dominate."[22] As mentioned, the slow drag combined a European American couple formation with dance movements drawn from African American group dancing of earlier periods—such as shoulder shakes, hip punches, angular limbs, and animated facial expressions. Interestingly, this analysis matches with Samuel Floyd and Marsha Reisser's views on ragtime *music*: that it had a white form but black melody, lyrics, and rhythms.[23] Unlike performances of the nineteenth-century quadrille or waltz by African Americans, the slow drag was a new creation—not an adaptation or appropriation.

This particular manifestation of embodied and dynamic hybridity would have long-lasting consequences for African American dance, culture, and people as well as stereotypes of them. The slow drag put hip movements from black group dances into a European ballroom relationship—what playwright George Houston Bass has poignantly called "a liberation of pelvic motion."[24] The result looked and felt like sexual coupling in a way that did not have precedence in recorded African American, or European American, dance history. Jazz historians Marshall and Jean Stearns wrote in 1966 that African dances prior to the slave trade did not have much physical contact between partners and that touching your partner's waist was considered obscene.[25] It is likely that this view remained largely unchanged during the plantation period, when slaves would have been exposed to few European-derived dances that involved a closed couple hold—only the waltz starting in the early to mid-nineteenth century, just a few decades before slavery ended.

Dance sociologist Katrina Hazzard concurs that it was the transition from the rural jook house to urban honky-tonks that finally transformed African American group-based dancing into partner dancing and thus cemented the relationship between sexuality and black social dancing. She writes that "hip-shaking and pelvic innuendo were now more of a statement to one's partner than to one's community."[26] The result offered dancers "a tremendous sex stimulation," according to Harlem Renaissance writer and dance anthropologist Zora Neale Hurston.[27] This shift, however, had serious consequences in terms of black stereotypes of the period. By bringing hip shaking—among other sensual movements—into a closed couple relationship, the slow drag fueled period assumptions about inherent black lasciviousness and hypersexuality, when viewed by outsiders.

In other words, the outside influence of European American dancing and its closed couple formation helped to support a longstanding association among white people between sex and black dancing—and by extension black people. Surprisingly, the expressions of sexual desire that have often led to the moral and aesthetic rejection of black dancing in white America for over a century were not part of the African American dance tradition prior to the Civil War. Instead, they were the result of a merging of black and white dancing traditions within the slow drag and dances like it. When sensuality morphed into sexuality on the dance floor as a result of a merging of these dance traditions, it was African Americans alone who bore the brunt of the political consequences. Yet, for African Americans, social dancing was not only about demonstrating sexual desire; it also offered them opportunities to create a home away from home.

DANCING TO BELONG

Despite its widespread practice and compelling history, the slow drag rarely appears in dance histories of any kind.[28] As mentioned in the introduction, most scholars of African American dance history jump from the cakewalk to the Charleston, and most social dance historians jump from the two step to the one-step. And yet, the slow drag was kin to both the cakewalk and Charleston and occurred on the same dance floors as two steps and one-steps. Its absence from our dance histories can in part be explained by its lack of commercialization. The slow drag wasn't captured in dance manuals; nor did performers tour the continent glamorizing it. It remained the "home cooking", so to speak, of African American dance of this period. And yet, it was a key part of competing empowerment efforts by different black communities in New York City during the early twentieth century.

From new migrants to young Harlem Renaissance artists, black working-class social dancing was a site of subtle and not so subtle political action.[29] It was how men and women performed who they thought they were and who they wanted to be seen as.[30] The body, at this time, was viewed as a potent site of performativity in black communities. Black fiction of the 1920s shows us how dance—in tandem with skin color, clothes, and manners—could demonstrate a person's class status. While some scholars have looked at the ways in which dancing negotiated *racial* identity among African Americans, here I want to explore its simultaneous relationship with *class* politics within New York City during the early twentieth century. In particular, as we will see, the slow drag enabled the construction and contestation of status during a volatile time in African American history when modernity's growing urbanization and industrialization imposed new forms of labor-based enslavement and burgeoning racism threatened livelihoods and lives.

For black migrants, social dancing was a response to their living and working conditions in New York. It offered them a space of freedom from overwhelming and backbreaking labor.[31] It provided them a means of expressing pain and finding moments of joy within their oppressive and, at times, violent circumstances. Most importantly, it presented them with a means of constructing community and, through it, identity.[32] A crucial aspect of this process was how social dancing symbolized and constructed "home" for these migrants. Drawing on the theorizations of sociologists and performance studies scholars, as well as the words of several artists who worked in Harlem during its Renaissance, this section shows that the slow drag facilitated black migrants' connection to an imagined home. Dance was one of the ways they mitigated and navigated their loss of grounding, safety, networks, family, and sense of self. In this way, it helped them pursue a means of integration and belonging in new environs.

Tera Hunter's historical research (1997, 2000) on the social lives of the South's urban black working classes of the late nineteenth and early twentieth centuries argues that dancing was a means of freeing the black working-class body from the oppression of harsh labor—that it signified freedom to African American men and women. Dancing offered freed slaves and their descendants a means of reclaiming their bodies symbolically from the slavery of the past and new forms of financial enslavement in the present. Her focus is the urban South, where the echoes of slavery could be felt strongly. In New York City, however, freedom from slavery

may not have been such a central focus. In this intense post-migration context, other needs might have taken precedence, like a need for emotional
expression and new identity formations through imagined connections
with home.

It is clear from Harlem Renaissance writings that dance certainly
served as an important emotional space for black migrants. Dancing's
pleasures enabled participants to find joy by escaping harsh living and
working realities; it also provided a means by which migrants could
acknowledge the pain and struggles of their current circumstances. Yet,
in post-migration locales, joy and pain were interconnected and had rich
symbolic value.[33]

Claude McKay's work, in particular, demonstrates migrants' complex
relationships with joy through his critical focus on the representation
of pain in embodied performance. His poem "Negro Dancers" portrays
how pain was the default emotion for movers until they were able to
discover some joy, in the moment, to express and share. He writes that
a band "drones out half-heartedly a lazy tune ... then suddenly a happy
lilting note is struck, the walk and hop and trot begin ... around the
room the laughing puppets spin to sound of fiddle, drum and clarinet,
dancing their world of shadows to forget. ... Dead to the earth and her
unkindly ways of toil and strife, for them the dance is the true joy of
life."[34] For McKay, dancing was a momentary escape from labor, hard-
ship, and oppression that enabled only fleeting, superficial expressions
of joy for participants.

Public representations of joy were problematic for other Harlem
Renaissance writers as well, many of whom emphasized the darker aspects
of Harlem life in their works. They saw joy as a mask for suffering or as
a demonstration of consent to oppression—or worse, as a sign that the
black working classes were not motivated to change their circumstances.
Langston Hughes, one of the key writers in this vein, did not shy away
from representing both the sadness and the violence that permeated
Harlem life at this time. In his poem "Song for a Banjo Dance," a dancer
is told to "shake your brown feet, honey" because the "Sun's going down
this evening—Might never rise no mo,'" while the "banjo's sobbing low."
Furthermore, his poem "Death in Harlem" demonstrates the violence that
could permeate black urban social dance spaces of this period. In this narrative poem, a character named Arabella is trying to seduce the Texas Kid
with her dancing, but when she briefly goes to the ladies room, another
woman named Bessie takes Texas onto the dance floor. This results in a
gun and knife being drawn and Bessie ending up dead on the floor of the

cabaret, while Texas takes yet another woman to bed that night. There is little joy in Hughes's representations of dancing.

At times, in fact, Hughes seems to resent the joy presented by some black performers, as he interpreted it as a misleading mask for their pain. His poem "Liars" criticizes those who "use words / as screens for thoughts / and weave dark garments / to cover the naked body / of the too white truth."[35] His "Minstrel Man" even queries how audiences could not see the soul-crushing suffering and pain behind jubilant black performances.[36] For Hughes, representations of joy that mask sorrow contribute to the oppression of black men and women as they deemphasize the pain that permeates their lives.

In addition to offering migrants a crucial space for emotional expression, albeit expression critiqued by several Harlem Renaissance writers, dancing provided black working- class men and women with a powerful means of establishing community and constructing identity in a new city—key needs for any migrant. Even in the 1920s, writers were already aware of this. Wallace Thurman wrote in 1927 that dance-based events were absolutely essential to the constitution of "low" Harlem, by which he meant the black working classes.[37] In a post-migration context, dance helped build such communities through its deployment of memory and remembrances of people and places left behind. Manhattan musician James P. Johnson recalled how, when he played for dance events during the 1910s, migrant dancers would often literally cry out for home while on the dance floor. He recalled to a reporter in 1959: "They were country people and they felt homesick." While dancing they would shout, "Let's go back home!"[38] Johnson's comments demonstrate how migrant dancers would call on the past to navigate the present. They constructed their sense of community and self through intentional linkages between North and South, then and now.

According to sociologist Paul Gilroy, under the conditions of migration, identity and belonging become no longer tied to a specific residence and become reliant on memory.[39] Expressions of memory in the form of stories, cooking, and behavior (for example) become key to identity-formation processes in migrants' new homes as a means of generating a feeling of belonging. In fact, in some African American migrant homes, foods associated with the South were called "letters from home," according to Katrina Hazzard.[40] Dance, of course, was especially well suited to remembrance processes for migrants, given that memory is inherently embodied and sensual.[41] We access memories of past occurrences through how they made us feel at the time. In this way, the slow drag could be more than an emotional outlet for them; through its frequent opportunities for individual soloing, it provided a space for migrants to remember their past as a means of reestablishing ties with the South and with other African American people in the United States.

Constructions of home are central to how migrants anywhere establish a sense of belonging and develop new identities for themselves. Sociologist Anne-Marie Fortier argues that "homing"—the work of establishing a feeling of home—is dependent on memory and the body's manifestations of it.[42] Home in this instance is not a fixed location—like an origin point or clear destination—but a construction in process that is reliant on our reclaiming of actions and objects that have the feeling of home, as we imagine it.[43] Home for black migrants in New York City could be embodied through many aspects of their lived experiences, including dancing, food, music, and religious expression; through these they could reclaim a sense of belonging—both to the past and present.

The slow drag, however, was not just a time machine; dancers were not trying to nostalgically live in an earlier time. Yes, this dance enabled dancers to call up movements associated with the past that were tied to specific places, people, and events, but it also combined these past dances with contemporary urban movement practices—such as the closed couple formation, references to sexual coupling, and new dance moves encountered in Manhattan. In other words, given its somewhat open improvisational structure, the slow drag offered a permeable border between past and present. It could evoke home defined as "the South" or a specific hometown, for example, while it could also connect dancers with their new home and feelings of modernity, urbanity, and contemporaneity. Past/present, new/old, and rural/urban were not exclusive notions; they coexisted in the slow drag. Such dance-based constructions of self and community, in the wake of dislocation, were crucial to the survival of new migrants.[44] In one evening they could move back and forth between the present and past, simultaneously remembering home and establishing a new one.

In this way, social dancing in black migrant communities served as a means of historical writing. A sense of history was grounded in a sense of home, and both could be expressed through movement. In his article on the plantation ring shout—a sacred improvisational circle dance that involves shuffling feet, clapping hands, and, when the spirit moves, solo dancing—Sterling Stuckey states: "The body very nearly was memory. ..."[45] Among slaves and their descendants who could not read or write, the body was where memories were housed. Bodily movement enabled recollection and historical connections to be made and maintained. In this way, dancing functioned as a form of oral history, an assertion of past experience and knowledge in the face of attempted erasure.

The issue of home was a complex one, however, given that migrants had left the South out of necessity—fleeing rampant violence, poverty, and racism. Sterling Brown's 1927 poem "Cabaret" critiques how black performers were forced by the entertainment industry of the time to embody and exoticize the South for audiences.[46]

> The chorus sways in.
> The 'Creole Beauties from New Orleans'
> (By way of Atlanta, Louisville, Washington, Yonkers,
> With stop-overs they've used nearly all their lives)
> Their creamy skin flushing rose warm,
> *O, le bal des belles quarterounes!*
> Their shapely bodies naked save
> For tattered pink silk bodices, short velvet tights,
> And shining silver-buckled boots;
> Red bandannas on their sleek and close-clipped hair;
> To bring to mind (aided by the bottles under the tables)
> Life upon the river—

Whether or not they actually grew up in Southern locations, African American performers were expected to wear bandanas, sing nostalgically of river life, and express a longing for home sweet home in Dixie. Strikingly, his poem juxtaposes such references with statements about the cruel living conditions in the South that had led to migration in the first place: serfdom, flooding, and violence.

> *(In Arkansas,*
> *Poor half-naked fools, tagged with identification numbers,*
> *Worn out upon the levees,*
> *Are carted back to the serfdom*
> *They had never left before*
> *And may never leave again)*

In this way Brown reminds readers that home, when referenced by choice through social dancing, was often a nostalgic construction that neglected the dangers that permeated migrants' prior lives. Nonetheless, dancing was a powerful symbol that forged connections that had been strained and broken. Such linkages were essential to migrants for building a greater sense of belonging in a new city.

For this reason, black migrant dancing was a step toward self-empowerment that helped define identities. Through its nostalgic cycling and recycling, this dancing asserted an African American heritage *and* its value simultaneously. It also performed a refusal to assimilate—despite the European influences on the movement. Dancers were not striving to perfect the gracefulness of a waltz, the prissiness of a quadrille, or the jauntiness of a two step (as black elites were, see chapter four). Instead, they were perfecting an amalgamation of rural and urban African American dance history and by extension culture—at a time when black men and women were widely assumed to have been stripped of all connection to their history and African-based culture by the slave trade and centuries of forced illiteracy.[47] Through their nostalgic dancing, migrants mitigated the loss of community connection that they felt so keenly, as they quietly pursued increased citizenship rights precisely when segregation was becoming more established legally and public racial violence threatened their safety.

EXOTIC *HARLEM*

As mentioned, many of the political and social leaders of Harlem, as well as the Harlem Renaissance movement itself, were not enamored with the slow drag. For many of them it represented all that they had overcome and were trying to erase from the memory of white America—poverty, ignorance, rurality, etc. That said, not all participants in the Harlem Renaissance viewed this dance negatively. While sharing a commitment to uplifting the race, the self-proclaimed "Niggerati" chose very different tactics than those who were driving the movement. Rather than pursuing greater status based on adherence to white middle-class norms and values, this small collective of younger artists chose instead to embrace black popular culture—including social dancing—as an example of "authentic" blackness.[48]

Artists in this subgroup (such as Langston Hughes, Zora Neale Hurston, Wallace Thurman, and Claude McKay) wanted, through their creative works, to reveal to the larger public "real" black culture and people. In their minds, these were best exemplified by the black working classes. The generational divide that distinguished this group from other Harlem Renaissance artists and writers is perhaps best demonstrated by the production and reception of a Broadway play called *Harlem* (1929), which was written by Thurman, in collaboration with journalist and playwright William Jourdan Rapp. This dramatic work featured the slow drag.[49] (See Fig. 1.3) In this case, however, the intention to celebrate the black working classes and their practices led to an inadvertent exoticizing of the subject matter that ultimately supported period black stereotypes and contributed to the closing of the play.

EDWARD A. BLATT *presents*

"HARLEM"

THE THRILLING PLAY OF NEW YORK'S BLACK BELT

By William Jourdan Rapp and Wallace Thurman   *Staged by* Chester Erskin

Harlem! . . . The City that Never Sleeps! . . . A
Strange, Exotic Island in the Heart of New York! . . .
Rent Parties! . . . Sweetbacks! . . . Hincty Wenches!
Number runners! . . . Chippies! . . . Jazz Love! . . .
Primitive Passion! . . . Voodeo! . . . Hot-stuff
Men! . . . Uproarious Comedy! . . . Powerful Drama!

APOLLO THEATRE
NOW PLAYING
Evenings Best Seats: $1.00; $1.50; $2.00; $2.50; and $3.00
Popular priced Matinees Wednesday and-Saturday

Figure 1.3 *Harlem* Playbill, 1920s (above and facing page). Paul Meltsner and Wallace
Thurman, *Playbill*: "*Harlem*: The Thrilling Play of New York's Black Belt" (New York: Apollo
Theatre, 1929). Courtesy of the Yale Collection of American Literature, Beinecke Rare Book
and Manuscript Library, Yale University (public domain).

HARLEM

What the New York Critics think of "HARLEM"

"There is more dramatic life in 'Harlem' than in three-quarters of the theatrical goods presently on display."
—George Jean Nathan, in Judge

▼

"The finest play since 'Porgy' . . . 'Harlem' packs a series of wallops, an abundance of compelling moments and so much of first rate play acting that it belongs high on the current stage menu."
—Walter Winchell, The Graphic

▼

"Something worth going to see and something worth thinking about afterward."
—Robert Littell, Eve. Post

▼

" 'Harlem' is a knockout; a glamorous, fast and colorful entertainment."
—Robert Coleman, The Mirror

▼

"High up near the top of Three Star Specials in dramatic wares is 'Harlem.' "
—Whitney Bolton, Morning Telegraph

Figure 1.3 (Continued)

Harlem arrived at the end of the 1920s after countless jazz musicals had featured African American dancing and dancers, but few of the realities of black American life. To counteract this, the producers cast the play almost entirely with nonprofessional performers and focused on a fairly simple story—a migrant family struggling to survive in New York City without losing their familial bonds and values from their prior home. Yet, the play dramatizes a rift between an older generation that valued community, religion, and family and a younger generation enamored of blues and jazz, always seeking pleasure and fun. These tensions were revealed through, among other things, an extended rent-party scene, which involved a great deal of sexualized slow dragging.[50] It was this scene that inspired the majority of commentary and criticism from the public and critics.

Thurman clearly wanted to incite debate about the black working classes with this play—in both black communities and America as a whole. Around the time of *Harlem*'s original production in New York, he drafted promotional articles to explain his artistic and political intentions to the public, clarifying why he wrote the play the way he did. In these pieces, he conveyed that it was important to him that his characters be "recognizably human," so they could "educate" audience members about the "concrete Negroes he has seen in the subway or [read] about." In addition, he said that he deliberately crafted characters that would not be "white folks' niggers."[51] Here Thurman was seeking to ameliorate American race relations—not by celebrating the talent of a few—but by revealing a perhaps previously unknown world to white America. He thought that knowledge would lead to interest and, perhaps later, to acceptance and respect.

Accounts of the play's dancing by critics at the time repeatedly emphasized the sense of "abandon" it created. Such responses were perhaps an indication of the explicit sexuality of the movement, which might have been interpreted as an *abandonment* of morality, restraint, propriety, reason, and control. Thurman's play directions tell the actors to

> . . . cement themselves together with limbs lewdly intertwined. A couple is kissing. Another is dipping to the floor and slowly shimmying belly to belly as they come back to an upright position. A slender, dark girl with wild eyes and wilder hair stands in the center of the room supported by the strong lithe arms of a long-shoreman. Her eyes are closed. Her teeth bite her lower lip. Her trunk is bent backwards until her head hangs below her waist and all the while the lower portion of her body is quivering like so much agitated Jell-O.[52]

Later in the script, Thurman reflects on the intended effect of the scene: "The dancing is lewdly abandoned and accompanied by much shouting. It is a virtual saturnalia of desire."[53] Although he does not use explicit language related to animality and primitivism here, as other authors did at times during this period, his choreographic choices validated stereotypes that would have adhered sexuality to blackness through movement, for white audience members especially.

This choice was a deliberate one, as Thurman apparently heightened the sexuality of the slow drag scenes in order to draw the attention of the press and increase box office returns.[54] During the development phase, producers forced Thurman (and Rapp) to push the slow drag scene to more of an extreme in order to satisfy audiences accustomed to flashy and sexy jazz musicals. So, they "decided to build their play around a [rent] party so as to give it the 'show qualities' that Broadway had indicated were needed for success."[55] The investors understandably wanted the show to make money and were perhaps less interested in Thurman's political goals. The highly sexualized result certainly drew attention to the play, but it also exoticized and eroticized the dancing of the black working classes represented therein.[56] Langston Hughes reported to another Harlem Renaissance poet, Arna Bontemps, in 1962 that the final result displeased Thurman immensely, so much that he felt the play was no longer his own work.[57]

Amplifying the sexuality may have led to a tidal wave of attention for the play, but it also led to its demise, as it inspired a multi-city letter-writing campaign by concerned black citizens who did not want their race represented in such a "denigrating" manner. The sexuality expressed in period black musicals and nightclub shows was not as much of a concern, evidently, as these kinds of performances did not claim to represent "real" African Americans in the way that Thurman's play did. Censors were repeatedly sent to productions in both Chicago and New York, and they requested revisions to the slow drag scene in particular. In the end, after a ninety-two show run on Broadway and successful tours to Detroit, Chicago, Toronto, and Los Angeles, *Harlem* was indeed shut down, mainly due to pressures from black elites. [58]

In his play, Thurman showcased the slow drag in a way that it had never been before and never likely would be again. Until this time, the dance had remained quietly within the quotidian realm, which is also how it was represented within the world of the play. It was not isolated, but integrated into the drama and deployed, not as entertainment, but as a means of delineating characters and furthering the plot. Thurman's portrayals, however, drew fire from all sides. European American audiences were not prepared for the slow drag, especially in exaggerated form with intense references to sexual coupling. Likewise, African American audiences were embarrassed to see the struggles of black migrants aired publicly, and they were concerned that the sexiness (exaggerated or not) of the dancing revealed to prying eyes would only reinforce longstanding stereotypes.

Here, as in so many Harlem Renaissance representations of the slow drag, the dance served as a form of folk art, meant to represent the raw artistic potential of African Americans. As such, it was a nostalgic construction, just as it was among New York City's black migrants. In *Harlem* (1929), though, the dance was used to hearken back to earlier in the century—given that by the time the play appeared, the slow drag had been in New York for decades. To many if not most black (or even white) elite audience members, it would have signified a past steeped in rurality, Southern-ness, primitivism, and a lack of civilization. During the 1920s, such qualities were inextricable from stereotypes about African American people, which was unfortunate given the stated progressive political aims of the original production. Nonetheless, the play did achieve its primary goal—it certainly did launch greater awareness of class differences in black communities.

DANCE INDUSTRY INTERVENTIONS

The slow drag, unlike its contemporary ragtime dances such as the turkey trot and one-step, never officially became part of the American ballroom industry's repertoire. It was never openly modified, codified, or commercialized. It is unclear why the dance escaped industry attention, except that it never really crossed over into European American social practices. Perhaps, from some perspectives, was it too sexualized or too black to be successfully "cleaned up" by white dance professionals? Maybe the name didn't capture the imagination? It is also possible that, because it wasn't footwork-based, the dance didn't lend itself to the ballroom industry's codification practices—a footprint map of a slow drag would have just looked like standing and walking. Slow drag dancers were connected from the knee up. It was the torso actions that really defined it, as well as the close relationship between partners—both of which were likely objectionable to the elite clients of ballroom dance professionals as well as very difficult to represent in a text

On the other hand, according to dance legend, blues *music* did inspire one of the most popular dances of the early twentieth century, the foxtrot—or at least one of the most popular versions of it. While there are many origin stories linked to this dance, the one that seems most relevant involved the famous modern social dancers Vernon and Irene Castle and their African American musical director James Reese Europe. The story goes that one night Europe was at the Castles' home and began playing "Memphis Blues" by

W. C. Handy for his own enjoyment.[59] Vernon heard the music and liked it, but found it too slow to dance to, at least at first. Castle eventually changed his mind and created a new dance product, which he called the Castle Foxtrot. The Castles later showcased their foxtrot in a musical called *Watch Your Step* in 1914, as well as a *Ladies Home Journal* article by Vernon Castle. The dance he described therein alternated between very slow steps and double time ones: "two slow steps (a glide, stride, or drag) followed by four quick ones (hop, kick, and stop)." As a whole, the Castle Foxtrot does not sound at all like an African American slow drag. And yet, the very slow steps that glide, stride, and drag are reminiscent of the slow drag's languid walk, as is the rhythmic play between the slow and quick steps described.

Importantly, these instructions describe the combination of a one-step with slow dragging movements—yet another hybrid creation. Vernon later told the *New York Herald* that the foxtrot is not really a new dance, "but had been danced by negroes, to his personal knowledge, for fifteen years." It seems likely that Castle is referring here to the slow drag, and not a foxtrot, which was not one of the original animal dances from African American communities. Perhaps Europe actually showed Castle the dance himself. Or maybe the Castles were already familiar with the slow drag through their dance experiences in New York City, which included occasional dance lessons with black professional performers.[60] In any case, in his dancing and commentary, Castle hints that the slow drag was likely the source of—or at least an influence on—his version of the foxtrot, which became a dominant iteration of this dance. This would mean that a (much abstracted) version of the slow drag, despite its low profile as a popular dance, eventually became the most widely practiced African American dance of the twentieth century.[61]

The slow drag, nestled within a version of the foxtrot, then, has likely traveled the world and attended many Western wedding celebrations and high school proms. Furthermore, reborn as a foxtrot, it became and has remained at the heart of the global ballroom dance industry throughout the twentieth century. This has been made possible, in part, by the foxtrot's connections with the blues, slow drag, and African Americans being forgotten or erased since the 1910s. The dance's associations with African American cultures were successfully hidden, despite Vernon Castle's public proclamations, from even contemporary practitioners—and even from dance historians since. Until I found the Castle quotes in the *New York Herald* and *Ladies Home Journal*, I myself, as a longtime social dancer and scholar of American popular dance, had no idea that this dance had any black connections. Given its appearance around 1914, several years after the ragtime era dances had first enjoyed popularity, it is possible that by then the ballroom industry had perfected its refinement processes and become more expert at controlling public dance discourses and thus perceptions.

Parallel with its radical refinement by the Castles into the foxtrot, the slow drag was openly embraced and in fact essential in African American communities across the nation—especially migrant ones. The foxtrot's popularity did nothing to diminish the slow drag's value to African Americans. Through its hybridity, the slow drag became a bridging dance for migrants that enabled them to remain connected with their prior home while endeavoring to forge a new one. Even though European partnering conventions were maintained in this dance, the movements themselves were derived from existing African American practices. These two contributions fused together came to embody modernity and urbanity in black communities.[62] In contrast, in New York City, among a small group within the Harlem Renaissance, the slow drag represented a rural past, cultural purity, and "the folk." In this way, simultaneously, the dance became a nostalgic representation of black authenticity that could be used tactically by these artists in citizenship efforts.

Interestingly, in both cases, the slow drag provided an important means of refusing assimilation into dominant white American culture. For migrants, it offered a vehicle for holding onto a black identity as they were moving into an alien environment that was overwhelmingly populated by people who looked like those who had terrorized them in the South. Simultaneously, the slow drag could also be a means of actualizing an African diasporic "racial feeling," to use Paul Gilroy's terminology, within a highly diverse black space.[63] Unlike the migrants, for the younger generation of Harlem Renaissance artists, folk forms such as the slow drag were used to confront the implicit, but common, Harlem Renaissance practice of elevating European-derived artistic values. While both groups were avoiding assimilation in their own ways, they were simultaneously seeking inclusion within America, on their own terms, through movement practices.

Even though they were not working in concert, New York's black migrants and the progressive sub-group of young Harlem Renaissance artists were both using the slow drag as a means of seeking greater empowerment through citizenship. Through its evocation of the South, this dance provided both groups with a means of valuing African American history and of grounding new articulations of modern black identity. The slow drag's repeated performance over time helped to strengthen a feeling of connectedness for New York's migrants and residents alike. In this way, it was a dance that helped mitigate the harsh impact of migration on black men and women. To them, it did not matter that the dance was actually an Afro-Euro-American hybrid dance form, only that it felt like home.

Jim's Place, the Tenderloin

Two A.M., Friday night/Saturday morning, October 1910

*A*rathskeller tucked just below a restaurant on West 35th Street near Broadway. A long flight of stairs leads into a raucous barroom. Toward the far back, a passageway opens onto a small dance floor ringed by crowded tables. A slightly elevated stage in the far corner features the evening's musical entertainment.

Glancing expectantly around the dark, smoky room, over the shoulders of her girlfriends from work in the shirtwaist factory, Lillian furtively scans for a partner. No one meets her eager gaze. In desperation she grabs one of her girlfriends and joins the other briskly moving couples on the dance floor. Neither girl looks at the other as they dance. Instead they focus on the young men standing at the edges of the dance floor. As Lillian expected, not two measures pass before a dashing pair pulls them apart.

Lillian's anonymous partner reaches for her waist, she grasps his shoulder, and their hands lock. After bouncing and rocking in place to the music, waiting for that ever-elusive beginning of the next phrase, they are off. They sway their shoulders and hips, left then right, in unison as their feet brush past one another, trying to keep up with the ragtime pianist's fingers. Step-together-step, step-together-step they go, barely landing on the pulse before the next bar begins. Soon they move in synchrony with the music, carving out wider and wider pathways to the left and right with rocking hips.

Lillian peeks up into her partner's eyes, but he watches the other couples, perhaps scouting new moves or watching vigilantly for any unexpected changes of direction. Ready for some fun, Lillian pertly inserts a slight backward kick at the *end of a phrase. Her partner smiles and slides a hand up to her shoulder blades. "Finally a turn . . . ," but before Lillian completes her thought, they begin whirling together, mapping out small circles in the spaces between their fellow dancers. Tightly gripping one another, cheek-to-cheek and chest-to-chest, they spin alternately left and then right.*

Their bodies remain pressed together after the turning stops, all the better to circle the crowded room with a few measures of skipping added to their two-step, double-time trotting on their tiptoes, and even some hops and foot-dragging slides to mark the end of a phrase. Lillian's favorite move, though, is halting midstream for a measure or two, forcing other couples to swerve to avoid them. During one such break, her partner suddenly leaps into a wide-limbed stance, fingers spread like claws. Lillian fearlessly mirrors his grizzly bear-like moves and turns around in a small circle, pitching herself from side to side. Seeing that she is game, her partner counters with his best turkey imitation: elbows flapping, feet flicking back every few steps, they circle in front of one another like agitated birds.

Once they resume their shared trotting, Lillian takes the time to gaze over the moves of the other dancers around her; they are wiggling and shaking their hips, shoulders, knees, and heads—hands clapping and slapping; no body part is left out. Then her eyes catch the movement on the raised platform where the small band—called Leroy's Boys—sits, or rather rocks, just a pianist, drummer, and a singer. The clatter of their heels alone was enough to electrify Lillian's limbs. The musicians' shoulders seem almost tied to their hips—punching, rocking, and sliding through the tune.

Riding high, Lillian decides to join in, emboldened by the knowledge that no one here knows her family or their friends from the synagogue. The next time she and her partner break away, instead of doing an animal dance, she rocks her hips and shoulders in opposite directions, upward and downward, then forward and backward. One body part follows the syncopations of the melody, while the other tries to capture the regular rocking of the pianist's bass line. Her head soon follows suit, bobbing first with and then against shoulder punches. Finally, mustering the courage to check her partner's reaction, she is relieved to find him laughing and rhythmically wiggling too. She steals his move, then he hers, and they challenge one another to move more wildly with each exchange. Gossiping and drinking nearby, Lillian's friends let loose shouts and whistles over the top of the piano music. What kind of trouble they would be in, if they did that at work!

By the time the pianist stops and the bartender calls for drinks, Lillian is exhausted and exhilarated. Flashing a quick smile to her partner, who had already grabbed another girl, she hobbles toward a chair. Lillian's friends barely wait for her to sit down before they rush over, hand her a beer, and demand the name of the dance she was just doing. After momentarily scanning the dense bar air for words, she laughs and proposes: "The Broadway wiggle?"

CHAPTER 2

༄

"A Colorful Nightmare"

Immigrant Ragtime Dancing
as Participatory Minstrelsy

For North American youth of almost any background, participating in African American dance forms is just part of growing up, or so it seems today. A century ago, however, such embodied cross-cultural adventures were only just becoming a widespread practice—one deeply linked with the emergence of ragtime dance and music in urban centers. To better understand this phenomenon, chapter two queries American youth dancing "black" during the ragtime era (1890s–1910s) through a specific case study: European immigrant youth in New York City. They were among the first to embrace ragtime dancing outside of black communities. My goal is to better understand how and why this historical moment launched cross-cultural dance exploration of this kind in America.

While ragtime certainly offered immigrant youth a means of release after a long day's labors and opportunities to socialize within their peer group, it was also intertwined with period cultural politics. As a symbol of modern American culture, ragtime drew these young men and women to it as a form of assimilation within their new homeland—much like the slow drag drew black migrants to it during this same period. But European immigrants and African American migrants sought belonging through very different ideals. What it meant to be American was a notion that was being actively constructed and intensely contested during this period, likely in reaction to the dramatic increase in immigration and migration. The predominant version of American identity in circulation valued whiteness over hybridity or any other racial category. Even though ragtime dancing was a hybrid dance form and strongly linked with African American culture, it was this "traditional" model of American identity (i.e., white) that ragtime most embodied for immigrant participants, as will be discussed here.

So how did ragtime come to be a symbol of modern American culture? As a hybrid dance form with both European and African influences, it was surely a controversial candidate for this role. This chapter suggests that it was through its connections with blackface minstrelsy that ragtime came to perform whiteness and thus American-ness for many participants. Through ragtime dancing, a new form of minstrelsy was launched, what I call "participatory minstrelsy." This new format substituted staged minstrelsy's seated spectators for performers who temporarily embodied markers of blackness through their own dancing to ragtime music. In this way, blackface minstrelsy did not die off during this period, but rather was given new life in a format that naturalized many of its original tenets in subtle ways. In other words, the legacy of blackface minstrelsy contributed to American youth's fascination with African American cultural practices throughout the twentieth century.

The chapter starts with an introduction to ragtime dancing, as well as the European immigrant youths who loved it. Then it addresses the history and practice of blackface minstrelsy, with an eye toward how its cultural work has been theorized in contemporary scholarship. Finally, it explores and explains how ragtime dancing operated like blackface minstrelsy, albeit in a much more subtle way. Aiding the assimilation efforts of immigrant youth, ragtime's participatory minstrelsy enabled these dancers to dodge their foreignness and stake a claim towards American-ness. Indeed, while relaxing with friends after work, ragtime dancers were able to shape their self-image and project who they wanted to be in the future.

RAGTIME AS RUPTURE

Ragtime dancing crystallized as a distinct social practice around the turn of the twentieth century. Sometimes called tough dancing, animal dancing, new dancing, halftime dancing, and modern dancing, this dance form was a complex of movement practices that accompanied ragtime music before World War I.[1] During this period, many individual dances waxed and waned in popularity. The cakewalk was the first formalized dance to ragtime music that briefly crossed over into mainstream European American dance practices in the 1890s. (See Fig. 0.2, introduction) It was followed by the "animal" dances (turkey trot, bunny hug, and so forth) during the early 1900s, which remained popular until World War I. This repertory was augmented by the so-called modern dances (one-step, foxtrot, and others) during the 1910s, which were adaptations of the earlier animal dances—as will be discussed in chapter three. In addition to these specifically named dances, there was a general movement style that was considered to be unique to ragtime dancing that involved syncopation, playfulness, torso undulation, and angularity, among other features. This style could even be applied to earlier European-derived dances, like the waltz and schottische, rendering them ragtime dances despite their nineteenth-century beginnings.

Of course, not everyone in America participated in ragtime dancing during this period. In fact, there was vociferous public criticism from many members of the middle classes, religious leaders, and professional dance teachers, who could not or would not accept ragtime's new bodily aesthetics. Such people associated this type of dancing with wanton sexuality, social vice, and delinquency among youth, and many worked to protect "nice young girls" from its perceived dangers.[2] One organization, in particular, led the way—New York's Committee of Fourteen (COF)—sponsoring extensive investigations of dance halls throughout the city, beginning just after 1900 and continuing for several decades. For the COF and other critics, ragtime was the embodiment of the dangerous changes that modernity was unleashing on American culture.

Despite the best efforts of its opponents, ragtime dancing was widely practiced among many different cultural groups, but everyone did not practice it the same way. There were profound regional, cultural, and class differences in the dancing in addition to inevitable changes over time. Ragtime dancing also meant something different to each specific group of participants because of their distinct dancing practices and histories. Nonetheless, there was a common style and repertoire that eventually came to be associated with ragtime during the first two decades of the twentieth century.

Ragtime dancing was a radical departure from the social dancing happening in New York prior to the turn of the century. Ragtime dancers held onto one another in close, intimate ways. All dancers improvised—both men and women. Participants made frequent use of gesture while dancing. They demonstrated boisterous movement qualities and angular bodylines. Finally, ragtime dancers engaged in a high degree of rhythmic play. In these ways, ragtime constituted a moment of rupture (i.e., discontinuity and transformation) within American dance history.[3]

During the ragtime era, the closed couple formation of late nineteenth-century European-style dancing became much more intimate.[4] This shift is evident in anti-dance reports that described how, when couples came in contact, their cheeks, arms, chests, and hips might be pressed together. One of the COF reports complained that, "Men and women held each other in a tight grasp, the women putting their arms right around the men. ... He [held] the woman right to him with both hands on her backside ... [there were] frequent hugs, 'feels' of breasts and posterior extremities."[5] The previous dance ideal was just the fingers of partners' hands delicately touching, with no torso contact whatsoever.

Further distinguishing ragtime dancing from earlier European American dance practices was its highly improvisational structure, which allowed for independent solo movements by both leader and follower—much like dancers did in the slow drag, as discussed in the prior chapter. Over the course of a single song, dancers could on numerous occasions break away from one another and make movement and timing choices individually, while retaining a partner connection with their eyes. A COF investigator reported that "some of the patrons ... turned themselves a loose [sic], and at intervals would stop and go through the most vulgar and suggestive motions."[6] Even though this particular investigator does not name the dance movements that were inserted, preferring instead to call them just "vulgar and suggestive," others indicate that the dances that filled out these solos often had animal names like the monkey glide, turkey trot, bunny hug, and grizzly bear. In addition to these recognized dances, there was a small arsenal of untitled embellishments—small kicks, hops, and foot stomps—that both men and women could add to their movements while still within a close embrace.

The animal dances in particular incorporated humorous gestures into ragtime dancing. In the turkey trot, dancers might flap their elbows; in the grizzly bear, they outstretched claw-like "paws" while rocking in a wide stance. In the bunny hug, they hopped while tightly embracing their partner's neck or perching paws under their chins. Of course, these are just the animal dances for which records remain. One can only imagine how many others were created spontaneously on dance floors across North America.

Ragtime dancers further animated their bodies with boisterous expressions of pleasure, desire, and playfulness. Their shoulders and hips moved as discrete units, providing an arena for rhythmic expression beyond the feet. Evidence of this can be found in a 1914 dance manual authored by the famous dancing couple Vernon and Irene Castle that delineated rules for so-called correct dancing. (See Fig. 3.3, chapter three) The famous couple reminds their readers *not* to "wiggle the shoulders," "shake the hips," "twist the body," "flounce the elbows," or "pump the arms."[7] These admonishments—which describe the animal dances quite well—suggest that ragtime dancers were incorporating rowdy movements of the hips and shoulders.

Further, ragtime dancers embodied angular lines as they moved across dance floors. The rocking and swaying that was integrated into traveling movements, such as the one-step and the two step, spread dancers' feet wide apart as they traveled, lowering their centers of gravity and creating a stronger sense of weight. This grounded bodily posture was adorned with surprisingly angular movements of the arms and legs, exemplified by the turkey trot and grizzly bear's jutting elbows, bent knees, and flexed feet. Furthermore, the pathways that couples carved out as they moved through space were similarly jagged; dancers abruptly switched directions, alternating between moving forward, sideways, and backward.

Even with the abundance of humorous gestures, the most characteristic feature of ragtime dance and music was its rhythmic play. Ragtime music was syncopated, and dancers as well as musicians incorporated sonic and visual accents on top of the music's regular pulse. Such accents—which could be embodied in spontaneous kicks, hops, dips, and stops—challenged the even beat of the bass line that undergirded the music. Together or as individuals, dancers could rhythmically meddle with the music's structure through their footwork, hip and shoulder movements, clapping hands, or arm gestures as they moved around the dance floor.

It is important to note, however, that some of ragtime's rupturous movement features would not have been completely unfamiliar to the European immigrant youths who are the focus of this chapter. For example, Eastern European Jewish folk dancing, like the folk dancing of many other European ethnic groups, shares a sense of play, the use of sonic accents (such as clapping and shouting), and a semi-structured improvisational style.[8] As a result of such similarities, ragtime dancing may have served as an important bridge between old and new worlds for Jewish and other immigrant groups.[9]

Despite these similarities, ragtime dancing radically differed from Jewish folk dancing both in terms of social context and movement vocabulary. No longer a multigenerational community event, ragtime offered immigrant youths a venue in which they could be free of many community standards of behavior. Dancers could touch each other publicly with more freedom and in unprecedented ways. Ragtime's movement qualities also projected a twentieth-century aesthetic of angularity and abruptness, in contrast to the roundness and smoothness of late nineteenth-century European dances that immigrants also danced in their ethnic communities. Unparalleled expressions of sexual desire and pleasure were made possible by the physical intimacy between dancing partners and the animated torsos that characterized the dance's style. Given these overwhelming differences, ragtime would have felt wholly modern and exciting to these young dancers.

HYBRID ORIGINS, BLACK ASSOCIATIONS

While group improvisation in Jewish immigrant dance may have supported a strong sense of community, as social historian Kathy Peiss has suggested, the individualized solo movements of ragtime dancing signaled independence, disorder, and even resistance. On a different level, ragtime dancing signified America and modernity to immigrant youth participants.[10] But which aspects of the practice facilitated those references? This section explores precisely how ragtime dancing facilitated the Americanization and modernization of these immigrant youth in Manhattan and suggests that racial associations were central to its significance.

Ragtime music, the inspiration for ragtime dancing, first appeared at the end of the nineteenth century in major cities of the American Midwest along the Mississippi River. Its earliest composers were African Americans like Scott Joplin, Ernest Hogan, and Joseph Lamb. Their music borrowed the structure of European-derived jigs and marches, but incorporated distinctly African American rhythms.[11] This music traveled first by way of musicians and later by way of sheet music into America's major urban centers of the period. According to James P. Johnson, a famous pianist of the period, New York embraced ragtime around the turn of the century, likely as a result of the general public's interest in the cakewalk.[12]

Ragtime also moved westward, causing some dance writers to mistakenly view the "Wild West" as its birthplace.[13] In fact, some period dance writers pointed to San Francisco's Barbary Coast, a key port for the American West, as ragtime dancing's site of origin.[14] One modern dancing manual told readers that "[t]he Turkey Trot (name to delight posterity) raced eastward from San Francisco in a form to which the word 'dancing' could be applied only by exercise of courtesy."[15] Although not as racially loaded a locale as the American South, San Francisco nonetheless had potent racial associations during the 1910s.

This location signified to American readers a crossroads, where eastern and western cultures precariously converged into a cacophony of racial and ethnic groups—African American, Chinese American, Native American, Mexican American, and "white" American. *Modern Dance Magazine* wrote of this far western city: "Before it was legislated into sobriety, the turbulent Barbary Coast was a colorful nightmare. . . . It set a wicked tempo to tempt the adventurous."[16] In this passage, "colorful nightmare" suggested dangerous racial mixing and "wicked tempo," the presence of African Americans specifically, given period black associations with rhythm.[17] Thus, when dance writers linked ragtime dancing with San Francisco's Barbary Coast, they also attributed it to a non-white space.

Ragtime music may have begun among African American musicians who were borrowing European American song structures, but it was enjoyed by audiences of many backgrounds. People danced to ragtime since its inception in the Midwest, but it did not coalesce into the social dance form just described until after the turn of the century in New York City. As discussed in the last chapter, in black communities, dancing to ragtime music often took the form of the slow drag—a walking partner dance that incorporated manifold torso undulations within a tight embrace. In urban white communities along the Mississippi, however, dancing to ragtime music probably looked quite different. Although few sources exist, initially dancers would have likely adapted their European American ballroom dance repertoire to the features of ragtime music—giving their two step and polka (for example) a little more rhythmic play, expressiveness, and perhaps a few solo moments, mimicking the structure of the ragtime music as well as the animated musicians who played for them.

Exposure to music or musicians alone would not have been enough to teach jook house animal dances to white Americans, however. Logic would suggest that this was the product of contact with not only musicians from black communities, but also dancers—either professional ones on stages or social ones in integrated dance halls. Historically speaking, dances that imitated animals had been a part of slave group dance practices and before that West African dance practices. According to dance historian Nadine George-Graves, after abolition, versions of these dances moved from jook houses to black traveling shows and, later, to musicals.[18] In addition, they were transported by black migrants as they traded rural homes for urban ones and Southern locales for Northern climes. As a result, animal dances would have been visible to participants and observers in African American social and theatrical entertainment spaces of the South and then the North during the final decades of the twentieth century.

Whether through black performers and/or black migrants, dances that imitated animals made their way to Manhattan where they became integrated into the social dancing already happening to ragtime music. The Tenderloin neighborhood, New York's "red-light" district before Harlem, was likely where this happened. Here European Americans and African Americans could socialize in dance halls, saloons, and clubs. Several COF reports confirm the integration of these spaces with the repeated phrase "white and colored" present.[19] One report from 1910 on the Douglas Club at 147 West 28th Street offered a little more detail: "One flight up, dance hall. Liquor sold without a license. The most outrageous affairs against all laws of decency take place there. Young factory girls enticed there to meet colored men."[20] "Factory girls" was a term for European immigrant women at this time, and so this report suggests that these young women might have been among the vanguard of cross-racial socialization in New York during the early twentieth century.

Given the circumstances of their creation, it would be a mistake to deem either ragtime music or dance an entirely black or a white practice. Both incorporated borrowings from multiple traditions from the very beginning. If anything, both were uniquely American and working class. Music researcher John Edward Hasse has also argued this in relation to the origins of ragtime music. He writes that it combined "African and European antecedents in a wholly new creation ... one of the first truly American musical genres ... allow[ing] Afro-American rhythms to penetrate to the heart of American musical culture, at a time when blacks were denied access to many avenues of American society."[21]

Ragtime dancing's mixed roots are further confirmed by analyzing the movement practice itself. On the one hand, a European-style couple formation dictates how the dancers come together; on the other, African-derived soloing traditions inform how they will separate. While a European American march provides the music's dominating baseline and thus the basic walking step of the dancing—playfulness, angularity, and expressiveness culled from African American expressive culture forms influenced what happened elsewhere in the body. Ragtime dancing integrated black and white dance traditions in America at a deep level, just as the music did. This was not a simple case of steps being stolen.

Despite this hybridity and ragtime's presence in integrated environments, it was interpreted by period participants and observers to be a *black* practice. I make this assertion based on numerous investigative reports, dance manuals, song lyrics, as well as the material presence of live black musicians at ragtime events. The link between ragtime and blackness was so strong, in fact, that anti-dance investigators frequently described ragtime with the epithet "nigger" in their internal documents.[22] This terminology was meant to be descriptive and, of course, pejorative. Its use indicates how commonly accepted it was at the time for ragtime to be associated with African Americans.

Secondly, two different dance manuals of the late 1910s published in New York used the term "negroid" to comment upon the purportedly black racial characteristics of ragtime dancing.[23] This now archaic term was perhaps an attempt on the part of dance writers to sound scientific or academic, and therefore knowledgeable, when discussing African-derived cultural practices. In any case, the casual use of this term in mass publications indicates that the general public was thought to likewise know that ragtime was black in origin—and also demonstrates how dance discourses helped inform the public's racial thinking.

Furthermore, these associations would have been reinforced in the dance halls themselves where African American musicians were frequently hired to perform ragtime. Although it is true that black musicians had often played at white dance events since there were slaves in the American colonies, in the 1910s, this became common practice in public spaces with the popularity of ragtime. As a result, there came to be enough black professional musicians to warrant an unofficial union to protect their interests: the Clef Club. Musician and writer (and later diplomat and activist) James Weldon Johnson wrote in 1925, reflecting on the 1910s, "Jim Europe was a member of the [Memphis Students], and out of it grew the famous Clef Club, of which he was the noted leader, and which for a long time monopolized the business of 'entertaining' private parties and furnishing music for the new dance craze."[24] Furthermore, American Studies scholar Reid Badger's critical biography of Europe confirms that African American musicians were in high demand during the 1910s in the network of small-scale commercial leisure spaces that comprised New York's famous nightlife. "The dramatic change in public attitudes toward social dancing specifically encouraged hotel and cabaret owners to seek black entertainers and musicians ... 'as whites turned with ever-increasing frequency to the more primitive steps of black culture'."[25] For this reason, prior associations between ragtime and blackness would have been strengthened upon entry into the dance clubs by seeing black musicians play ragtime music.

Finally, the songs performers sang in these spaces often used a stereotypical black dialect and referenced rural Southern locations—areas of the United States that were marked as black as a result of centuries of slavery and decades of minstrel shows set in a fictionalized Dixie.[26] (See Fig. 2.1) The association between blackness and Southern-ness would have only been strengthened in the early twentieth century by escalating migrations of African Americans from the South into New York. At this point in American history, and arguably throughout the U.S.'s existence, African Americans were inextricable from the South in the minds of people living in the North. And so songs sung in black dialects that referenced the South—often by live African American musicians—would have underscored for attendees that ragtime was black every time they went out dancing.

Given these factors, the black associations of ragtime could not easily have been missed by European immigrant youth.[27] As newcomers, they would likely have been curious and inquisitive about such things, especially given their own positioning as ethnically "other" in America. If they were unsure or confused initially, their thinking could have been shaped by their work peers, as well as other youths present in the clubs. These young immigrant men and women only slept in ethnic enclaves; the rest of their time

The Mississippi Dippy Dip

Lyrics by - Ballard MacDonald
Music by - W. Raymond Walker

It was at a rag-time ball, Down at Wat-er-mel-on hall,
Fid-dles ring-ing, all the dark-ies sing-ing,
Out up - on the floor the boys and girls were wing-ing,
Mus-ic stopped to take a rest, Then Miss Mandy did re-quest,
M I dou-ble S I, dou-ble S I, double P I.
That Mis-sis - sip-pi dip,
That Mis-sis-sip-pi dip-py dip-py dip.

Chorus
There's that tune that I've been wait-ing for,
Swing me, hon-ey, right a-cross the floor;
Go on, let her rip, don't you slip, don't you trip,
John-ny, get your gal for the Mis-sis-sip-pi dip;
Just put your arms a-round me tight-er Hon',
Ev-'ry step I take's a light-er one,
You've got to come from Dix-ie,
If you want to do that Mis-sis-sip-pi dip-py dip-py,
Mis-sis-sip-pi Mis-sis-sip-pi dip-py dip.   dip.

Won-der why does my heart beat, Keep-ing time with both my feet,
Go on gli-ding, keep your feet a sli-ding,
Feels as if up - on the wings of love I'm ri-ding,
Hon-ey aint that mus-ic great? From that ev-er lov-ing state,
M I dou-ble S I, dou-ble S I, double P I.
That Mis-sis - sip-pi dip,
That Mis-sis-sip-pi dip-py dip-py dip.

Chorus
There's that tune that I've been wait-ing for,
Swing me, hon-ey, right a-cross the floor;
Go on, let her rip, don't you slip, don't you trip,
John-ny, get your gal for the Mis-sis-sip-pi dip;
Just put your arms a-round me tight-er Hon',
Ev-'ry step I take's a light-er one,
You've got to come from Dix-ie,
If you want to do that Mis-sis-sip-pi dip-py dip-py,
Mis-sis-sip-pi Mis-sis-sip-pi dip-py dip.   dip.

Figure 2.1 Ragtime Lyrics, 1910s. W. Raymond Walker's "The Mississippi Dippy Dip" (New York: Jos. W. Stern & Co, 1911). Courtesy of the Sam DeVincent Collection of Illustrated American Sheet Music, National Museum of American History, Smithsonian Institution Archives Center (public domain).

was spent in culturally integrated environments. Public discourse, reinforced by what they saw and heard in the dance halls, would have quickly taught them to see ragtime's racial connotations.

During the period of ragtime's popularity, hybridity was not really a conceptual possibility; the 1910s American worldview was constructed in black and white terms. As a result, ragtime's actual hybridity would not have been perceptible to participants. From a European American perspective, any presence of black inheritance would have rendered this dance and music entirely black—just like any person of mixed race in the United States during this period would have been—based on the "one-drop rule" for racial identity that operated at this time.[28]

In light of the subjugated position of African Americans at this cultural moment, the question remains, then, why were these European immigrant youths participating in dances they thought to be black? Why were they among the first in the United States to allow their bodily movements to transgress a racial divide? Today cross-cultural dance exploration has been normalized as part of American culture, but in 1900, it would have been a radical choice. What did these young men and women have to gain by engaging in cross-racial dancing?

BLACKFACE LEGACIES

The short answer to these questions is *American-ness*. Dancing ragtime offered European immigrant youths a means of constructing themselves as white, which was essential to being considered American at this time. Their whiteness, in turn, was made possible by ragtime dancing's adaptations of the conventions of the minstrel stage as theorized by social historian David Roediger, cultural theorist Richard Dyer, and political scientist Michael Rogin. With this in mind, this section discusses ragtime's historically interconnected relationship with American minstrelsy.

Ragtime dancing certainly lacked the directness of nineteenth-century blackface minstrelsy. Nonetheless, it was an inheritor of its conventions, perhaps because of the proximity of the two performance forms. Music researcher Ingeborg Harer has suggested that ragtime music and dance originated on minstrel stages, where European American and African American performers in blackface drew upon and mimicked black performance styles. She writes, "what later, in the last decade of the 19th century, was labelled 'ragtime' was played much earlier at minstrel shows, disseminated by itinerant musicians ... and performed at the same time as dance and song." In a sense, Harer has located another working-class entertainment site where black and white aesthetics merged, importantly, at an earlier time than usually attributed to ragtime.[29]

Thriving in the decades immediately before ragtime dancing crystallized, blackface minstrelsy was an early form of American musical theater and vaudeville in which performers darkened their skin with burnt cork and acted out black stereotypes for comic effect with, of course, racist implications. Ragtime dancing, with its cross-cultural embodiments of blackness, was recognized as a new development soon after minstrelsy's popularity began waning in North America. In fact, music historian William Schaefer has argued that the emergence of ragtime music led directly to the decline of white minstrel performance. He attributes this to ragtime's demonstration of the artistry of African American musicians and composers and the control it offered them over their own images in American popular music.[30]

Yet the increased respect that ragtime may have afforded African American musical artists was certainly tempered, at the very least, by market concerns. In order to be successfully sold to mainstream consumers, ragtime music was strategically linked with minstrelsy in several ways, which will be discussed shortly. Hence, there were implicit limits, largely determined by black stereotypes, placed on self-representation by African American artists during this period in a variety of arenas, including music, dance, and theater.

Even the Fisk Jubilee Singers, an internationally renowned African American choir from Nashville, Tennessee, were initially understood through the framework of minstrelsy during the late nineteenth century, according to cultural theorist Paul Gilroy. Reviews referred to their performances as minstrel shows and commented that they were "genuine negroes"—a phrase borrowed from minstrel posters of the time. Moreover, the quality of their performances was measured against the quality of minstrel troupes. According to Gilroy, they were "forced to compete on the new terrain of popular culture against the absurd representation of blackness offered by minstrelsy's pantomime dramatization of white supremacy."[31] To counter the specter of minstrelsy, however, the singers stressed the seriousness and religiousness of their work and its historical roots in slave culture.[32]

Even as stage minstrelsy became less popular, several of its conventions carried over into ragtime music and dance. For example, ragtime sheet music covers often displayed images strikingly reminiscent of blackface performance. (See Fig. 2.2) Figures were adorned with large, bright-red lips, exaggerated formal wear, and depicted in grotesque poses. Backgrounds included images of watermelons, switchblades, and chickens. All of these features indelibly linked ragtime with the minstrel stage and its egregious representations of African Americans.[33]

Figure 2.2 Ragtime Sheet Music Cover, 1900s. Harry Von Tilzer's "Abraham" (New York: Harry Von Tilzer Music, 1904). Digital image from the University of Colorado Digital Sheet Music Collection. Courtesy of the American Music Research Center at the University of Colorado (public domain).

In addition, the lyrics of many ragtime songs continued several traditions of theatrical minstrelsy. They sometimes featured the same caricatured "black" dialect used by minstrel performers—full of "dat" and "dere," misconjugated verbs, and missing word endings. (Figs. 2.1 and 2.3) Ragtime songs were also set in vaguely Southern locations, such as barnyards and Dixie, or more specific ones, like Tennessee and Mississippi, also in a manner reminiscent of minstrel shows. Finally, ragtime songs at times

That Fade-Away Dance
Novelty Song

Words by - Artur A. Hyden
Music by - William T. Pierson

She said to him, "My dear, won't you teach me
To do dat dance, so cream-y and peach-y?
It's called de Fade - a - way; I'se got to learn today!
Ev-'ry time dat mu-sic starts a - play - in', I starts sway-in!
Oh, please come on dear, let's get busy,
An' sway a-roun' an roun' till we're diz-zy!
Dat tan-ta-li-zin' tune will drive me clear in-sane;
While de mu-sic lasts let's dance dat lov-in strain."
Ah'm cra-zy fo' dat

Chorus
Fade - a - way dance! Hol' me tight!
Yes, dat Fade - a - way dance! Do it right! Do it right!
Dere's some-thin' hyp-no-ti-zin' bout dat dream-y air.
When you feel your sen-ses slip-pen; you don't care.
Keep on gli-din'; gli-din', do dat dip; do dat dip;
Keep on sli-din', sli-din'; don't you slip, don't you trip.
Hear me pray-in' dat de or-ches-tra will nev-ah stop.
Hold me, fold me; don't you let me drop!
Ah could dance dat mel-o-dy all night an' day,
Dat Fade - a - way, Fade - a - way dance!
Ah'm cra-zy fo' dat dance.

Oh, come on hon', an let us get danc-in';
Dat dream-y mel-o-dy am en-tran-cin'.
Dat am de Fade - a - way, de la-tes' dance, to-day.
Lis-ten to dat tune di-vine, now ain't dat some-thin fine!
Oh, come on hon', now don' be un-easy,
Dat mus-ic sure am lur-in' an' teas-y.
Dat ev-er lov-in' Fade - a - way's done got me, man!
Mis-ter lead-er, don't stop play-in' wid your band,
dat mes-mer-i-zin'

Chorus
Fade - a - way dance! Hol' me tight!
Yes, dat Fade - a - way dance! Do it right! Do it right!
Dere's some-thin' hyp-no-ti-zin' bout dat dream-y air.
When you feel your sen-ses slip-pen; you don't care.
Keep on gli-din'; gli-din', do dat dip; do dat dip;
Keep on sli-din', sli-din'; don't you slip, don't you trip.
Hear me pray-in' dat de or-ches-tra will nev-ah stop.
Hold me, fold me; don't you let me drop!
Ah could dance dat mel-o-dy all night an' day,
Dat Fade - a - way, Fade - a - way dance!
Ah'm cra-zy fo' dat danc

Figure 2.3 Ragtime Lyrics, 1910s. William T. Pierson's "That Fade-Away Dance" (Washington, DC: W. T. Pierson, 1918). Courtesy of the Sam DeVincent Collection of Illustrated American Sheet Music, National Museum of American History, Smithsonian Institution Archives Center (public domain).

utilized the racial epithets of minstrelsy, referring to people as "darkies" and "coons."[34]

These conventions did not, however, leap directly from minstrel stages onto ragtime dance floors. There was an important bridge between them, called "coon" singing or shouting, which began around the turn of the century.[35] Coon shouts were popular songs, typically sung in a bluesy manner in nightclub settings by matronly (non-black, often Jewish) women, such as Sophie Tucker and Fanny Brice. The singers at times wore blackface, and the songs they sang relied heavily on exaggerated black dialect, sexual innuendo, and references to an idealized South. Coon singers, who were frequently first- or second-generation European immigrants (just like the dancers at the center of this chapter), performed African American inspired music while audiences sang along, thus providing an important means of embodied participation for all present.[36] The audiences' limited embodiment of blackness, through singing along with coon singers, in many ways primed the American public for ragtime dancing's more fully embodied engagement with black-mapped performance practices.[37]

Whether or not ragtime music and dance originated on minstrel stages or coon shouting venues, we know that ragtime and minstrelsy shared imagery and rhetorical devices. There was a relationship between them that was clearly visible and audible to the public. Furthermore, to state the obvious, minstrelsy was steeped in black associations given the nature of its humor. Given that ragtime and minstrelsy were linked in the public mind, ragtime was permanently connected with not only cross-racial mimicry but also African American culture in particular.

RAGTIME DANCING AS MINSTRELSY

Theatrical blackface minstrelsy was made possible by several key components, all of which also appear in ragtime dancing to differing degrees, though much more subtly. Its key components are (1) temporary embodiment of markers of black otherness; (2) parodic impersonation of the black "other" as constructed by stereotypes; and (3) non-normative, transgressive behaviors, often sexual, facilitated by these markers.[38] This section discusses not only how minstrelsy constructed American-ness and how minstrelsy has been addressed in dance research previously, but also specifically how ragtime dancing transformed minstrelsy into a more participatory activity for the twentieth century.

David Roediger, Michael Rogin, and Richard Dyer have all argued that blackface minstrelsy, in its nineteenth-and-twentieth-century iterations, was a means of articulating a white American identity for recent European immigrants in the United States.[39] Roediger, for example, writes that "the simple physical disguise . . . of blacking up served to emphasize that those on stage were really white."[40] He argues that donning markers of blackness reinforced the whiteness of performers by highlighting differences. Blackface's juxtaposition of two racial groups did not blend them; on the contrary, the over-the-top exaggerations and distortions, easily shed once offstage, instead reinforced the binary nature of period racial classifications. Dyer writes, "One function of the exaggerations of blackface . . . was to make very clear and sharp the difference between black and white races."[41] Such scholarly work illustrates that blackface was a distancing mechanism that served, paradoxically, to separate nonblack performers from the very racial identity that their performances seemed to embody.

In this way, foreignness could be eclipsed. Period racial binaries excluded all but white or black conceptualizations of race. Indeed, during this period in U.S. history, white and black were viewed as opposite and mutually exclusive categories. Moreover, race carried more weight than nation of origin in figuring differences.[42] The power of this racial binary was at the very heart of blackface minstrelsy. As Rogin explains: "Blackface is a form of cross-dressing, in which one puts on the insignias of a . . . race that stands in binary opposition to one's own."[43] Thus, minstrelsy's black disguise colored its wearer white and, by doing so, obscured other social differences like being of foreign birth or having foreign-born parents. So-called foreigners could use the binary thinking of mainstream discourses to their advantage, to advance assimilation agendas in particular. This, in part, explains minstrelsy's popularity among American immigrants since the 1830s.

Although many respected scholars have limited their research to more traditional forms of minstrelsy, in which performers wore blackface makeup on theatrical stages beginning in the 1830s, a few have recently expanded their definition to other circumstances that did not involve burnt cork. Popular culture scholar Linda Mizejewski writes about "café au lait" lighting effects within Ziegfeld Follies performances and how they were used to mark white-skinned performers with a temporary "duskiness" that indicated blackness and enabled minstrel conventions to continue in a new context.[44] In dance studies, Juliet McMains has compared the use of tanning cream in ballroom dance competitions to minstrelsy's burnt cork in terms of its signaling of otherness, liberation from social mores, and engagement with Latin stereotypes.[45]

Dance scholar Susan Manning's work has been especially important in this regard because she examines how even choreographic choices can mark white dancers' bodies in a metaphorical way with a temporary black-ness.[46] She writes:

> This representational convention I have termed *metaphorical minstrelsy*, a con-vention whereby white dancers' bodies made reference to nonwhite subjects. In contrast to blackface performers, modern dancers did not engage in imper-sonation. Rather, their bodies became the vehicles for the tenors of nonwhite subjects. Modern dancers did not mimic others but presented an abstraction or personification of others—Oriental, Indian, Negro.[47]

What is especially interesting here is that Manning feels that movement marks the body in a similar fashion to makeup or lighting—that it can color the dancer visually but without changing the appearance of skin color. For this author, minstrelsy isn't always dependent on parody, but simply the indication and embodiment of a racial other through multiple visual cues.

Clearly Manning's arguments concerning metaphorical minstrelsy pave the way for mine relating to participatory minstrelsy. Ragtime dancing enabled movers to embody markers of blackness temporarily. Instead of burnt cork, these dancers moved in ways that were understood to be black at this time. Two already-referenced dance manuals published in New York toward the end of ragtime dancing's popularity offer an illustration of which movements would have signaled blackness to viewers. Edward Scott's *The New Dancing As It Should Be* boldly stated that "there was also a good deal of talk about the TURKEY TROT, with its degenerate negroid *mouvement des hanches*."[48] Likewise, A. M. Cree's *Handbook of Ball-room Dancing* admonished readers to "avoid dipping the shoulders, rolling the body, and pump-handle action with the arms; such Negroid actions are very unseemly."[49] Here Scott and Cree identify what constituted 1910s black dancing, at least from the perspective of dance professionals of European descent: movements of the buttocks and shoulders, as well as vertical axis dips, sequential rolls through the torso, and angular move-ments of the limbs.

Because ragtime dancing was a quotidian practice rather than a the-atrical one, its mobilization of minstrelsy's elements could be subtle and undramatized. The dancing itself could be made more or less explicitly black by increasing or decreasing the elements named above. These bodily markers of blackness looked very different from "blacking up," of course, but nonetheless served as clear signals of otherness to period participants.

In addition to being increased or decreased, these dance choices could easily be added and removed through the improvisational structure of rag-time dancing—thus rendering them temporary, a key aspect of minstrelsy.

As mentioned earlier, temporariness highlighted racial separateness, like the incompleteness of the burnt cork makeup, which was applied to leave a frame of white skin to remind observers of the artifice of the performer. This ever-present white frame indicated to viewers that the makeup could be easily removed, that the blackness was temporary, and that it was their white privilege to *choose* to be black or not; only non-African Americans could remove markers of black identity.[50]

As discussed before, ragtime dancing involved a basic walking step that could be deviated from by simultaneous soloing. It was within these solo moments that the dancing understood as black could be deployed most easily and frequently. Freed from the framework of the closed couple formation, dancers had room to liberate their torsos, change levels, syncopate creatively, and be more angular with the lines of their limbs. Importantly, these dance interludes were temporary, as the structure dictated that dancers eventually and always returned to the basic step. With each solo, dancers could demonstrate their ability to put on and take off the movements that marked their bodies as black—just like immigrant minstrel performers did with their burnt cork makeup and its ever-present white frame.

Two other key components of minstrel performance are parody and impersonation. Although it is true that ragtime dancers were not engaged in comedy routines as traditionally defined, their dancing was nonetheless comedic. The playfulness that imbued their soloing certainly made fun of themselves (and others) as they tried on the movements of others through torso gyrations, increased groundedness, playful timing, and surprising angularity, for example. However, in the animal dances in particular, as Nadine George-Graves (2008) has argued, ragtime dancers generated stereotypical renderings of African Americans relating to animality, primitivism, and sexuality. Goofy monkey glides, sexy bunny hugs, and rough-and-tumble turkey trots were meant to be hilarious and were licensed by the perceived blackness of the dancing. Certainly ragtime dancers were not identifying with actual black men and women here, but rather stereotypes of them. In this way, they engaged in a form of comedic misidentification through their dancing.[51]

The final key component of minstrelsy is transgression—representations of otherness liberate participants from everyday behaviors. The overwhelmingly playful and sexual ethos of ragtime dancing that worried the COF and other moral guardians testifies to its escapist function. Bodies pressing against bodies on crowded, dark dance floors with shouts of hilarity flying over the music as dancers imitated different animals for each other—in 1910s New York, this was highly transgressive behavior. Ragtime dancers could be licentious and ridiculous in ways that were not possible off the dance floor, and these behaviors were made possible by dancers' embodiments of blackness—just like immigrant, coon-shouting women and blackface minstrel performers could be sexual in public thanks to the perceived black content of their singing and/or comedy. They were not being "themselves" when they behaved non-normatively; they were pretending to be someone else. This was part of ragtime's immense allure, its liberating potential.

Through its adaptation of these minstrel components, ragtime dancing's embodiments of blackness—what I am calling participatory minstrelsy—differentiated and distanced immigrant dancers from African Americans and thus implicitly empowered them to lay claim to a white racial identity. In a world steeped in binary understandings of race, participants could mark themselves as white by dancing in ways that were constructed as black. Being seen as white was essential in order to be embraced as American at the beginning of the twentieth century. Thus ragtime's minstrel elements offered new European immigrants a powerful means of learning and claiming American-ness in the face of rampant xenophobia.

Ragtime dancing transformed staged minstrelsy into a more participatory phenomenon, which had the effect of heightening the social impact of these cross-racial performances while at the same time rendering their cultural work more covert. Dancers internalized cross-racial mimicry, engaging bodily with stereotypical renderings of African Americans and enabling the implications of minstrelsy to become naturalized in potentially powerful ways that have continued into the twenty-first century.

By 1910, blackface minstrelsy as a theatrical form was becoming less and less popular. In its place, and as an inheritor of its cultural work, ragtime dancing emerged as a new, subtler version of minstrelsy. Participants moved instead of watching others move—thus taking into their bodies the signs and significations of the practice's racial implications in a deeper way. Ragtime's racial mimicry in turn was key to its popularity as it created a space for novel ways of moving that felt modern and American to participating dancers—because they could temporarily feel "black." Besides its thrilling speed and creative opportunities, ragtime dancing was pleasurable in part because of its racial associations.

EUROPEAN IMMIGRANTS AND AFRICAN
AMERICAN MIGRANTS

Ragtime was not simply the form of social dancing that happened to be practiced at the time of overwhelming European immigration and African American migration. With its cross-cultural features, it was danced because of intense demographic pressures. Immigrant youth needed to seek whiteness and its privileges to position themselves as *not* black—or rather, *not* the most maligned group in New York City.[52] During the early twentieth century, because of their perceived difference, foreigners were excluded from organizations, jobs, unions, churches, and schools. The participatory minstrelsy that ragtime dancing put into motion through its temporary embodiment of black dancing ironically asserted the unqualified whiteness of European immigrants. It symbolically differentiated and separated them from African Americans and, in so doing, blotted out their foreignness. In short, it rendered them Americans—offering them a racial safe haven of sorts.

While ragtime dancing's cultural borrowing could be seen as indicating a desire for racial integration, other evidence suggests that this was likely not the case. Integration was not taking place between immigrants and African Americans in other social arenas of New York City. During this period, these groups were not allied, even though they shared working-class economic conditions and in spite of the advantages and leverage such an alliance might have afforded. Instead, immigrants excluded African Americans from their trade unions (to protect their jobs) and neighborhoods. Racial tensions abounded between recently arrived immigrants and African Americans, at times erupting into race riots, especially near the end of ragtime's popularity. On many fronts, not just on ragtime dance floors, immigrants struggled to separate themselves from African Americans.

Although the movement technique of ragtime dancing *integrated* European American and African American dance traditions, as practiced by immigrant youths, it served to symbolically *separate* black from white. The temporariness of dancers' cross-racial excursions underscored their privilege to take blackness on and off, and hence their whiteness. Moreover, through this performance of separation, immigrant ragtime dancers were able to enact a challenge to the marking of their bodies as foreign by American society—in this way, bodily movement was mobilized to complicate hegemonic body-based categorizations.

After a long day of working in a factory, these young men and women wanted to relax in clubs, saloons, and dance halls—far from the prying eyes of their old-world parents and community members. Here they could drink, laugh, sing, and move sexily, playfully, and raucously to ragtime music. Dancing in this way made them feel more adult, more modern, and, most importantly, more American. It helped bond their youth culture and glossed over feelings of "difference" that might have troubled them. For these reasons, ragtime dancing played a key role in immigrants' sense of belonging, and thus assimilation, during the first decades of the twentieth century.

Immigrant ragtime dancers, as well as the migrant blues dancers discussed in the prior chapter, used social dancing as a means of self-empowerment through assimilation—the former into mainstream "white" American culture and the latter into an urban African diasporic culture. These two distinct populations *both* chose to meet modernity's challenges by embodying tactical constructions of self, and other, through movement. In addition to the pleasure of escape, physical exertion, socialization, and self-expression that dancing practices offered these populations, who were experiencing the stress of relocation, they also provided participants a crucial means for constructing feelings of sameness and belonging, and thus, identity formation.

Danse Chateau, Times Square

Four P.M., Saturday, March 1914

A cabaret adjacent to King's vaudeville theatre on Broadway near 43rd Street. Well-heeled ladies, both young and old, sip tea and nibble cake in keen antic- ipation. Tiny round tables ring the vast white dance floor. Well-coifed young men lurk near the edges of the room joking quietly among themselves, wondering how much they will earn from this crop of ladies. Their dark suits contrast sharply with the soft hues of the "Moroccan" décor. The band, on the other hand, blends in well with their white and gold-trimmed sultan-like, silken costumes. Only their dark-skinned faces, peering out beneath their turban, betray their pres- ence—carefully nestled behind the far corner's faux palm trees.

From her perch in the middle of Manhattan's most cosmopolitan of crowds, Lillian leans forward from her seat to catch the eye of Leroy, the band's pianist. He nods and then noiselessly pokes his fellow band mates to attention. Deep breath in, deep breath out. Timidly Lillian rises to clasp Matteo's, or rather Matthew's, nearby hand. As if on air, they majestically walk toward the center of the dance floor where they are greeted by the pianist's opening bars, as well as the eager gazes of all those present.

On cue, they turn to face one another, reaching up onto their tiptoes as if they might very well take flight. Their hands meet in a dispassionate embrace. At first, a neat trot with the straightest of legs. Glide, glide, glide, not clop, clop, clop, Lillian mutters under her breath, trying to remember the choreography.

A sleek pivot, then freeze 2-3-4. Double time to zig . . . then zag . . . knees aching, toes cramping, Lillian smiles vaguely somewhere over Matthew's right shoul- der. Whoa, the dip. Just a slight bend of the knees, but always a surprise if she *is daydreaming. And another and another. A smattering of applause awards their feats.*

Slide left—just the foot, 2-3-4. And right. Matthew grimaces briefly at her rogue hip that seems to want to punctuate the 4. Lillian follows him, from wide smooth circles into figure eights, from a closed position into a flirtatious skater's hold. Tap together front 1, right 3, front 1, right 2, freeze 3-4. Again. Not exactly syncopation, but certainly not an old-fashioned two step either.

Trotting toward the home stretch. Hop together, flick kick. Just a dash of fun. Pivot, pivot, pivot, pivot—judiciously leaning away as their momentum supports them. And . . . they unexpectedly release into a deep gracious bow. Gripping each other's hands tightly for balance, they work to catch their breath and smile at the same time.

As the music fades away, Leroy broadcasts, "Ladies and gentlemen, the Marvelous Maxwells! Modern dancing's most refined representatives! Currently starring in A Summer's Day at the Victoria Theatre." Applause surges through the air as Lillian and Matthew bow humbly, yet glamorously, over and over again. As the enthusiasm fades, Matthew clears his throat and carefully says, "Please join Mrs. Maxwell and I on the dance floor. . . ." Before the ever so slightly accented words are out of his mouth, the eager tea-sippers are about them, circling the star dancing pair.

On cue, a small army of matronly chaperones emerges from the wings to hastily introduce the female patrons to the waiting young men, each woman matched with a (hired) prince charming of her own. Leroy and his band launch into their rendition of "Too Much Mustard" as the Maxwells guide the crowd around the dance floor—modeling the very steps they had just performed, with a few embellishments of their own—a sudden stop, fast turn left then right, and a few jaunty skips. The ladies barely notice. Their hands are full just staying on the beat and off their partners' toes. After a few rotations of the dance floor, Lillian and Matthew slip away, grab a pair of shabby garment bags, and race over to the Victoria Theatre for their evening show. No time to be social; they were on stage in a couple of hours.

CHAPTER 3

ↄ\ᴑ

"The Ugly Duckling"

The Refinement of Ragtime Dancing and the Mass Marketing of Modern Social Dance

Of the original [turkey] 'trot' nothing remains but the basic step. The elements that drew denunciation upon it have gone from the abiding-places of politeness . . . it prefers to be known as the One-Step. And in the desire for a new appellation it is justified, since no history ever so vividly recalled the fable of the ugly duckling.[1]

Troy and Margaret West Kinney, *Social Dancing of To-Day* (1914)

In their 1914 dance manual, the famous American dance writers and illustrators Troy and Margaret West Kinney use the fairytale of the ugly duckling as a metaphor for the transformations occurring in social dance of early twentieth-century America. In that famous 1843 story by Hans Christian Andersen, a duckling is deemed unattractive by the other ducks because it looks different. By the end of the story, however, the little brown bird is transformed into a beautiful white swan. In a similar fashion, ragtime dancing and its turkey trot needed to change before they could be profitably marketed. Specifically, they needed to be whitened in order to appeal to a conservative, white clientele. While dance writers of the period might attribute such changes to natural aesthetic progression, they, like the dominant notion of beauty suggested by the ugly duckling story, were deeply connected with aesthetic values that were distinctly racialized.

Indeed, the turkey trot could not become the One-Step, nor could ragtime dancing become "modern" social dance until contemporary conceptualizations of race partnered with innovative mass-marketing and production strategies of the early twentieth century.[2]

During the 1910s, the ragtime dancing of European immigrants and other members of the working classes became assimilated into the white middle class's modern social dance, which expressed a nostalgia for a simpler time when migrants and immigrants were a less pressing demographic force. The changes that dance professionals made to the dances to make them more marketable enacted a type of essentialism that asserted white racial dominance. In this way, social dancing modeled, and perhaps influenced, what was happening in America's melting pot, which merged, absorbed, and diluted difference.

This chapter begins with a clarification of how I am using the terms "ragtime" and "modern" dance, as twentieth and twenty-first century dance writers rarely agree on their definitions. Following this, for non-specialists, I provide a detailed description of the differences between ragtime and modern social dance practices to better understand the "refinement" process in detail. The remainder of the chapter explores the impact of both commercialization and 1910s racial discourses on the creation of modern dance—as it was a *partnership* between commodification and racialization that transformed ragtime dancing into modern dance.

RAGTIME DANCING AND MODERN DANCE

While ragtime dancing grew out of community practices, as discussed in chapter two, what came to be known as modern social dance (hereafter denoted simply as modern dance) was crafted from existing ragtime movements by 1910s social dance professionals in combination with existing European American ballroom dances with roots in the Baroque and Renaissance periods.[3] Modern dance coalesced in urban cabarets, dance academies, and publishing houses of New York City during the mid-1910s. (See Figs. 3.1 and 3.2) It was designed for and largely practiced by that city's European American middle classes before being exported across the United States and Europe, where it flourished in urban centers until jazz dancing took hold in the early 1920s.

Through modern dance's popularity, many professional dance partners—for example, Vernon and Irene Castle and Maurice Mouvet and Florence Walton—achieved national and even international fame with the assistance of media coverage, dance manuals, sheet music, films, and touring musical

Figure 3.1 Professional Modern Dancers, 1910s. "The Turkey Trot, Grizzly Bear and Other Naughty Diversions: Whether Objectionable or Not, They Are Neither Pretty Nor Artistic— Originated in Far Western Mining Camps and Found Their Way to the Stage," *New Bedford Sunday Standard* (February 4, 1912). Courtesy of the New Bedford Free Public Library (public domain).

Figure 3.2 Modern Dancers, 1910s. "Where the Turkey Trot and Tango Have Killed the Waltz," *New York Times* (April 20, 1913), Picture Section, Part 1. Courtesy of ProQuest Historical Newspapers: New York Times (1851–2010) (public domain).

theatre shows. (See Fig. 0.3, introduction) Even though it was far more formalized than ragtime dancing, modern dance never became a single, codified technique. In practice, it included a range of related movements and styles—all of which shared a commitment to so-called refinement. Several new dances and dance steps contributed to its lexicon. The one-step and foxtrot are perhaps the best-known modern dances. The tango, *maxixe*, half and half, Apache, Boston, and hesitation were also quite popular, especially among professional performers.[4]

Since modern dance was derived from ragtime dancing, they shared many similarities, including a similar improvisation structure.[5] Both utilized basic steps in a closed couple hold that consisted of simple walking movements. Both enlivened their basic steps with variations that invoked a sense of play and created a space in which dancers could feel they were being creative. Modern dance and ragtime dancing's variations provided contrast in terms of level, spatial path, speed, and rhythm. In both of these practices, rhythmic play was a distinguishing feature.

That said, modern dance and ragtime dancing differed in radical ways. Indeed, as discussed in the last chapter, ragtime embodied play, angularity, casualness, inventiveness, and abruptness. Generally speaking, it had six key features: Partners (1) held onto one another in intimate ways; (2) improvised; (3) frequently gestured; (4) used boisterous movement qualities; (5) deployed angular body lines; and (6) engaged in a high degree of rhythmic play. In contrast, modern dance was defined by an almost opposite approach to each of these six distinct features. The differences between modern dance and ragtime dancing were thus much more pronounced than the similarities in terms of aesthetics, body part usage, partnering, and variations. Ragtime mobilized an aesthetic of rupture, whereas modern celebrated one of restraint. The former was a celebration of change, difference, discontinuity, and disruption. Even though a rather intimate version of a closed dance position was deployed as dancers traversed the floor, ragtime dancers frequently broke apart to solo dance. As they did so, they divided their torsos into discrete parts, such as shoulders, waists, and hips. In addition, the use of accented movement frequently departed from ragtime music's steadily rocking bass line. Finally, angular bodylines proliferated as limbs jabbed into space. In contrast, modern dance valued control, containment, organization, rules, and inhibition. Couples danced in a united way, as a single unit, and *with* the rhythmic structure of the music. Together, dancers governed their collaborative bodily movements in service to smooth, graceful lines of the body and through space. Their variations were brief and few and therefore did little to disturb the self-control they exuded.

Ragtime dancing encouraged dancers to use their entire bodies by mobilizing shoulders and hips and animating their faces and limbs. This activation of multiple body parts meant that ragtime was more weighted and effortful than modern dance. Ragtime freed the torso and limbs to express sexual pleasure and desire; conversely, modern dance's aesthetic of restraint inhibited the torso and thus suppressed sexuality. Modern dance imbued participants with the appearance of innocent playfulness— which may have, nonetheless, felt subversive, as these dancers were adults embodying at times childlike behavior.

When dancing together, ragtime dancers grabbed each other around the neck, hips, and waist, and they pressed their torsos together and pushed apart for solo improvisations. Thus they moved with greater physical connection between partners than modern dancers, and as a result, they directed much more energy toward one another. Importantly, owing to this more flexible couple formation, followers could insert variations into ragtime's basic steps and choose solo movements when opportunities came about. Both partners could also invent steps while on the ragtime dance floor. In contrast, modern dance's discourse insisted that followers submit to leaders and that students learn correct dancing from dance professionals. This meant that teachers and performers, not dancers, were privileged to be creators of dances and dance steps. It also meant that modern dance reasserted a male-centrism on the social dance floor—even though (or perhaps because) teaching dance during the early twentieth century had, according to dance historian Linda Tomko, the potential to "empower ... women to claim a new professional identity" and dancing in public spaces "afforded women a certain autonomy."[6]

Compared with modern dance, then, the variations within ragtime dancing were much more disruptive in nature and integrated throughout the dancing experience, despite their common improvisational structure. Ragtime's timing changes were much more uneven and sudden, floor patterns more unruly, and level changes more pronounced. In addition to periods of solo dancing by both dancers, some of ragtime's smaller variations, such as single hops, kicks, or stomps, could be added by either the leader or follower to any basic step, which added yet another layer of rhythmic complexity to a couple's dancing. As a result of this multileveled deployment of variations, ragtime's improvisations did not reinforce dichotomies between restraint and rupture, control and freedom. Instead, because of its mixture of these concepts, ragtime celebrated the possibility of varied movement and individual expression throughout the dancing experience. Modern, on the other hand, offered pleasure in control through its clear demarcations of order and disorder, sexuality and propriety, and male and female roles, as well as in the brief escape and transgression from these roles.[7] Such transgressions were tightly managed, however, and limited to short and very specific moments immediately followed by a return to restraint. Thus these two related dance forms theorized radically different values and relationships among the body, pleasure, and society—although both, of course, did involve a tremendous amount of fun for participants. Their sources of pleasure, however, were different.

In short, what had been full-bodied dancing became restricted to the lower limbs; what had celebrated pleasure and sexuality became reserved playfulness; what had emphasized invention, difference, and individuality came to emphasize uniformity. Post-refinement, the spirit of ragtime could be found only in modern dance's brief variations, which interrupted its repetitive patterns and provided dancers with a momentary break from perpetual restraint. For a historian, the variations within modern dance are like sediments that testify to this dance form's process of creation—both in terms of its commodification and its racialization. They, briefly but safely, offered modern dancers a taste of ragtime dancing's kinesthetic pleasures.

SELLING DANCING

The transformation of ragtime dancing into modern dance was influenced by far more than aesthetics, despite the frequent references to beauty and artistry in modern dance publications. The radical changes made to ragtime also were grounded in both commercial interests and race politics, which will be discussed shortly. This section focuses on how dance professionals drew upon innovative mass-production and marketing strategies of the early twentieth century to reformulate ragtime dancing into a product that could be more easily sold to a wider, and wealthier, American public that envisioned itself as refined. In particular, it explores how the mass-production principles of Taylorism can be found within modern dance's practices and teaching modes, especially their codification, simplification, and emphasis on control.

Unlike a watch, car, book, or even a piece of music, social dancing as an improvised bodily practice does not lend itself to mass production or broad marketing, at least beyond a local scale. However, if a dance is defined by its choreographic design, then that dance can conceivably be sold. Such codification has historically been central to the commodification of dancing. Furthermore, such commodification requires a detailed and accessible textual representation of the dance, someone to teach the choreography, or both. Even so, social dancing, more than most theatrical dancing, poses additional challenges to commodification efforts. While it might be possible to learn a few dance steps by rote, developing an understanding of how those steps fit together (i.e., their improvisational structure) is much more difficult. Such knowledge has to be gained through practice, with teachers or partners. In this way, the learning of social dance actually requires human contact and ongoing participation to be successful.

The ephemeral and improvisatory nature of social dancing did not stop 1910s dance professionals from trying to mass-produce and market it to the American public. Their efforts in this regard transformed ragtime dancing practices into a modern dance product that was much easier to teach, learn, and sell en masse. As already described, earlier iterations of ragtime dancing required extensive improvisation and embodied creativity—skills not easily learned other than through shared bodily experience. Thus, even more than the average social dance practice, ragtime dancing was a difficult product to create. Its central skills could not be easily taught to large classes of students, and its improvisational structure could not be adequately explained in quick and easy how-to-dance manuals.[8] Indeed, ragtime dancing needed to be radically changed in order to become saleable to more than a few consumers at a time. Moreover, for this experiment to work, its entire ethos had to be altered from one that valued individuality to one that engendered conformity.

At the time of the rising popularity of modern dance, mass production was a preoccupation in a number of industries. Approaches to optimizing industrialization were being theorized most notably by Frederick Taylor, who championed hierarchical knowledge management, retraining of workers, and rational control of all aspects of production processes.[9] In these three ways, he sought to transform existing production methods into a scientifically streamlined and efficient model.

Applications of Taylor's principles can be found to varying degrees in modern dance and its burgeoning industry. Moreover, they account for some of the key differences between ragtime and modern dancing. I am not suggesting that modern dance teachers read Taylor's books and articles, but that they participated in a cultural climate that was absorbing and adapting his ideas as part of a broader modernization process.[10] Indeed, the Western world was becoming increasingly modular in its structures and thinking during the 1910s.

Taylor's scientific management system emphasized hierarchical knowledge management as the basis of efficient control of production. His system dismantled open, flexible workspaces in which artisanal workers were highly skilled, largely self-managed, and educated via apprenticeships; in their place, he advocated for rigid, ordered, and stratified workspaces in which managers controlled workers who carried out very specific tasks. In this scheme, only managers understood the entirety of the production process. According to Taylor's logic, the resulting commercial product (and its production) would be more predictable and reliable in its quality, thus raising profits.

Prior to the modern dance industry, ragtime dancers were in a sense self-taught and self-managed creative agents. With the advent of modern dance, though, dance knowledge came to be increasingly managed by teachers. In the process, dancers surrendered much of their creativity and choice-making to a fixed lexicon of dance steps to be learned in a piecemeal fashion—much like artisans who went to work on an assembly line would have.

To accomplish the "de-skilling" necessary for greater manager control, Taylor's scientific management method required the retraining of all workers according to the new rules and standards of production. Surviving 1910s dance manuals repeatedly insist that dancers be retrained, in order to leave behind their old ways of dancing and learn the new, correct way to dance—which was defined by the author's principles and rules. This emphasis on retraining enabled much stronger control over the movement and thus the dancers and dances as commodities.

As might be expected, the best-known aspect of Taylor's work is his emphasis on control over all phases of the production process. For him, maximum efficiency can be achieved only with clear rules and precise standards so that all actions are regulated and planned. He therefore sought to find the one best method for doing a particular task by watching workers and analyzing their movements in order to break down the process and compartmentalize the actions involved.[11]

Following a similar pattern, modern dance professionals pursued the standardization of ragtime dancing by making the dances simpler in structure and fewer in number in order to make their teaching more efficient. Articles and manuals repeatedly celebrated modern dance teachers' standardization of social dancing. A manual from 1918, written by Vivian Persis Dewey from Kenosha, Wisconsin, offers an example:

> After a stormy and chaotic period of dance revolution, and constant changing, dancing has once more become settled. The one-step and fox-trot have become standardized, and the steps are now sane and practical. . . . The good dancers in all parts of the nation are dancing certain definite steps.[12]

Compared with both late nineteenth-century ballroom dancing and early twentieth-century ragtime dancing, modern dance used just a few basic step patterns that were remarkably simple. Modern dance's one-step and foxtrot consisted mainly of stiff walking directly on the beat. Even more complex dances, such as the hesitation and Boston, only added pauses to this pert walking. Over the course of the 1910s, moreover, the number of dances in circulation dropped dramatically. For instance, manuals written in 1919 tend to contain half as many dances and dance steps as those published in 1914.[13]

As a result of Taylor's ideas, it was during this same period that the use of replaceable components came to be typical in manufacturing production. This allowed for assembly-line construction, use of the same parts in several products, and easy component replacement. For modern dance professionals, the variation served as a kind of replaceable part that could be simply inserted into basic steps at the whim of the leader. In some cases, it could even be inserted into a number of dances, not just one. Maurice wrote in 1915:

> Most of the Tango steps are easily applied to the fox trot by a slight change in rhythm. The Cortez, the Promenade and the Scissors can all be done with good effect. For that matter, many people use some of the Maxixe figures very well, and truly it does not matter much what actual steps one uses....[14]

Variations were not only easily incorporated; they came to be seen as interchangeable as well. In a way, they became yet another dance commodity to be packaged and sold.

Taylor's emphases on hierarchical knowledge management, retraining, and rational control all served the purpose of empowering managers. In the dance industry, dance teachers assumed this gate-keeping role with aplomb. Importantly, this happened at a time when the necessity for dance lessons and teachers might actually have been questioned on the basis of ragtime dancing's affirmation of social dancers as independent creators. A Taylor-like emphasis on control, however, enabled modern dance teachers to exert greater influence over social dancing practices through a strategic highlighting of correct technique and a de-emphasis on independent choice-making by dancers. A St. Louis, Missouri, dance academy owner, Frank Leslie Clendenden, wrote: "Insist your pupils take the correct position, which is graceful; they will like it in time.... Control is the greatest point to consider in all our new dances."[15] Although this statement could be interpreted as stressing a dancer's control over his or her own movement, it also underscores the necessity for teachers, as managers, to regulate their students' dancing practices, both in terms of their physical movements as well as its meanings and values.

In these ways, modern dance professionals redesigned ragtime dancing to suit America's burgeoning consumer culture. They codified dance steps, reduced the number of dances, developed interchangeable variations, lessened opportunities for improvisation, and fostered uniformity and order by augmenting teacher control. In so doing, they diminished the degree to which modern dance embodied ragtime's self-expression, spontaneity, and individuality. Nonetheless, and ironically, these were the very qualities—repackaged as freedom, fun, and personality—that dance professionals used to market modern dance to the American public.

RACE PURITY AND REFINEMENT

Although the commodification of ragtime through Taylor's principles is compelling on its own, to stop here would neglect half the story. Ragtime's transformation into a commercial product would not have been complete without defusing its racial threat. Ragtime's mixed heritage and perceived blackness rendered it extremely problematic for an American public that valued homogeneity, white hegemony, and neat racial categories—despite (or perhaps because of) the country's growing proportion of immigrants and migrants. As a result, the refinement process also had to remove ragtime's references to blackness by containing its exuberant physicality and sexuality, among other aspects. Although such changes had little to do with the ease of mass production per se, they had everything to do with the difficulty of mass-marketing a product with black associations during the 1910s.

As discussed in the last chapter, ragtime dancing was strongly influenced by African American social dancing practices of the late nineteenth century, and the music was typically performed in clubs by African American musicians, even in segregated white settings. Ragtime dancing did not appear, though, to be simply an appropriation of African American dancing by European American dancers;[16] there did not seem to be outright stealing of steps. Instead, ragtime dancing was the result of an integration of dance traditions created by working-class people of different cultural backgrounds—including European immigrants and African Americans—occasionally dancing and socializing in proximity and together in cities across the United States. And yet, ragtime was perceived as black, a mapping consistent with the so called one-drop for black racial identity that operated during this period, which deemed anything and anyone tinged with blackness to be totally black.[17]

The refinement process needed to strategically remove ragtime's blackness in part because *black* was not yet openly marketable in dominant American culture, as it would become in limited ways in the 1920s. This problematic marketability can also be linked to ragtime's references to miscegenation and thus its threat to dominant ideologies of race purity and the idealization of American national identity as white. One of the primary ways ragtime alluded to miscegenation was by mixing black movement with white bodies. When European Americans practiced ragtime, it created a cross-cultural bodily experience for those dancing and those watching.

For the many U.S. urban dwellers accustomed to European American couple dancing and whose understanding of black movement practices was informed by minstrelsy, ragtime was recognizable as a miscegenated dance form. Its practice, then, would have signaled a co-mingling of black and white cultures, the result of which was understood as black. While immigrant dancers temporarily embraced this blackness through participatory minstrelsy as a way of asserting their American-ness, members of the middle classes sought to avoid it, and thus further distance themselves from the poor.

The miscegenations of ragtime matter because at this time in U.S. history, the issue was of great concern, affecting people's lives at both individual and national levels. Race purity was idealized, and it was an accepted truth that the races had to remain separate for social order to be preserved. Boundaries between cultures had to appear to be clear, fixed, and unbroken. Cultural theorist Richard Dyer writes in his book, *White*: "[I]f races are conceptualized as pure (with concomitant qualities of character, including the capacity to hold sway over other races), then miscegenation threatens that purity" and also the power that purity provides.[18] Within this paradigm, miscegenation in any and all manifestations must be prevented to preserve the purity thought to be key for maintaining race-based hierarchies (and hence white racial dominance).

On multiple levels, ragtime dancing practices provided powerful reminders of increasing diversity and decreasing white racial dominance.[19] The blackness of ragtime in particular presented a challenge for dance professionals who wished to create a dance form that could be mass-marketed to a white majority that feared the loss of their dominant status. The miscegenation associated with ragtime would have heightened broad social fears relating to white "race suicide," owing to the dancing's multilayered enactments of racial mixing between black and white cultures.[20] Visible reminders of miscegenation eventually had to be eliminated, which was most easily accomplished by erasing ragtime's blackness, which for many meant its hip movements, sexual innuendos, and animal imitations (as will be discussed below). In this way, dance professionals' use of the term "refinement" reminds us of the word's broader connotation: the removal of contaminants and purification. The repeated use of this term in period dance writing betrays how deeply connected social dance practices were with early twentieth-century concerns relating to race purity.

REFINEMENT'S WHITENESS

In a climate where race purity resonated with national identity on multiple levels, it is not difficult to understand why ragtime dancing might have been tough to market. In order to be sellable to the general public, the dancing not only had to be codified, but also whitened. However, when describing the changes they made to ragtime, dance professionals rarely discussed race explicitly. Their word choices nevertheless communicated racial connotations in indirect ways. Furthermore, dance writers often relied upon origin stories and explanations for the refinement process to convey the whiteness of modern dance and to distance it from ragtime's black linkages.

The writings of dance professionals unambiguously embraced refinement as a pathway toward enhancing artistry, morality, and health. It was viewed as a means of improving one's self. For example, Charles J. Coll and Gabrielle Rosiere's 1922 dance manual declared in its introduction:

> Dancing ... promotes social morality and when properly administered the community is socialized, humanized.... The manifold advantages derived from dancing as an exercise, the great delight it affords as a recreation, its refining influence on manners, are becoming each year more fully recognized. Parents should be anxious to give young people an opportunity to become accomplished in the graceful art.... To be aesthetic, to love what is beautiful, is to perceive through the senses.... Dancing is a form of expression and an exquisite one....[21]

As much as dance steps and technique, dance teachers were selling self-improvement and, through it, social mobility when they represented modern dance as refined.

Even though direct discussions of race were rare, class was openly referred to in dance manuals. Here, cultural theorist Stuart Hall's assertion—also referred to in the introduction—that "race is thus, also, the modality in which class is 'lived,' the medium through which class relations are experienced, the form in which it is appropriated and 'fought through,'" is salient.[22] In numerous instances, race and class are often expressed and experienced through one another. In this case, through an open rhetorical engagement with class concerns while simultaneously adjusting the movement's racial implications, we can perceive that dance discourses in early twentieth-century America were used to police racial boundaries in indirect ways.

Besides marketing values that were tacitly white, another way in which race was subtly communicated in the literature of modern dance was through narratives of origin, which were found in the opening pages of dance manuals or peppered throughout articles about social dancing in the mainstream press. Such stories elevated modern dance by connecting it with a "white" origin of some kind (such as Greece or Rome, key locations in the rise of Western Civilization) and/or implicitly denigrating ragtime dancing by attributing it to racially questionable roots (such as the "Wild West"), as discussed in chapter two.

Modern dance writers also obliquely indicated modern dance's whiteness and ragtime's non-whiteness through the ways in which they described ragtime's transformation into modern dance. When the Kinneys wrote about the refinement process, as already discussed, they compared it to the story of *The Ugly Duckling*. The ugly duckling, according to its traditional telling, begins life ugly and brown. The story ends with the duckling reaching maturity, finally becoming white, beautiful, and accepted by those like him. By linking the refinement of ragtime dancing with this fairy tale, the Kinneys allude to the white ideal to which modern dance held itself and also remind readers that ragtime should not be understood as white. They also suggest that brown was infantile and white was mature (not to mention elite). In effect, through this metaphor, they constructed ragtime as modern's "other."

Thus dance professionals seem to have been arguing two contradictory points—that modern dance was a refinement of ragtime *and* that these dances had different origins. While it is possible that they only strategically used the concept of refinement to link their product with ragtime and its illicit allure, a close comparison of ragtime dancing and modern dance practices supports their familial relationship, as will be explained in detail in the next section.

Furthermore, modern dance's teachers, performers, and writers acknowledged ragtime as their other when they policed the boundaries of so-called proper dancing. In this way, their language suggests a linkage between the two, rather than ragtime being simply a separate but competing form. For example, the Castles' manual ends with this: "*Drop* the Turkey Trot, the Grizzly Bear, the Bunny Hug, etc. These dances are ugly, ungraceful, and out of fashion [my emphasis]." (See Fig. 3.3) By using the word "drop," these famous dancers acknowledged that social dancers were, in fact, doing ragtime, and perhaps even preferring it. Certainly modern dance professionals wanted to assert a clear separation between ragtime and modern in order to sell their product, but their fervent efforts and the language they deployed actually testify to an intimate relationship between the two.

EMBODIED DISCOURSES OF RACE IN MODERN DANCE

Despite such thinly veiled discursive clues to the refinement process's racial implications, its whitening agenda is most evident upon closer examination of the differences between the movement practices of ragtime dancing

CASTLE HOUSE SUGGESTIONS
FOR CORRECT DANCING

Do not wriggle the shoulders.

Do not shake the hips.

Do not twist the body.

Do not flounce the elbows.

Do not pump the arms.

Do not hop—glide instead.

Avoid low, fantastic, and acrobatic dips.

Stand far enough away from each other to allow free movement of the body in order to dance gracefully and comfortably.

The gentleman should rest his hand lightly against the lady's back, touching her with the finger-tips and wrist only, or, if preferred, with the inside of the wrist and the back of the thumb.

The gentleman's left hand and forearm should be held up in the air parallel with his body, with the hand extended, holding the lady's hand lightly on his palm. The arm should never be straightened out.

Remember you are at a social gathering, and not in a gymnasium.

Drop the Turkey Trot, the Grizzly Bear, the Bunny Hug, etc. These dances are ugly, ungraceful, and out of fashion.

Figure 3.3 Modern Dance Manual, 1910s. Vernon and Irene Castle, "Castle House Suggestions," *Modern Dancing* (New York: Harper and Bros., 1914), 177. Courtesy of an American Ballroom Companion: Dance Instruction Manuals, ca. 1490–1920, Library of Congress, Music Division (public domain).

and modern dance. Indeed, an analysis of the technical changes made to ragtime in order to create modern dance reveals that the refinement process was working toward race purity by removing black movement references, even as it was also attempting to commodify a dance practice in order to improve its marketability.

As indicated by 1910s dance manuals, ragtime dancing's black associations were demonstrated through movements of the whole body, especially
the buttocks and shoulders. In particular, vertical axis dips, sequential rolls
through the torso, and angular movements of the limbs activated the body
as a whole. Two dance manuals mentioned in the last chapter that were published in New York toward the end of ragtime dancing's popularity illustrate
this clearly. Edward Scott's *The New Dancing As It Should Be* remarked that
"there was also a good deal of talk about the TURKEY TROT, with its degenerate negroid *mouvement des hanches.*"[23] Likewise, A. M. Cree's *Handbook
of Ball-Room Dancing* told readers to "avoid dipping the shoulders, rolling
the body, and pump-handle action with the arms; such Negroid actions are
very unseemly."[24] Here these authors were telling readers which movements
were considered black at the time, from their perspectives.

Crucially, these depictions of black movement coincided precisely with
what modern dance industry professionals removed from ragtime in order
to transform it into modern dance—its animation of the whole body
through a loosening of the torso and freeing of the limbs. Time and time
again, 1910s dance writings admonished readers:

> Don't sway your body from side to side.
> Don't sway your hips from side to side.
> Don't throw your shoulders from side to side.
> Don't rag—don't wiggle.
> Don't bend your knees or hold them stiffly.
> Don't poke your head over your partner's shoulders.[25]

Through such instructions, teachers effectively instruct dancers not to dance
ragtime, to remove black dancing from their bodies, and to instead perform a
white racial identity. Modern dance constructed the expectations for a white
dancing body through an absence of blackness and, through this process, reinforced existing associations between blackness and primitivism or, in other
words, anti-modernity. In this formulation, white signals progress and tech-
nological advancement, whereas black signals primitive and "the natural."

In a similar way, dancers were expressly told how to dance modern
through an aesthetic of bodily restraint largely culled from late nineteenth-
century European-derived ballroom dancing, a dance form that epitomized
whiteness in America at that time. A 1914 dance manual by Philadelphia
dance impresario Albert W. Newman conveys this aesthetic succinctly:

> The style of dancing to-day is a smooth gliding step, using the ankles and
> the knees moderately…. Any oscillation of the body is considered vulgar….

> Remember that although one may use the feet accurately, unless the general bearing
> is graceful he or she cannot be considered an accomplished dancer.[26]

This language is startlingly similar to dance manuals printed twenty years earlier, a time prior to the massive influx of non-Northern European immigrants and African American migrants.[27] Ironically, *modern* dances—a name that suggests an embracing of the contemporary—in many ways embodied a *nostalgic* view of America at a more homogeneous, seemingly simpler time, not unlike the blues dancers discussed in chapter one.

Modern dance was, in effect, designed to be reminiscent of social dancing that was seemingly free of nonwhite influences. When modern dance professionals instructed dancers what to do and not to do in these ways, they also communicated how to dance white and how *not* to dance black. By dancing according to these particular values—by restraining the torso and limbs—modern dancers strived to embody a construction of a pure white racial identity. In their effort to express modernity in movement practices, dancers essentially embodied the incommensurability of black and white and reified the black/white binary that dominated racial thinking of the time.

Consequently, dance professionals played an important role in the definition of socially constructed physical markers of racial difference—even though their language only directly addressed issues of modernity, aesthetics, and class. Their labors provided dancers with a means of performing an elevated social status whenever they entered the dance floor, at a time when social mobility seemed increasingly possible. Importantly, their dominant aesthetic values were rooted in Western European understandings of beauty. Thus the very pursuit of class status, defined in these terms, meant that modern dancers and dance professionals helped define a new and subtle means of reinforcing white hegemony through and over the body.

While enjoying an evening out on the town, modern social dancers in early twentieth-century America could perform whiteness and re-inscribe the value of racial purity simply by avoiding movement associated with African Americans—such as shoulder-shaking, knee-lifting, or hip-wiggling. This was appealing because ragtime's merging of black dancing and white bodies alluded to miscegenation precisely when increasing heterogeneity was feared. For this reason, ragtime dancing could not be easily sold with its black associations intact; it needed to be whitened and indeed controlled through simplification and codification before it could be mass-marketed as "refined" modern dance. Such changes became even more crucial if this dance form was to be embraced as a means for performing an elevated social status. In this way, early twentieth-century paranoia related to white "race suicide," coupled with concerns over the nature of American identity, helped shape social dance practice and an emerging ballroom industry.

These prejudices relating to African Americans in particular and racial difference more generally worked in partnership with emerging mass-production processes, which dictated that ragtime's improvisations should be diminished. Indeed, commodification reduced this dance form's repertoire, homogenized its variations, eliminated solos, and sharply reduced physical contact between dancers. For this reason, modern dance, as the refined version of ragtime dancing, provides us with another valuable case study for how racial subjugation can be central to the economic and industrial development that often defines modernity.

That said, through the creation of modern dance, these dance professionals launched modern ballroom dancing and the industry that lives on today, which continues to be a vital profession for vulnerable groups—the working classes, new immigrants, and young women.[28] This industry offers those who might lack formal education opportunities for professional advancement, financial reward, and international travel. Ballroom dance teaching and performance still has the power to lift individuals out of poverty and launch them on the path towards a more cosmopolitan lifestyle. Furthermore, modern ballroom dancing itself, owing to its codification, is highly accessible and, for this reason, has the capacity to bring people together in shared movement synergy around the world. To this day, it retains the broadest reach of any social dance that has ever existed.

Grand Lodge of the Fraternal Brotherhood, Harlem

Eight P.M., Saturday, February 1920

A large, stately ballroom lit with countless candles and adorned with wide swaths of white organza. Big round tables ring the space, set with flowers and elegant china—here families and friends sit chatting over coffee and dessert while observing the dancing nearby. The dance floor is full but not packed, with couples of all ages dressed in formal attire—tails for the men, of course, and softly draped shimmering ball gowns for the women. At the edge of the dance floor, several young men stand near an elegant older gentleman. He whispers directions into the young men's ears, one at a time, while simultaneously smiling and nodding at couples whirling by and patrons sitting at tables.

Nervously, Dorcas finally succumbs to her mother's insistence that she take a turn around the dance floor. Watching feels more comfortable, given that she has only had a couple of lessons, but she also knows it was fruitless to resist. She lifts her spine and gently presses her shoulders back—this part of her dance lessons she can at least remember—as she follows a few paces behind her mother. She heads straight across the room toward the dancing master, whose greying hair and slightly faded lapels give him away. Within a few moments, a handsome young man stands before her extending his hand, with a warm half smile gracing his face. It is as though a mail-order prince charming arrived.

With a nod, Dorcas accepts his kind offer and walks slowly toward the edge of the dance floor. Here they stand coolly, their outreached gloved hands just touching one another's palms and backs. They look away from one another, each over the other's shoulder, toward the couples whirling by, waiting for a point of entry.

Fortunately the music is for a pert schottische, one of the few dances covered in her lessons so far. But Dorcas's mind is racing. Is it on the "one" or the "and" that we step out? Do I swivel my head when we change direction, or is that too "common," as mother would say? She vaguely remembers there is a turn involved in this dance, but where it happens and which foot it starts on escaped her. Thank goodness she has gloves on to conceal her moist palms.

Prince Charming meets her eyes to confirm she is ready before sliding one foot out into the circle. Dorcas echoes his movement. It is as if her body remembers things she doesn't. Soon they are skipping and sliding together first in one direction and then the other. Like a gust of wind changing directions, they shift in synchrony. Together they seem to sweep the dance floor, jubilantly arching one way and then the other. She only needs to submit to her partner to feel like the most graceful woman in the room.

After her partner senses she had mastered this basic step, he cautiously introduces a turn, which brings them even closer together. Rather than skipping and sliding, he begins hopping in a tight circle every other beat, first on one foot and then the other. This is not the most elegant of turns, but Dorcas enjoys the synergy of their shared efforts enormously. Like a top, they softly spin together in their own little world in the midst of the other dancing couples. At this moment of relative ecstasy, it suddenly occurs to her that she should seek out a review of her performance by checking the expression on her mother's face. A quick scan over her partner's shoulder finds her mother seated nearby with friends, her eyes glued on Dorcas. It is hard to read her face—pride, concern, pleasure, and attentiveness are all present simultaneously. Dorcas breathes a sigh of relief just as the song is ending.

As she and her partner walk back toward her mother, she stops him for a moment to ask his name so she can find him again. "The name is Charlie, miss," he replies, his eyes scanning the floor boards. The rush of the dancing emboldening Dorcas, she then asks over lowered lashes, "Charlie, do you teach dancing somewhere?"—thinking how lovely it would be to dance with him more often. Dating is clearly not an option, given his profession, but dancing together might be. He replies, "Tonight is my first night working with the professor, miss, but I hope to work at his studio one day"—then he pauses before adding softly— "Normally, at night, I dance downtown in different shows. Jazz, you know?" At this confession, she gives Charlie a wistful smile as she turns to continue their walk toward mother.

CHAPTER 4

✧

"The Eclipse"

Ballroom Dancing, Bodily Code-Switching, and the Harlem Renaissance

The schottische, a late nineteenth-century ballroom dance, was renamed "The Eclipse" and performed at the opening of Professor Charles H. Anderson's New Select School of Dance in Harlem's Imperial Elk's Auditorium in 1925, at the height of the Harlem Renaissance.[1] The Eclipse and ballroom dances like it were central to Anderson's ambitious plans to "revive the almost lost cause of the terpsichorean world, and place it firmly once more on the ground where it belongs."[2] He was just one of several African American social dance teachers who opened small businesses proffering European-derived ballroom dances—*not* ragtime or modern dances—in the wake of massive northward migrations into Manhattan. Their clients were African American elites (and would-be elites) who wanted to learn the bodily codes of "respectability," which were linked with white ideals.

This chapter discusses Anderson as an example of the ways in which Harlem created a fertile environment for black professionalization through social dance teaching during the 1920s.[3] It will then query the social mobility fostered by ballroom dancing in black communities during this period through a consideration of cultural politics. Following this, the chapter counterbalances these assessments with an exploration of dancers' experiences and how they may not have matched media representations—focusing in particular on how black ballroom dancing did not always follow the rules of

European-influenced ballroom dancing. Finally, I propose a new way of understanding the complex significations of black elite dancing of this period, what
I call bodily code-switching, that is rooted in Henry Louis Gates's notion of
"signifyin(g)'" and W. E. B. Du Bois's "double consciousness."

SOCIAL DANCE IN THE HARLEM RENAISSANCE

European-derived ballroom dances such as the Eclipse were the only forms
of social dancing represented in New York's black periodicals of the 1910s
and '20s, which catered to the approximately 70 to 80 percent of Harlem's
population that was literate. While the *New York Age* and *New York Amsterdam
News* covered stage entertainments almost exclusively, the NAACP's *Crisis*
rarely, if ever, discussed dance. (See Fig. 4.1) Only the *Inter-state Tattler* (also
known as *The Tattler* and *The Hotel Tattler*) addressed black social dancing with
any regularity, and it was devoted to the ballroom dancing of Harlem's so-
called respectable classes, which included both the growing middle and small
upper classes—what I call, for the sake of simplicity, the "elites", who were
united in their disdain for the working classes and hunger for upward mobility. *The Tattler* was Harlem's society magazine from 1924/5 to 1932. Based
on such sources, one might believe that African Americans in Manhattan did
not dance ragtime or jazz socially—even though much of New York City and
America did. Indeed, at the height of the ragtime and jazz crazes, when songs
were proclaiming "Everybody's Doin' It," well-to-do Harlemites were *not*, in
fact, doing it—instead, they were learning traditional ballroom dances like
the schottische, which first appeared in the middle of the nineteenth century
and, by the 1910s, had long been considered old-fashioned. In fact, I have
encountered only one ballroom dance manual published between 1900 and
1930 that provides instructions for this dance.

The African American dancing of European American social dances during
the ragtime and jazz eras might be regarded as quaintly nostalgic at best or
traitorous at worst. Yet this dancing was not an attempt at reverse minstrelsy
or white mimicry as cultural theorist Homi Bhabha's understanding of mime-
sis might suggest, but can be more productively considered an example of,
what literary theorist Henry Louis Gates would call, "repetition with a signal difference."[4] Even though surviving images and newspaper sources present the social dancing as European-influenced, interviews with participants
decades later indicate that Harlem's new residents also "ragged" their ballroom
dance steps, thereby generating more complex racial references. In this way,
the social dancing of black elites referenced white ideals while, importantly, it
also offered a mode of interrogating them through implicitly interventionist
dance moves in a manner reminiscent of the cakewalk of decades earlier.[5]

In this way, Harlem's elites engaged in what I call bodily code-switching, which is a particular type of mimicry.[6] With more earnestness than humor, they subtly critiqued the strictures of European-style ballroom dancing *and* the black stereotypes of the dominant white cultures that surrounded them. They also demonstrated their assimilation and mastery of white cultural norms. Their dancing embodied the complex politics of respectability within Harlem in the 1920s, as well as the ideology of hope that fueled it. Harlem's elites and aspiring elites sought not only social mobility for themselves but also for the race. In addition, they announced their desire to be included in modernity and not be grouped with those "left behind" any longer. Through ballroom dancing, they helped construct black Harlem of the time, its social relations and divides, as well as a modern black identity.

By looking at black periodical sources alongside interviews, it becomes clear that the dancing of white ballroom dances by Harlem's elites was an intricate political choreography. On the one hand, it offered participants an important means of learning and then performing the physical markers of their new hard-won class status. On the other, through its occasional engagement with black movement influences, such as those discussed in chapter one, this dancing also provided a means of brief nostalgic reconnection with a pre-migratory home—given that many of the new members of the black middle classes were migrants who had been able to achieve a degree of success in Manhattan. Moreover, by dancing ballroom with "black" inflections, these participants aimed to imagine a post-migration black community by constructing a shared racial "feeling," to borrow sociologist Paul Gilroy's term, which will be discussed later in the chapter. In this way, they echoed the efforts of Harlem Renaissance leaders who endeavored to establish a "New Negro" identity through other artistic forms, such as literature, poetry, sculpture, and painting—but rarely dance.[7]

Looking beyond the dancing itself toward the industrial structure that enabled it reveals that the *teaching* of these dances to this particular population provided migrant men with an important source of financial support during their transition to New York City and offered them an attractive alternative to the physical labor that other migrants were doing. If regarded as a labor network, the work of these men eventually constituted a new micro-industry that would provide a pathway into the American black culture industries that would grow steadily throughout the twentieth century. Finally, the teaching of European American dances to Harlem elites provided migrants with a path to professionalization and a means of earning respect. By considering the teaching of white dances to black people from the perspective of economic concerns in this way, we can move beyond simplistic judgments about cross-cultural borrowing and appropriation toward a more complex understanding of how dance can intervene in social relations, cultural politics, and human experience.

THE SOCIAL LIFE OF COLORED AMERICA.

Figure 4.1 Harlem Ballroom Dance Event, 1910s (above and facing page). "The Life of Colored America—II: The Bachelor-Benedicts' Assembly, New York City, Jan. 2014," *The Crisis* (May 1914), 234–235 (public domain).

II.—THE BACHELOR-BENEDICTS' ASSEMBLY,
NEW YORK CITY.

Figure 4.1 (Continued)

PROFESSOR ANDERSON AND BLACK HARLEM

As a means of illuminating this moment in dance and American history, this section focuses on Professor Charles H. Anderson. His experience is likely representative of others for whom less documentation has survived, although it is difficult to estimate how many other African American dance teachers were working in Harlem.[8] His career provides an example of how micro-industrialization and professionalization were possible during a time of unprecedented growth in black New York. Anderson was a Southern migrant who went from being a street performer to a central figure in Harlem's ballroom dance world by slowly adapting to changing times and tactically building his career. Anderson's success was possible because his work helped to establish Harlem "society," along with its new class system, and contributed to community-based racial-uplift efforts.

Throughout his career, Anderson worked within the interstices of black New York—seizing opportunities as they emerged—as it shifted from downtown to uptown. During the ragtime years, he struggled, but once he reached a degree of professional stability as a dance teacher and dance hall manager, he tried to leverage his success to solidify the new profession of social dance teaching for other African American men. The popularity of dancing during the jazz years, on the other hand, which paralleled the rise of black Harlem and the "New Negro" movement, offered Anderson an opportunity to grow his businesses rapidly—although he resisted the allure of jazz for many years. During this era, instead, he endeavored to appeal to Harlem's growing middle-class members, who were seeking to perform in publicly visible ways their education, cosmopolitanism, and elevated class status. In these ways, he was among Harlem's first batch of black entrepreneurs who effectively adapted to emerging opportunities and prevailing notions of class.

Anderson began his dance career with no formal training shortly after he migrated to New York from Lynchburg, Virginia, around 1900.[9] After spending a few years dancing (likely some version of tap dancing, sometimes called a "breakdown") in the lobbies of railroad stations for passersby, he began formally teaching ballroom dance around 1905, a few years after his brother Jack began hosting a regular dance "class" in the Tenderloin entertainment district at the West 53rd Street Hall—much like the one described in the opening vignette in chapter one.[10]

Anderson was a popular teacher who, out of necessity, became involved in dance hall management. During these years, his classes—which were eventually held at the Palace Hall (50th Street and 7th Avenue)—functioned as undercover dance halls. As mentioned in chapter one,

New York City laws at this time, which were influenced by middle-class progressive-era reformers, made it very expensive and difficult to run a legitimate, licensed commercial dance venue. It was much easier to get a license to run a dance academy without alcohol, than an entertainment hall with it. As a result, dance classes and academies—explicitly positioned as separate from alcohol-serving establishments—became a main venue for social dancing in Manhattan. Of course, these locales were usually located above or below a bar, so dancers could easily refresh themselves.[11]

Anderson's dance events were sometimes known as the "Blue Ribbon Classes," a name likely chosen to indicate that participants were winners, first class, highly prized, or certified in some way. According to a COF report from 1910, Anderson's classes were held in a hall perched over a basement bar and involved five to six hundred dancers. For this reason, he employed four other teachers as instructors to assist him with the management of these events—William Vaughn, Moses Mims, and Mr. and Mrs. Frank Stewart. The dancing he promoted during this period was what he called ballroom dancing, a term that brings to mind European-derived partner dances of the nineteenth century, which explains perhaps why he was later referred to as an "old school" teacher in the 1930s Harlem Works Progress Administration (WPA) Report.

Anderson tried to leverage his success to help other dance teachers. He worked to found a professional association that would support black ballroom dance teachers in New York. The WPA report tells us that in 1907, Anderson helped launch the Metropolitan Association of Dancing Masters. It had five members at its inception, all of whom were men—J. Hoffman Woods, William Vaughn, William Banks, Charles H. Anderson, and Charles Alexandria.[12] Archival evidence does not tell us how long this organization lasted, if it grew to include many more members, or if it eventually merged with another group, but its numbers suggest that there were perhaps fewer than a dozen teachers like Anderson operating at this time in Manhattan. Its very existence, however, indicates a surge in the popularity of dance teaching as a profession among New York's African Americans—as well as their exclusion from the two dominant American dance organizations at the time: the American National Association of Masters of Dancing and the International Masters of Dancing. The dances these men specialized in were quadrilles, schottisches, polkas, lancers, varsouvianas (a type of waltz), and prances. These were not only nineteenth-century European-derived round dances, but several of them emanated from more than fifty years before—thus reinforcing the teachers' conservative self-positioning in terms of repertoire.

The ragtime craze was a challenging time for all black performers, as white dancers were more often than not the public face of the period's social dancing, as will be discussed in the next chapter. Limited surviving evidence suggests that Anderson was unable to grow his dance hall teaching business for African American clients during the 1910s, ragtime's period of popularity. Instead, he added occasional exhibition ballroom performances and private coaching for elite white clients to his repertoire of professional activities. For example, he and his wife danced so-called society dances in a 1914 film called *Uncle Remus' Visit to New York*—one of the first "race" (all-black) films to be produced. According to a WPA report, they also performed at large-scale theatrical events in Manhattan, including one sponsored by the *New York Times*.

In an effort to continue his work as a dance professional, Anderson had to cautiously expand his teaching repertoire beyond nineteenth-century ballroom dance to eventually include ragtime. The Harlem WPA report tells us that Anderson offered *private* ragtime dance lessons to white socialites like Gertrude Vanderbilt and professional modern dancers like Irene Castle and Joan Sawyer. In fact, Anderson told his WPA interviewers that Mrs. Castle encouraged him to "go South to teach dancing"—perhaps she meant as part of her touring show.

Interestingly, Anderson's work with ragtime luminary Joan Sawyer was reported in the black press. Articles in the *Chicago Defender* and the *New York Age* both mention that he had been contracted to teach Sawyer a dance called the "Congo Schottische," which she later performed on Broadway.[13] Given that the schottische was a decidedly old-fashioned dance by 1914, this public acknowledgment of Anderson's work would likely have enhanced his reputation among his African American elite clientele who valued nineteenth-century dancing.[14] Anderson's genre expansion into ragtime dancing—which enabled him to acquire a few white elite patrons—occurred discreetly, then, and was not part of his public teaching or performing in black communities. This may have protected his reputation as a society dance teacher in the long term.

Like many black New Yorkers, Anderson moved uptown around 1916. There he became part of the generation that established Harlem as a national and global black capital. Black Harlem, from the very beginning, was devoted to uplifting the race, as well as self-improvement for those who aspired to a better life. A. Philip Randolph, a labor organizer, civil rights activist, and long-time New York resident, described the difference that Harlem made in the following way:

> There was a certain standard, social standard, in the life of Negroes in Harlem then.... You had a little gloss. There was a greater sense of respectability within the Negro group. They were trying to do things, trying to achieve status for the race.[15]

Moving uptown or up from the South to Harlem seems to have inspired a hope for the future—a sense of upward mobility. Such notions permeated all of Harlem's cultural activities and in particular its social dancing. As a result, a market developed for "respectable" dancing that Anderson was able to take advantage of and eventually dominate. The growth of his dance businesses was directly tied to the ideology of hope that infused Harlem during this time.

In Harlem, Anderson hit his stride professionally, and his businesses rapidly diversified and expanded. During this period, he returned to focusing exclusively on black elites and would-be elites. The growth of Harlem as a black capital and nexus for modern African American identity provided Anderson with the opportunity to help build Harlem culture, as well as its new class system. Furthermore, he became central to local racial-uplift efforts and thus provided a means of social mobility for aspiring individuals, as well as "the race." In these ways, Anderson contributed to the construction of black modernity during this period. Anderson's success, however, was dependent on his ability to meet his clients' needs and match his teaching to prevailing discourses of class.

At first, Anderson went back and forth between seeing clients in his new private dance studio near 7th Avenue and 136th Street and producing large events in rented commercial spaces like casinos, ballrooms, and fraternal lodges.[16] He promoted dance contests for the general public as well.[17] To run these events successfully, he had to go beyond his existing staff members and hire over twenty temporary instructors, inviting those interested to apply the day before the event. The fact that there were likely twenty-five dance instructors operating at one event suggests that perhaps dozens of men were working within this profession at the time.

Later in the 1920s, Anderson had to adjust his practices to match Harlem trends. He began to hire single women and called them instructresses and hostesses, not teachers.[18] In this way, he paralleled practices at Harlem's other music-dance venues, like the Cotton Club and Small's Paradise, which were famous for their employment of attractive, young African American women as performers in their revues.[19] Indeed, these women were central to spectacles downtown, as well as successful black musicals like *Shuffle Along* (1921) and *Dixie to Broadway* (1924).[20] Anderson's advertisements during this period stress the presence of numerous "beautiful hostesses" at his events, and in one advertisement, an attractive young woman in a glamorous pose is featured.[21] It seems that by the late 1920s, Anderson could no longer rely solely on his own respected reputation to draw people to his events; he had to hire these women as examples of youthfulness, sex appeal, and modernity—all key values in Harlem of the 1920s.

Anderson also eventually found ways to embrace the Jazz Age, at least superficially, in order to keep and grow his business clientele. Interestingly, *Tattler* articles tell us that around 1924 Anderson entered into a partnership with another teacher named Darling Mack, who taught stage jazz dancing, as well as social dance. His advertisements claimed to "train you direct for all Broadway revues."[22] Together they hosted large events with huge orchestras that were designed to draw hundreds of participants.[23] For his largest events, Anderson also began to include vaudeville and/or Broadway headliners to entertain the crowd during the orchestra's intermission. In these ways, Anderson used the opportunities that were available to him and gave the public the impression that he was keeping up with the times.

In terms of the dancing, though, Professor Anderson did not waiver in his commitment to European American ballroom practices throughout the jazz era. According to WPA reports, he remained rooted in nineteenth century ballrooms with schottisches, waltzes, quadrilles, polkas, and lancers. It was not until the mid-1920s that he slightly expanded his repertoire to include foxtrots—a dance that would have been considered new ten years prior. Despite white America's widespread interest in black dancing throughout this period of time, Anderson, according to his own promotional literature, did not teach the turkey trot or Charleston. He kept teaching—and presumably his clients kept dancing—old ballroom dances that were no longer even danced at fashionable European American dance events.

Despite his staffing and partnership shifts, Anderson's clientele did not change much over time. His language choices and the location of his advertisements tell us that his clients continued to be the African American elites, despite his late, superficial embrace of jazz. Throughout the 1920s, Anderson frequently published in the *Inter-State Tattler*. Promotional articles therein called his school of "select dance" a "refined institution" in a "wholesome and clean" atmosphere.[24] Authors refer to Anderson as a "commanding presence"[25] and an "old master" with the "courtliness and urbanity of a gentleman of the good old school."[26] Anderson himself refers to his clients as the "most fashionable and colorful" and the "elite of dance."[27] Nowhere in print does he directly link his dancing with the new trends like ragtime, jazz, or indeed anything considered modern—in stark contrast with most white professional social dance teachers of the period. Instead, Anderson's niche was classiness defined conservatively and nostalgically.

In contrast, the advertisements and writings of white dance professionals in *Fellowship Magazine* and *Modern Dance Magazine*, for example—which were dedicated to social dancing during the 1910s—used the words "modern" and "new" over and over again. They stressed the freedom that ragtime dances offered to participants and the individuality and personality that could be expressed through them. These ideas adhered to an emerging model of self-fashioning that developed in the early twentieth century, in part a response to the social changes brought about by dancing and other forms of expressive culture.[28] Anderson and his compatriots chose not to follow suit, perhaps because they could not do so. They were not in a secure enough economic position to embrace the contemporariness enabled by ragtime and jazz dancing. This choice is evidence of the continued perilous situation for African Americans during this period, even among the few with economic advantages. A conservative stance was clearly safer for all involved.

In this way, Anderson continued in a pattern established during the cakewalk era, twenty years earlier, when professional dancers like Aida Overton Walker endeavored to represent themselves as "refined" (i.e., professional and sophisticated). According to theatre historian David Krasner and cultural historian Karen Sotiropoulos, Walker tactically tied these concepts with conservative understandings of morality.[29] Both performers and African Americans were seen by outsiders to be naturally amoral, and she meant to change that view, by offering the public a positive alternate model. In this way, she was part of her generation's racial-uplift efforts that predate the Harlem Renaissance ones. Importantly, she framed her agenda in a collective sense, according to Krasner, not in an individual one, by which he means that she spoke in terms of the entire race. He argues that to do otherwise would have been perceived as threatening to black men, as well as white folks in general.[30]

Through Walker's approach, in particular, we can perhaps better understand Anderson's tactical repertoire choices. The embracing of the newness and modernity of ragtime and jazz also meant expressing the empowering notions of freedom, individuality, and personality these forms embodied. This could have put Anderson and his clients in a risky position in terms of public representation. They might have easily been seen as "uppity," or at least, not knowing their place. By remaining conservative in their dance repertoire—by dodging the controversial associations with ragtime and jazz—they threatened far fewer people with their dancing and perhaps ensured greater longevity for their careers and the profession.

DANCING HOPE

Professor Anderson was, of course, not only selling dance knowledge, but also the ideas that the dancing referenced. Dancing European American ballroom dances provided the new black elites with a way to demonstrate their "distinction," to use Bourdieu's notion, from the black working classes, who did not have the financial means to properly learn the dances from a teacher.[31] Ballroom dancing, as both a luxury good and cultural product, had the power to articulate social differences within Manhattan's black communities. In this way, specific bodily movements could express dominant aesthetic values for consumers with sufficient economic means who wished to elevate their social position. It is important to note, however, that these values were rooted in dominant Western understandings of beauty. Thus the very pursuit of class status, defined in these terms, meant that dancers and dance professionals helped to subtly reinforce white ideals within black communities.

The possibility of dancing in pursuit of upward mobility was facilitated by the ways in which social position was being redefined in black urban communities during the opening decades of the twentieth century. Elite standing was being delineated in broader and more flexible ways than it had been in the past. As a result, a black middle class was burgeoning within what had been, more or less, a two-caste socioeconomic system throughout the nineteenth century. Hence social mobility in black urban communities became more available, which in turn created a space in which social identity needed to be and could be expressed in various body-based ways—including social dancing. In this climate, respectability emerged as a crucial concept that was tied to economic growth, or at least its promise. Indeed, an ideology of hope came to permeate the embodied cultural practices of Harlem's elites and aspiring elites during the Renaissance.

After the Civil War, a tiny black upper class and a vast black working class were separated by a negligible middle class. According to historian Kevin Gaines, nineteenth-century black upper-class status was closely tied to proximity with white Americans through employment and/or blood relations.[32] As a result of the association between family lineage and social standing, among African Americans, lightness of skin color became a marker of elite status in black communities and, by inversion, darkness of skin color an indication of lower status—thereby creating a "mulatto elite" in the words of historian Alessandra Lorini.[33]

Around the turn of the century, however, the lightness of a person's skin color began to be less indicative of social status in black communities—thereby lending greater permeability to class divides. Freed from biological imperatives, the potential for social mobility increased. During the opening decades of the twentieth century, black social status began to be more determined by profession, education, and outward behavior than it had been previously. Lorini has argued that it was not until the 1920s that "class lines of the black urban community followed those of the white class structure," by which she means that class status was less dependent on skin pigment and more dependent on wealth.[34] She explains that a new black bourgeoisie of business and professional men, who were "gradually assuming upper-class status and either merged with or replaced in status the older [black] upper class,"[35] manifested during the early twentieth century. Indeed, during this period, the traditionally light-skinned members of the black upper class were forced to make room at the top for a critical mass of newly wealthy African Americans who had recently achieved business and professional success, *after* their migration out of the South.

In addition to the changing composition of the small black upper class, a black middle class began to flourish during this period according to Gaines. Although a certain degree of occupational and material achievement was associated with this socioeconomic cluster, he argues that what truly distinguished this group from the black lower classes was their fierce aspiration toward respectability.[36] This notion, although appropriated from white culture, encapsulated an effort toward greater empowerment that strategically positioned members of the black middle classes above the black working classes. It likewise positioned the black middle classes in alignment with their white counterparts, through their shared investment in a particular notion of respectability. In this way, the black middle class challenged racial prejudice and asserted their assimilation within America. It was also a means of survival. And, it was the increased flexibility of social boundaries in early twentieth-century black urban communities that made this kind of aspiration even possible.[37]

Although not necessarily realistic, the *possibility* of significant economic improvement was enough to inspire members of Manhattan's African American communities to hope for a better future than they had allowed themselves to hope for in the past, whether they came of age in the North or the South.[38] Lorini echoes this view, writing that "[t]he presence of a small wealthy black aristocracy and a growing number of nouveau riches became a strong point of reference for the black middle class, who could dream about imitating their success."[39] In Gaines's view, such hopes or dreams could propel former members of the black lower classes into the rapidly expanding black middle classes. While I agree with Gaines that an ideology of hope was likely at the heart of the early twentieth-century black middle class, this group's social dancing practices suggest that hope alone was not enough. Aspiration had to be outwardly demonstrated—embodied—through social practices such as dancing in order for hope to be truly a part of middle-class-ness. Ragtime and jazz dancing, though, were not good candidates for the expression of aspiration by members of the black middle classes. Their dancing preferences tell us that European-derived ballroom dancing embodied *their* hopes much better.

NOT DANCING RAGTIME AND JAZZ

The European-ness of Harlem's ballroom dancing certainly facilitated the public performance of social distinction, but so did its distance from ragtime and jazz. As discussed in the previous chapters, these particular dances were among the first African-influenced social dances to become widespread American social practice, and they constituted the predominant dancing in American urban centers during the early twentieth century. It seems, however, that ragtime and jazz were too publicly linked to stereotypical blackness to be useful to the new black middle classes in their performances of distinction. Even though the blackness of ragtime music and dancing was not always explicitly acknowledged outside of black communities, their racial associations were nonetheless indicated by references to the South, use of black dialect, and syncopated rhythms in the music, as well as angular body shapes, emphasis on hip movement, and the mimicry of animals in the dancing, as discussed in chapter two.

Despite the purported "chic-ness" of the "Negro" during the 1920s in particular, blackness was still widely and stereotypically linked with poverty, illiteracy, etc. Such an association could clearly not be risked by the newly privileged. According to Harlem poet and critic Lorenzo Thomas:

> The African-American intellectuals who launched the "New Negro Movement" at the turn of the century were acutely aware of the pariah status being imposed upon their people ... the black leadership tried to counter [increasing hostility and legalized racial segregation], in part, by demonstrating yet again the humanity and aptitude of black people. Often this meant drawing their attention to the former slaves' mastery of Western cultural standards.... W. E. B. Du Bois, editor of the NAACP's *Crisis* magazine beginning in 1910 penned numerous accolades for African American performers of European classical music....[40]

In this context, then, black elites' preference for European-derived ballroom dancing over ragtime and jazz can be understood as a means of demonstrating their humanness, as well as their potential to meet Western ideals, thus qualifying them for full American citizenship. In short, in the face of very real hostility, ballroom dancing for these participants functioned as propaganda and insurance at the same time.

DODGING THE BODY

Besides publicly avoiding ragtime and jazz, it was also important for the European American ballroom dancing of black elites (and would-be elites) to be distanced from the body itself and its physicality, sensuality, and sexuality. Although difficult to imagine—a form of dance being distanced from the material body—in Anderson's promotional articles, movement and/or the body is rarely mentioned at all. One article refers to the dancing as "beautiful," while another calls it "formal"—but that is it. In fact, in Anderson's published commercial representations, more time is spent describing the teachers than the dancing—"famed for their faultless dress and demeanor," for example. Only one of the promotional articles I located is accompanied by an illustration of any kind, which is a photograph of a woman standing and looking at a flower. Anderson's advertisements contained only text and rarely named the dances taught or the type of music to be played. The result of these choices was that the excitement, energy, effort, sensuality, and pleasure of dancing was not conveyed; it was instead omitted, which implied that Anderson and his patrons' dancing was calm, controlled, and almost cerebral.

This was all in stark contrast to the marketing practices of the European American ballroom industry, which was busily selling refined versions of ragtime and jazz to the American public. These white dance professionals frequently used sketches and photographs of moving bodies to advertise themselves. Their proffered dance practices were named carefully (as ragtime, modern, or new dancing, for example) depending on the intended audience. Articles describing social dancing evidenced a fascination with the moving body; the prose lingered over its new patterns, energy, and practices. Early issues of *Modern Dance Magazine*, for example, included not only images of what to do and what not to do on the dance floor, but also articles debating the right way to dance. Here is a passage from one of the articles:

> The old Turkey Trot was an exaggerated and crude swinging of the body from side to side, accentuated by throwing the feet out from side to side. As the New Dances developed, and the individual dancer acquired more poise and grace, the feet were kept close to the floor, and the swinging and jumping of the body transformed into a gliding, waving movement.[41]

Here we can see the attention to the sensual body and its movement that was starkly lacking in writing about dancing in the black press. This level of physical description was avoided in all the public self-representations of Anderson and the dancing he promoted.

This aversion to the body and its physicality is reminiscent of sociologist Norbert Elias's argument that the body was at the center of European conceptualizations of civilization.[42] In *The Civilizing Process*, he asserts that since the Middle Ages, social etiquette—as a performance of one's degree of civilization—has demanded a gradual denial of bodily needs and functions. As a result, things like spitting, body hair, and expressions of sexual desire (for example) became increasingly relegated to private realms. Thus, perhaps in an effort to reinforce the civilization of themselves, their clients, and their movement practices, Anderson and other dance teachers tactically obfuscated the materiality of the dancing body in the representations of their work.

THE BODY IN THE HARLEM RENAISSANCE

Interestingly, this choice to obfuscate the body also parallels the uplift efforts of Harlem Renaissance leaders who were deeply invested in a "New Negro" theatre, literature, and art—but notably not dance. Social dancing, if African in influence, was not openly supported by the conservative leaders of this movement. Their balls included European-derived ballroom dancing, according to representations in black publications of the time. (See Fig. 4.1) Only the younger generation of Harlem Renaissance artists discussed in chapter one, as part of their rebellion, created work that represented the importance of African American social dancing in black communities—Langston Hughes's *Not Without Laughter*, Zora Neale Hurston's *Their Eyes Were Watching God*, Wallace Thurman's *Cordelia the Crude*, and Claude McKay's *Home to Harlem*, among many others.

In fact, the NAACP's journal *Opportunity* did not mention African American concert dance until 1934—near the end of the Harlem Renaissance—according to dance scholar Susan Manning.[43] The first few concerts of such dancing were not even reviewed in New York City's black periodicals—which signaled a lack of approval from Harlem's leadership. On the other hand, the arguably less sensual "New Negro" theatre and music productions did regularly receive comment.[44]

The first concert of African American dance to be openly approved of by Harlem Renaissance elite was Asadata Dafora's *Kykunkor* of 1934, which appeared on Broadway and achieved a measure of commercial success downtown. Appearing at the very end of the Renaissance, this work was celebrated by one of its founders, Alain Locke, as an ideal for its integration of African folk materials, artistic use of drums, and restrained sexuality.

Locke had a complicated relationship with the performing arts of the Harlem Renaissance. On the one hand, he saw their potential to demonstrate the development of African American culture; on the other, through his reviews, he sometimes imposed a Eurocentric value system on African American artists. According to poet and cultural critic Lorenzo Thomas, "Nevertheless, the Eurocentric element of Locke's thought led him to the scenario that would produce symphonies from jazz in much the way that 18th- and 19th-century European composers 'elevated' and refined simple folk airs into chamber music and symphonic motifs."[45] And so it was likely that Dafora's theatricalization of African folk dance and music—as a means of demonstrating artistic development—most appealed to Locke.

Here we find indications of the rocks and hard places between which dance operated during this period in uplift-oriented black communities. On the one hand, as Manning argues, it needed to be perceived as authentically black to be valued; on the other, it needed to be judged as artistic by white Western standards, but without seeming derivative of white models or expressive of "natural" black talent. Furthermore, the dancing could only deploy the body in non-sexualized ways, or it risked being aligned with popular dance practices like jazz and ragtime, which were *not* considered art by the Harlem elite. Black popular dance's associations with sexuality and entertainment rendered most dance and movement suspect among those invested in improving wider perceptions of African Americans. For these reasons, representation of the black body was a tense topic of consideration during the 1920s within Harlem. Nonetheless, the professional activities of Anderson and his compatriots can be viewed as an extension of the Harlem Renaissance project, given their efforts to positively transform representations of African American men and women through what they viewed to be artistic practices, ballroom dancing.

BODILY CODE-SWITCHING

Thus far, this chapter has addressed the *representations* of black elite dancing by early twentieth-century African American dance professionals, but the question remains whether the *experience* of dancers parallels the surviving evidence. Interviews with artists who were active during this time period in New York tell us that a more complex situation emerged on dance floors. Jazz researchers Marshall and Jean Stearns interviewed pianist Sidney Easton in the 1960s, who remembered that, when dancing ballroom dances, "the colored people used ... lots of solo work and improvised breaks by each dancer putting together steps of his own."[46] His description is echoed by stride pianist James P. Johnson who remarked in a 1955 interview that within a 1910s Manhattan dance "school":

> The "pupils" danced sets, two-steps, waltzes, schottisches. ... I played for these regulation dances, but instead of playing them straight, I'd break into a rag in certain places. ... The dances they did ... were wild and comical—the more pose and the more breaks, the better.[47]

In this way, these musicians testify that, in certain contexts, ragtime and jazz movements were inserted into ballroom dancing by African Americans. Perhaps toward the end of public events or in lower-class venues like buffet flats[48]—safe spaces to temporarily deviate from white norms and values—ballroom dancers strayed from their lessons with Anderson and his colleagues.

Easton and Johnson indicate that black ballroom dancing of the early twentieth century often contained instances of simultaneous soloing, also known as breaks, that briefly departed from the restrained aesthetics of European-style ballroom dancing, which emphasized grace, linearity, control, and lightness. These discrete moments—just as in the slow drag and ragtime dancing—were clearly improvised and individualized according to the personal repertoires and creative choices of each dancer. Dancing that involved "poses" and "breaks," as described by Johnson, sounds a lot like the cakewalking of the nineteenth century, especially if it was also "wild" and "comical." Given the structure of popular music of the early twentieth century, it is likely that these breaks aligned with the repeated choruses of songs. Whenever they happened, in these moments of freedom, dancers could stretch their limbs, play with rhythms, and express silliness. They could exude positive energy, flirt, draw attention to themselves—feel as though they were at home.

While such dancing could be seen as a means of reconnecting with a pre-migratory sense of home, as with the black working classes discussed in chapter one, in this case, it also helped construct a modern African American identity through what I describe as bodily code-switching. As mentioned earlier, New York City had been home to several black communities for centuries. After abolition, successive waves of migration northward, and the subsequent relocation to Harlem from downtown in the 1910s, an urban, modern, and diasporic black identity was in the process of emerging—called the "New Negro" by many.[49] According to Locke, a founding father of the Harlem Renaissance:

Here in Manhattan is not merely the largest Negro community in the world, but the first concentration in history of so many diverse elements of Negro life. It has attracted the African, the West Indian, the Negro American; has brought together the Negro of the North and the Negro of the South; the man from the city and the man from the town and village; the peasant. ... Each group has come with its own separate motives and for its own special ends, but their greatest experience has been the finding of one another. Proscription and prejudice have thrown these dissimilar elements into a common area of contact and interaction. Within this area, race sympathy and unity have determined a further fusing of sentiment and experience. So what began in terms of segregation becomes more and more, as its elements mix and react, the laboratory of a great race-welding. ... In Harlem, Negro life is seizing upon its first chances for group expression and self-determination.[50]

Rooted in shared experiences of dislocation, prejudice, and visible difference, but with disparate homelands and cultures, Harlem's black residents used dancing to generate a powerful, unifying "racial feeling," as described by Gilroy. For this influential sociologist, a sense of racial belonging is generated by performative everyday behaviors that communicate a feeling of racial belonging, both to oneself and others.[51] In particular, for Gilroy, music and other "kinesics" such as dance have the ability to say what cannot be said about black experiences, consciousness, and self-understanding and, as a result, help construct unity among diasporic black peoples.[52]

And so through these solo moments in which African diasporic dance movements were improvised within the larger strictures of European American ballroom dances, over time, shared feelings of unity were generated that came to be central to modern black identity. We cannot know if it was the orderly white patterns that were being momentarily escaped from or the insurgent black expressions of difference that made the dancing feel like home—or if it was simply the space and time to remember the past or imagine the future. In any case, such dancing, along with other cultural practices within Harlem, brought into being a feeling of shared modernity, blackness, and belonging that was much needed after migration, but very different from race-based feelings associated with prior constructions of home.

With their dual embrace of European distinction and black difference, Harlem's elites had the opportunity to reference white ideals and also comment upon them through their embodiment of black cultural references. One way to view this hybrid type of performance is as a form of mimicry, which post-colonial theorist Homi Bhabha has suggested can be a key part of civilizing processes that normalize the hierarchical power structure. For him, mimicry can convey only a partial similarity that reminds all those involved of the difference between the original and the copy—a "strategic failure" of a sort that continually marks the other and their performances of self as inappropriate.[53] To read black elite ballroom dancing as simple mimicry, however, does not allow much room for the dancing to be used as a means of empowerment by the dancers, which was surely part of the appeal.

Another way to interpret Harlem's black ballroom dancing is as a form of self-reflexive, intertextual "signifyin(g)" that revises white ballroom practices by asserting an "authentic" black difference.[54] Literary theorist Henry Louis Gates Jr. has suggested that it is common within African diasporic artistic practices to find repetition, imitation, and revision as creative approaches. He calls this practice "repetition with a signal difference" and argues that it defined these artists "both with and against [white] concept[s] of received order."[55] Such work, for Gates, asserts a relationship between European and African cultural traditions and thus the dual heritage of black Americans. Signifyin(g), with its intersecting layers of meaning and political agenda, fits well with the social practice of ballroom dancing in New York's more privileged black communities.

The signifyin(g) of Harlem's ballroom dancing differed somewhat, though, from the complex significations of the nineteenth-century cakewalk, which, as discussed in the introduction and chapter one, mimicked the grand marches of white ballroom dancers for comic effect.[56] (See Fig. 0.2, introduction) While cakewalking was rooted in parody, impersonation, and caricature, early twentieth-century ballroom dancing in Harlem was neither ridiculous nor even comedic in its appropriations of white dance. That is not to say that parody was not also present at times, just not in the European-derived ballroom dancing sections. It was present, nonetheless, in the solo moments that drew upon a cakewalking vocabulary, in which white dancing and dancers could be implicitly critiqued for their "dicty" (pretentious) ways, for example. So on the one hand, European American ballroom dances (and by extension people) could be emulated, but on the other, they could also be ridiculed—just in different moments of the same dance.

Indeed, black ballroom dancing can be seen as an intercultural *bricolage* that was tactical in its political maneuverings—simultaneously resisting and appeasing both black and white expectations of them.[57] W. E. B. Du Bois, one of the leaders of Harlem's elite during this period coined a term that addresses this type of experience, what he called "double consciousness." For him, this described the modern African American experience of feeling black while also needing white Americans' approval. He indicated that modern African Americans were forced by their conditions to see themselves through the expectations of an "other" world. He writes in *The Souls of Black Folks*:

One ever feels his two-ness,—an American, a Negro; two souls, two thoughts, two reconciled strivings; two warring ideals in one dark body, whose dogged strength alone keeps it from being torn asunder. The history of the American Negro is the history of this strife,—this longing to attain self-conscious manhood, to merge his double self into a better and truer self.[58]

In many ways, the ballroom dancers among Harlem's elite rendered visible Du Bois's groundbreaking concept through their tactical dancing choices, which is ironic, given his suspicion of dancing as a "moral degrader".

Building on Bhabha, Gates, and Du Bois, as well as Krasner's assessment of the cakewalk, the social dancing of Harlem's elites might be viewed as a tool used by the participants. Dancers were not earnestly trying to be white and failing through their dancing, as in Bhabha's model, but instead practicing a subtle form of embodied "signifyin(g)'" through bodily code-switching. By moving between two dance traditions at will—that vary greatly in terms of attitudes toward time, space, and energy, for example—dancers aligned themselves with and critiqued both, without rejecting either. This embodied bilingualism would have been invaluable for navigating Harlem's shifting cultural landscape after migration and during the Harlem Renaissance when one's body was viewed as a performance of one's place in the world.

Instead of a rejection of one culture or the other, black ballroom dancing in the first decades of the twentieth century asserted a biculturalism and thus a fresh model for American identity formation. In effect, dancers laid claim to inclusion in both communities and thus critiqued the white rejection of black culture, as well as the assumption that one can belong to only one culture at a time. Their dancing could have reminded those present of the relationships between black and white cultures that were the foundations of American experience at all class levels. This model for black identity formation is exemplary of Gilroy's conceptualization of Western modernity, which is dependent on intermixture and hybridity—what he calls cultural syncretism.[59] From his point of view then, danced cultural mixing would have also signaled both modernity and Western-ness, two key components of upward social mobility at this time.[60]

INDUSTRY IMPLICATIONS

During the Harlem Renaissance, dance became an important means of professionalization—thanks to the efforts of entrepreneurs like Charles H. Anderson—that had long-term impact at individual and social levels for African Americans. Ballroom dance teaching offered a novel means of financial support to new migrants at a vulnerable time in their lives, when they had left behind much of their family, community, and work. Through its embrace of respectability, this form of teaching also offered a means of garnering respect for teachers, as well as "the race." Most importantly perhaps, these men (and a few women) were able to build a new profession that benefited themselves and also future generations of black dance professionals at a time when manual labor was the primary means of earning income in black communities.

Indeed, dance teachers such as Anderson were able to capitalize on the Harlem middle classes' desire to distinguish themselves from the working classes and unite themselves after waves of migration and uptown relocation. These dance professionals offered participants opportunities to learn and perform European-style ballroom dancing, as well as a safe space in which to continue to privately embody African-derived dance moves when they wished. They also enabled Harlemites to work against stereotypes relating to a perceived lack of civilization among black Americans. Dancers were able to demonstrate a mastery of Western dance forms and thus, symbolically, their eligibility for inclusion and assimilation within modern America.

Importantly, these dance teachers were able to establish dance teaching as a profession. This is especially significant given the few professional opportunities available to African Americans at the time. According to U.S. census data from 1930, only 2 percent of U.S. "Negroes" were engaged in work that could be classified as a profession. This status occupies the top of the employment classification structure and denotes not only financial remuneration but also the acquisition of skills and knowledge through training, the implementation of technical standards, and the practice of businesslike behavior in the workplace. This document states that the largest recognized professions among African Americans in New York City in 1930 were "actors and showmen" and "musicians and teachers of music."[61] The more esteemed professions—law and medicine—welcomed almost no African Americans. Within this context, the professionalization of dance teaching augmented a very brief list of professional jobs truly open to African Americans in New York City during the early twentieth century.

The labor of these innovative dance teachers eventually led to the establishment of dance schools, which provided employment for more and more black men and eventually women in Harlem. Although not previously identified as one of the micro-industries that blossomed in early black Harlem, dance was indeed part of Harlem's economic growth. Much like the beauty and food industries that created opportunity and wealth for some, dance

Figure 4.2 Professional Ballroom Dance Partners, 1930s. Promotional Image. Courtesy of the Fredi Washington Collection, Schomburg Center for Research in Black Culture, New York Public Library (used with permission by Ronald Seymour).

teaching was also a vital new industry of this time period, but on a smaller scale—although it might have actually *employed* more people. Given that Anderson employed close to twenty-five people at one time and that he was the most successful ballroom dance entrepreneur in Harlem at the time, my best guess is that fifty to one hundred people, primarily men, worked in Harlem's social dance industry during the Harlem Renaissance.

Such professional developments were limited in their impact on the lives of female migrants, however. Evidence suggests that black women were not able to position themselves as independent dance teachers until the 1930s when they created employment opportunities as children's dance teachers in so-called kiddie dance schools.[62] Perhaps hiring women of color by the hour for their physical expertise would have too closely resembled prostitution and risked the legitimacy of the profession of ballroom dance teaching in black communities.

Ironically, at the same time that ragtime and jazz brought black movement into American social dance practices on a mass scale, a new profession and industry was launched in Harlem for black dance teachers that was predicated on a rejection of these border-crossing dance forms. Harlem ballroom teachers could not risk being publicly associated with such controversial practices given the fragility of their own and their clients' newfound (and desired) social position. Just like the white dance professionals of the ragtime era, black ballroom teachers had to carefully and cautiously navigate the racial implications of the dancing they proffered in relation to prevailing class- and race-based discourses. As a result, African American social dancing remained eclipsed by European American ballroom dancing, at least among the elites of Harlem, during the early twentieth century. (See Fig. 4.2)

Fourth Floor of the Dobson Building, Theatre District

Ten P.M., Monday, September 1922

An office at the end of a hallway, sparsely furnished with two chairs and a small table on which sits a (borrowed) Victrola. The steady hum of the street below can be heard through the windows, which are open to let in the cool air from outside. The floors are dusty and worn looking, especially in the center of the room, where they have been scuffed thin. The walls are empty at the moment except for a few stray nails, and there is no sign on the door, just a number. A nicely dressed man quietly sits in one of the chairs rubbing his hands together while his mind wanders. He is alone, waiting.

Even though this isn't his first time, James is nervous. By day he opens the front door to the building; by night he "borrows" an empty office to teach dancing. Only the building manager—to whom he slips five dollars per week—knows. He could lose his job, or much, much worse, if found out. Yet, even if James had the money, it is doubtful that the building would officially rent to him anyway. . . . Well, in any case, this is a start, somewhere to begin. And it is a chance to dance again—or rather teach dance, which is almost as good. Clearly, he isn't going to be hired to dance on Broadway these days—too old, too dark—so this is his best option.

His 9:30 p.m. appointment is late. Should he stay? Probably better to wait, since late money is better than no money, as his wife would say. And they really need this starlet's five dollars ... an elevator dings and high-heeled shoes can be heard making their way toward him—finally! Soon enough, she is in the doorway, bejeweled and in fur even though it is September—clearly she has a "patron" already. Her manager follows her in and plops down in the empty chair with a huff and lights a cigarette. He has other things he would rather be doing tonight, but Mary can't be expected to come here alone.

"Good evening, Miss Porter," James says carefully, "I am looking forward to working with you." She replies: "Yeah, thanks, umm ... me too ... well, uh, here's my song." Mary quickly hands him a record without looking at him directly. Maybe she is as uncomfortable as he is? Could this be the first time she has been this near to a black man?

"My pal Lillian told me you know how to make a song pop"—she flicks her shiny red nails to show what she means—"what I really need is a new step that's gonna grab folks' attention, you know," Mary says. She turns to finally face him. "Lemme show you what I've got so far. ..." She tosses the fur to her manager and moves to the middle of the floor, pauses, and then snaps her fingers to indicate that James should start the record. He starts the music for her, taking his time. While she kicks high, flails her arms, and tries to wiggle her hips, James keeps his face carefully composed. If he smiles, she might think he finds her attractive. If he frowns, she might be insulted and leave. Best to look as neutral as possible if he wants to keep her business.

"Well, Miss Porter," James says when the song finally ends, "That looks nice, real nice, ma'am. . . . I would hate to mess with such a great routine, but I might have just the right step for you. It would just perk that audience up—I know it. Make them remember your name." Mary squeals her pleasure at such a thought and insists that he show it to her right away. At the racket, the manager looks up from his recently begun nap, sees she is happy and not upset, and puts his chin back on his chest.

Where to start? He can't teach her how to dance in one evening. What can he give her to do, that she actually can *do? James strolls over to the Victrola slowly, waiting for inspiration. The song starts as he is walking back to her. Then it comes to him, a basic shimmy! Easy and shocking at the same time—perfect.*

"Alright, Miss Porter, follow me. ..." He stands in front and a little to the side of her, resting his hands on bent knees. Quickly looking back over his shoulder to make sure she is with him, he then pops one shoulder forward and the other one back, repeating the movements real slow. "Like this?" she asks. He sees she is on the right track, more or less. So he speeds up. "A little faster now, Miss Porter." He tries to get her in tempo with the song, but she struggles with her balance because her hips don't seem to know how to follow her shoulders yet. "Alright, then, almost there—now, can you take your hands off your knees, Miss Porter?" He turns to face her, careful not to look her in the eye or directly at her body for too long. She holds her arms away from her torso awkwardly, but then looks at how his arms rest loosely by his side and tries to match him. Not too bad for a first try.

"Very good, Miss Porter. Let's find a place to put this in. What do you think of the chorus?" She nods, while still rocking her shoulders—not the best movement combination. He strolls back over to the Victrola with a small smile on his face, hands in his pockets. They were going to be there for a while ... if only he could charge by the hour.

CHAPTER 5

᳗

"Marvelous, New, Dirty Steps"

Appropriation, Authenticity, and Opportunity
in Broadway Jazz Dance Teaching

During the 1920s, while Professor Charles Anderson was busy building his dance teaching business in Harlem, catering to black elites and their interest in ballroom dance, a small group of African American men slowly built parallel businesses downtown. These entrepreneurs did not avoid or reject the most popular dance form in America at that time, jazz, or its black associations. Instead, they seized the opportunity to market it as "authentic" black dance, to Broadway performers in search of new and exciting steps to enliven their routines.

A quick glance through the pages of the nascent *Dance Magazine* of the 1920s reveals numerous jazz dance routines with names such as "High Yaller," "Pickin' Cotton," "The Savannah Stomp," and the "Hula-Charleston," each represented by a specific white Broadway performer. (See Fig. 5.1) Looming just behind each dancer, however, is a dark dancing figure that remains nameless and faceless.[1] Although only a shadow, this image stands as a strong reminder of the numerous, unacknowledged black dance teachers who taught and choreographed for white Broadway— who supported the popular theatre of this vibrant time in important ways, while also establishing a new profession for themselves and many others who followed.

Unlike the modern dance teachers of the 1910s, who proffered *refined* versions of black dancing to the public, African American jazz teachers did not

HIGH
YALLER

Music: *Moanin'*
Low by Ralph
Rainger, last 8 bars
repeated.
(Harms, Inc., N. Y.)

Routine Described
by Ray Moses

ILLUSTRATION I

Introduction

Imitating the negro walk, slow, slouch, lazy and undulating:

	COUNTS
Take 8 steps forward, stepping on first count of each bar and undulating up and down on the next three	1–32

8 Bars

Figure 1

In place, facing audience, arms at sides:

	COUNTS
As in Illustration I, lift left leg out sideways, bring it down beside the right	1–4
Repeat with right leg	5–8
Repeat faster with left leg	9–10
Repeat again with right leg	11–12
Repeat again with left leg	13–14
Pause	15–16
Repeat entire figure, beginning with right leg	17–32

8 Bars

Figure 2

Arms as in Illustration II, alternate hands circling out from the wrist every two bars, first right hand, then left:

	COUNTS
Stamp right foot slightly to the right	1–2
Drag left foot up to right foot	3–4
Stamp right foot to the right again	5–6
Drag left foot up to the right	7–8
Stamp left foot slightly to the left	9–10
Jump into the air landing with left foot on half-toe crossed in back of right	11–12
Pivot left on left foot dragging right foot behind, finish facing front	13–14
Stamp right foot, then left	15–16
Back-brush with right foot	17–18
Stamp left foot, then right	19–20
Back-brush with left foot	21–22
Stamp right foot, then left	23–24
Forward-brush with right foot, then heel tap with left foot	25–26
Back-brush with right foot, finishing with right foot crossed in front of left	27–28
Dragging left foot behind, pivot on right foot to the right to finish facing right-stage	29–32

8 Bars

Figure 3

Chorus of music: facing right-stage:

	COUNTS
Slide forward with left foot, hands on hips, as in Illustration III	1–2
Drag right foot up to left	3–4
Repeat steps in counts 1–4	5–8
Facing up-stage (back to audience), slide forward with right foot	9–10
Drag left foot up to right	11–12
Slide forward with right foot	13–14
Stamp with left foot, then right	15–16
With feet flat and slightly apart, move hips around in a circle to the left	17–24
Move hips around in a circle to the right	25–32
Repeat entire figure	33–64

16 Bars

Figure 4

Snake hips: feet slightly apart, weight on left foot, right foot raised on half-toe, left hip out, fingers snapping rhythmically—Illustration IV:

	COUNTS
Move right foot, knee and hip around in a circle to the right, finishing with position reversed: weight on right foot, left foot raised, etc.	1–4
Repeat circular movement to the left finishing in reverse position	5–8

ILLUSTRATION II

	COUNTS
Repeat movement in counts 1–4 faster	9–10
Repeat movement in counts 5–8 faster	11–12
Repeat movement in counts 9–12	13–16
Repeat entire figure to the opposite side: beginning hip movement to the left	17–32

8 Bars

Figure 5

Negro strut: hands clapping syncopated rhythm, 4 times in each bar, on counts 1, 1-and, 2-and, 4-and:

	COUNTS
With weight on right foot, step forward on ball of left foot	1–2
Slide left foot slightly backward, changing weight to left foot	3–4
Repeat action in counts 1–4, with right foot	5–8
With arms in position as in Illustration V, hands trembling from wrist:	
Repeat steps in counts 1–4	9–12
Reverse arms (left arm forward, right arm back), hands still trembling, repeating steps in counts 5–8	13–16
With arms exaggerated as in Illustration VI, hands trembling, repeat steps in counts 1–16	17–32

8 Bars

Figure 6

Exit right-stage, back to audience—Illustration VII:

	COUNTS
Step left with left foot, raising arms up	1–2
Slide right foot up to left, lowering arms slightly	3–4
Repeat until off stage, raising arms higher and more excitedly each time	5–32

8 Bars

30

Figure 5.1 Blues Dance Instructions, 1920s. Ray Moses, "High Yaller: A Blues Number from 'The Little Show' Conceived and Danced by Clifton Webb," *Dance Magazine* (October 1929), 30–31. Courtesy of the Jerome Robbins Dance Division, New York Public Library for the Performing Arts (public domain). [images from microfilm]

A Blues Number from The Little Show Conceived
and Danced by Clifton Webb

Photographs by
Edwin F. Townsend,
posed by Clifton Webb

ILLUSTRATION III

ILLUSTRATION IV

ILLUSTRATION V

(At left) ILLUSTRATION VI

(At right) ILLUSTRATION VII

Figure 5.1 (Continued)

write manuals, open their own cabarets, or appear on sheet music covers. Rather, they had to remain unseen—or at least publicly unacknowledged by the Broadway performers and producers they assisted—while they quietly opened studios, gave lessons, taught routines, and choreographed for theatres and clubs all over Manhattan.[2] In so doing, they developed new ways of working within a subordinating system of appropriation between black and white performers of the period that had its roots in the ragtime era.

After discussing the relevant terminology and historiography, this chapter situates the teaching by black jazz dancers within the contexts of period musical theatre and earlier instances of black dance teaching. It then focuses on the studios that were founded by early jazz dance teachers, examining their working conditions and interpreting their labor tactics in relation to writings on "black invisibility."[3] Following this, I sift through some of the material and political consequences of this new career path, with the assistance of contemporary race theorists George Lipsitz and J. Martin Favor. I then turn my attention to some of the surviving remnants of choreography by these black jazz teachers while seeking to identify what "authentic" black movement (their dance product) might have looked like on musical theatre stages of the era and within Broadway jazz studios founded during this pivotal period.

TEACHING BLACK DANCING

Teaching dance from black communities through paid lessons did not become a career possibility until African American dancers launched studios in the Broadway theatre district of Manhattan at the height of the Jazz Age (roughly 1920–1930). There were certainly isolated incidents of formal dance teaching by black dancers prior to this point during the cakewalk and ragtime dance crazes. But, as will be discussed, these incidents did not constitute a defined career path.

During the 1920s, the terms "dance coach" and "dance director" were quite common within New York's entertainment industries.[4] Nonetheless, I deliberately use the titles of teacher and choreographer throughout this chapter in order to emphasize what those jobs actually entailed. I also use the term "professional" in order to highlight black dancers' decisions to teach and choreograph as a career. In these ways, my terms seek to query period hierarchies and distinctions made between not only black and white dancing and dance professionals, but also between theatrical dance and popular dance forms.

Although African American professional dancers had worked in Northern cities for more than a century, hardly any earned significant income as *teachers* of black dancing. As discussed in the previous chapter, before the 1920s, the very few African American men working as professional dance teachers taught European American dance. Black dancing was rarely taught formally in either the black or white communities of New York City. Rather, dance steps and stylings were learned more casually through observation and participation at African American religious, social, and familial gatherings.[5]

The teaching of black dancing and the gradual professionalization of such teaching have received scant scholarly attention in the humanities: a chapter in the Stearns' *Jazz Dance* (1968), a brief section in Brenda Dixon-Gottschild's *Waltzing in the Dark*, and a conference presentation by Constance Valis Hill.[6] For all of these authors, the issue of credit (or lack thereof) is addressed but dealt with quite differently. Marshall and Jean Stearns seem to regard the lack of credit afforded to early black dance teachers as more understandable than Hill and Dixon-Gottschild do. *Jazz Dance*'s chapter on Buddy Bradley, the most renowned of these teachers, opens with an anecdote about a white dancer named Clifton Webb who took credit for Bradley's choreography in programs, press interviews, and magazine articles. The Stearns wrote, "Did Webb remember Buddy Bradley? He did not mention him—but then neither would many others in the same position.... Nobody saw anything wrong in such an arrangement. The coach had been paid."[7] Their writing emphasized the irony of white Broadway being dependent on black dance teachers, rather than the inequities—short and long term—that resulted from this arrangement.

In contrast, Dixon-Gottschild and Hill comment directly on the injustice of white dancers taking credit for and profiting from black dancers' work. These authors were writing thirty years after the Stearns, following the black power movements of the 1960s and '70s, when dance scholarship was beginning to grapple with the erasures of black contributions to a variety of dance forms in America. A quote from Katrina Hazzard's *Jookin'* exemplifies this:

> Between 1877 and 1920, African Americans saw their music and dance adopted (poorly) by the white theater, the recording industry, and the newly emerging popular culture industry, while they suffered systemic exclusion from those markets. The songs of Mae West, Sophie Tucker, and Tin Pin Alley, Ann Pennington's black bottom, and the dances of Vernon and Irene Castle transformed black culture into something that white Americans could safely partake of. They led the white invasion of cabarets and the outright exploitive commercialization of African American entertainment of the next three decades.[8]

Many scholars of black dance treated any appropriation of black culture with abhorrence during the 1990s, not just Hazzard. Although Dixon-Gottschild and Hill do not use language as strong as Hazzard, their writings likewise critique white dancers and producers succeeding at the expense of professional black dancers and teachers—even if it was an accepted practice at the time.

While productive and important in many ways, this particular view of appropriation may have actually prevented a more in-depth consideration of the black dance teaching of the 1920s until now. If appropriation is primarily viewed as a way in which black dancers are victimized, then there is no motivation to look for ways in which many black dance professionals might have actually *used* the system of appropriation to their (limited) advantage when they began teaching the white representatives of jazz dancing. Any tactical moves would have been rendered invisible.

My work takes a position on appropriation that is somewhere in between the Stearns and the 1990s scholarship of Hill, Hazzard, and Dixon-Gottschild. I take very seriously the material ways in which a system of appropriation limited black performers' opportunities for career advancement. I also recognize the repercussions of an appropriation system that reinforced the longstanding view that black labor existed for white profit and pleasure. At the same time, it was within this same system that the careers of teachers of black dancing were launched. Without forgetting the costs, my work brings to light how some individuals found ways to gain some benefits within an oppressive system, albeit to much smaller benefits than the white dancers they taught. Building on the work of Hill, Hazzard, and Dixon-Gottschild, this chapter inquires into the cultural work accomplished through the appropriations they discuss.

PRECURSORS

More than any other factor, the superficial but overt embracing of blackness that occurred during the Jazz Age established fertile conditions for professional black dance teaching. The black associations of jazz dancing and music did not need to be veiled as they had been with ragtime; rather, they were celebrated—the more *authentic* the better. In the 1920s, the "Negro" was now chic. In New York City—which hosted the most developed theatre business in the country—this meant that all-black musicals returned to Broadway theatres en masse, after approximately a decade in Harlem, and scores of downtown residents traveled uptown to patronize Harlem clubs that offered dancing and music by black performers. Indeed, there were more performing opportunities for black dancers during the 1920s than ever before.[9]

But this alone was not what enabled the professionalization of black dance teaching. It was the even more plentiful performance opportunities for *white* dancers who could dance jazz that were the catalysts for this new profession. White jazz dancers were the primary clients of the Broadway jazz studios, not professional black performers. Furthermore, it was white celebrity women who were most able to market black dances (such as the shimmy, Charleston, and black bottom) directly to the American public through films, magazines, sheet music, and theatre shows. Black *dances*, not black *dancers*, were the real stars of the Jazz Age—a fact that may have limited the success of any visibly black dancers, but simultaneously enabled the careers of jazz dance teachers working behind the scenes. From the perspective of white audiences, it was *Ann Pennington's* Black Bottom, not Ethel Williams's (a popular African American professional dancer of the 1910s and 1920s) and certainly not Buddy Bradley's.

While these developments created the possibility of professionally teaching black dancing by generating an interest in putting explicitly black moves on white dancing bodies, relationships between black and white performers established during earlier decades laid the groundwork upon which the Broadway studios were built. Indeed, there were antecedents to the professionalization of black dance teaching in two prior dance trends that introduced mainstream America to black social dancing—the cake-walk craze of the 1890s and the ragtime craze of the 1910s.

The late nineteenth-century cakewalk provides the first extant evidence of African Americans teaching black dancing for pay. As discussed in the introduction, their clients were the fashionable elite of New York City, such as Mr. and Mrs. William K. Vanderbilt, for whom learning to cakewalk was an entertaining novelty.[10] During this period, black professional dance teams like Charles Johnson and Dora Dean, and Aida Overton Walker and George Walker were able to openly market the cakewalk to America through periodical articles, sheet music, and musical theatre performances.[11]

This practice was revived after 1910 when the turkey trot, bunny hug, and monkey glide enraptured Manhattan's ragtime social dancers. Yet the people who sought lessons in black-associated dancing during this period were less likely to be white socialites like the Vanderbilts and more likely to be white professional dancers. The ragtime dance craze was also notably different from the cakewalk craze because its primary representatives were white dance teams (like Vernon and Irene Castle, and Maurice and Florence Walton), even though the dancing continued to be partially derived from African American sources.[12] As white dance teams rose to great heights of stardom from 1910 to 1920, black performers receded into the background—relegated to Harlem theatres and segregated vaudeville circuits that paid far less than Broadway. James Weldon Johnson has poignantly described this period as "the term of exile of the Negro from the downtown theaters of New York."[13]

During the ragtime dance craze, which limited the financial success of black performers, the occasional lessons given by black professional dancers to white performers sometimes developed into ongoing relationships, what I will call "private teaching." It is unclear, however, how widespread this practice was from 1910 to 1920. In her 1961 Stearns interview, Ethel Williams (mentioned above) remarked that after winning several dance contests around Manhattan and briefly performing at Bustanoby's cabaret in the Broadway theatre district during 1914, "Mrs. Castle [called at my home] and asked me to teach her some steps."[14] Unfortunately, Williams does not go on to say if she accepted the offer, although it is possible that she passed this opportunity along to her dance partner Johnny Peters. According to Noble Sissle, a musician and composer who worked with the Castles, Peters was "the fellow who was responsible for inspiring Mrs. Castle and others." He explained: "Mr. and Mrs. Castle simplified some of these steps so that the society people could do them but they got much of it from [him]."[15] Sissle's statements indicate that Peters, an African American professional dancer, coached the Castles, the foremost white representatives of modern dance.

Furthermore, Sissle's recollections suggest that the Castles were not the only professional dancers that Peters coached. His reference to "Mrs. Castle and others" indicates that the Castles' arrangement with Peters was not an isolated incident. It seems that the private teaching of white performers by black dancers actually began during the period of 1910 to 1920, and black dancers provided some of the ragtime dance craze's stars with their innovative steps. This teaching was not yet plentiful or lucrative enough, however, to support the opening of dance studios as would happen later.

THE BROADWAY JAZZ STUDIOS

The Broadway jazz studios opened during a period of widespread interest in and commercialization of black-associated dances, but with comparatively limited opportunities for African American performers. The studios seem to have emerged out of the private teaching that began during the ragtime craze, perhaps inspired by the studios opened by white professional ballroom dancers between 1910 and 1920. Ned Wayburn's famous downtown studio, in its catering to Broadway stars and hopefuls, might also have been an important model for the jazz studios.[16] Ultimately, these studios provided a way for African American dance teachers to coordinate their efforts and pool their resources, thus paving the way for the professionalization of black dance teaching.

It is difficult to estimate the number of black dancers who transitioned to being teachers during the 1920s. Using the research of the Stearns, Dixon-Gottschild, and the Harlem WPA Writers Project, I was able to identify nearly twenty of them by name, including Eddie Chavers, Buddy Bradley, Frank Harrington, Herbert Harper, Charlie Davis, Ernest Carlos, Mabel Horsey, Willie Covan, Lawrence Reed, Leonard Harper, Elida Webb, John Bubbles, Clarence Robinson, and Roland Holder. The invisibility that was necessary for black dance professionals to make a living as teachers and choreographers in Jazz-Age Manhattan has unfortunately precluded many others from becoming part of the historical record.

Financial backing was an absolute necessity for opening a dance studio in the downtown theatre district of Manhattan.[17] No professional performer, black or white, could have made enough money to set up and then sustain such a business as it grew over time. Even the Castles needed society backing to set up their Castle House studio, and they were the most renowned dance couple of the 1910s. The Stearns even suggest that author, arts patron, and socialite Carl van Vechten financed a Broadway dance studio.[18] Unfortunately, they do not explain the nature of the financial arrangement between van Vechten and the studio talent (i.e., who was primarily profiting).

Van Vechten was probably not the only entrepreneur who viewed such studios as an investment opportunity. Black dance teaching was certainly a growth business during the 1920s as white Broadway endeavored to mimic black Broadway's dancing style, following the tremendous success of the musical *Shuffle Along*, which ran from 1921 to 1924. In addition, individual Broadway theatres and producers may have had a hand in launching at least a few of the studios—especially given how much they had to gain by their presence in the downtown theatre district.

Based on the Stearns interviews and the New York City WPA Writers Project, it seems that a dancer named Charlie Davis was among the first to open a Broadway studio that taught black dancing. Noble Sissle reported to the Stearns that "[Davis] danced for years and then when white dancers tried to learn some of these dances, he opened a studio."[19] His studio became a haven for white dancers who wanted to learn black dances.[20]

While Davis's studio was among the first, Billy Pierce opened the most successful studio in 1925. It was Pierce who was memorialized by James Weldon Johnson's *Black Manhattan* of 1930. Johnson wrote:

> Billy Pierce, though he is not on the stage and his influence has been exerted almost entirely through the white performer, cannot be omitted [from the historical record].... Mr. Pierce conducts a large and successful studio where he teaches dancers the art of tapping out intricate Negro rhythms with their feet.[21]

By the end of the 1920s, instructors who worked in Pierce's studio were teaching some of the best-known stars on Broadway, including Mae West, Gilda Gray, Ann Pennington, and even Fred and Adele Astaire. They were also creating choreography for the most profitable Broadway revues, such as the Ziegfeld Follies, George White's Scandals, and the Greenwich Village Follies.[22]

Contrary to Johnson's claims, however, Pierce actually did not dance or teach dancing; according to Thaddeus Drayton (one of the teachers at the studio), Pierce was more of an "impresario."[23] Drayton's clarification of Pierce's role indicates that the manager/teacher model (i.e., someone with business or management experience presiding over several dance teachers) may have internally structured some Broadway jazz studios. With regard to financial arrangements, Drayton told the Stearns that Pierce split the revenues with his teachers.[24] In their chapter on Buddy Bradley, the Stearns claim that dance instructors at some schools were paid as little as fifteen dollars per week, no matter how many routines they choreographed or how many students they taught.[25] In comparison, Pierce's arrangement with his teachers seems quite generous.

Drayton mentions that Pierce hired only men at his studio. This is confirmed by Dixon-Gottschild, who notes that "this was a male dominated profession," adding that Elida Webb was "one of the few women" actively teaching at the time.[26] It is difficult to know why this was the case—why women were excluded from this new dance profession. Given the period connections between prostitution and dance, it might have been too risky to hire women for their physical (i.e., dance) expertise. These studios were just getting off the ground and clearly needed to be cautious.[27]

One of Pierce's most popular teachers was Buddy Bradley. His extensive client list brought the studio much of its fame and income. In fact, we know more about Bradley than any other African American dance teacher of this period because of his extensive interviews with the Stearns and successful career abroad, where his name was actually printed in programs and he was given public credit for his work. With Bradley we have the benefit of knowing many of the shows on which he worked, while we must speculate about his compatriots who remained in New York. Indeed, his archival trail offers an example from which we can cautiously generalize about the experiences of other African American dance teachers of this period, while keeping in mind, of course, that he was much more successful than most.

Bradley, as part of his job at Pierce's studio, was hired to privately teach stars, as well as to "group" scenes for musicals, a task I choose to describe as choreography. In one of his numerous interviews with the Stearns, he described his job simply: "They call me to patch them up," referring to shows.[28] He did much more than his humility implies, however. An advertisement in a 1927 *Tattler* announced to Harlem:

WANTED
16 Peppy Brown Skin Girls
Ziegfeld Productions—Long Broadway Run Assured
Free Dance Instructions by
Buddy Bradley
All Casting Under Personal Direction of Billy Pierce[29]

This advertisement tells us that Bradley and Pierce—as well as possibly other 1920s black dance teachers—worked closely with the Ziegfeld Follies and other big musical and revue producers, such as Lew Leslie and George White, on both casting and choreography.

Bradley and the other African American dance teachers of the 1920s were not just choreographic handymen who might be called upon to fix problems. They were choreographers in every sense, though they did not receive credit in the program or a seat in the audience on opening night. This caveat implies that a key job requirement of 1920s black dance teachers was a tactical invisibility to white audiences—a fact that demonstrates the superficiality of the Jazz Age's celebration of "Negro" chic.

Bradley's invisibility as a choreographer to the white theatre-going public was reinforced by his absence from the theatre once the show opened. As Drayton once told the Stearns, "They'd let [Bradley] rehearse and when the show opened he was out."[30] Although it is possible that Bradley "was out" due to his own hectic work schedule, Drayton's phrasing alludes to a forced absence, perhaps due to a desire by producers to take full credit for Bradley's choreography or their aversion to the show being associated with an actual African American.

Of course, Bradley was not actually invisible; white audiences simply did not see him. In Harlem and the Broadway theatre district, he was not only visible, he was sought after for his expertise. The previously mentioned *Tattler* advertisement indicates that Bradley and Pierce had name recognition in New York's black communities despite their invisibility to Broadway audiences—otherwise Ziegfeld would have had no reason to name them in the advertisement. Furthermore, these men were well known within Broadway circles, as is made evident in Pierce's recurring advertisements in *Dance Magazine* during the late 1920s, which was a periodical

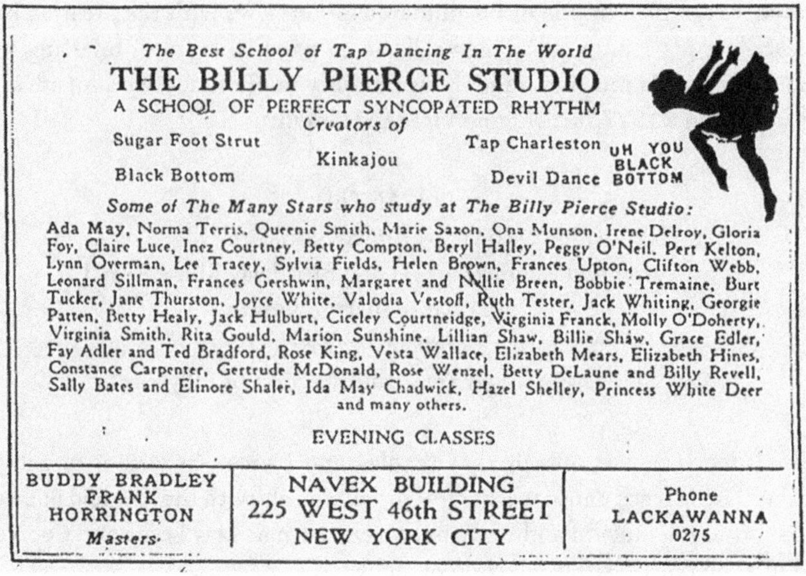

Figure 5.2 Broadway Jazz Dance Studio Advertisement, 1920s. "The Billy Pierce Studio," *Dance Magazine* (December 1927), 6. Courtesy of the Jerome Robbins Dance Division, New York Public Library for the Performing Arts (public domain).

geared to clientele that included Broadway performers and those who wanted to be. (See Fig. 5.2) For example:

> The Billy Pierce Studio
> A School of Perfect Syncopated Rhythm
> *Creators of*
> Sugar Foot Strut, Black Bottom ... Tap Charleston, Devil Dance
> ***
> Buddy Bradley and Frank Harrington
> *Masters*[31]

Such ads did not run every month, but only once or twice a year. Nonetheless, they indicate that Billy Pierce and Buddy Bradley (as well as Frank Harrington it seems) were actually quite visible to aspiring and professional dancers downtown.

INVISIBLE MEN

African American professional dance teachers were invisible only to the audiences who paid to see their work. But who required this? Whom did it benefit? Dixon-Gottschild offers us a theory of invisibility within black American performance that is drawn from her extensive research on twentieth-century theatre and dance. She writes: "the Africanist presence ... has suffered from sins of commission and omission; it has been invisibilized, to coin a new word."[32] Dixon-Gottschild views invisibility as a choice on the part of white performers and producers—not black. Her language implies a deliberate pilfering and erasing of black contributions. She insinuates that black dance professionals were acted upon, rendered invisible by others who stood to profit from their labors.

Novelist Ralph Ellison, who was living in Harlem during the 1930s, attributes black invisibility to white observers, not necessarily competing performers. In his 1947 *Invisible Man*, he wrote: "I am invisible, understand, simply because people refuse to see me ... they see only my surroundings, themselves, or figments of their imagination—indeed, everything and anything except me."[33] Ellison reminds us that *not seeing* can be a habit and is not always the result of deliberate erasure. Rather, his book describes the conditions—the white ignorance, the force of habit, and the white objectification and dehumanization of black people—that made the ignorance of black contributions (and therefore people) possible. His understanding of black invisibility shows us how white audiences may not have recognized the black men and women who contributed to the white jazz performances they were seeing, while at the same time knowing that jazz dancing was a black phenomenon.

How else could white jazz dancers have learned their craft? If they did not directly learn through lessons, then they certainly learned moves from observation in black clubs or theatres. Mae West confessed as much in her autobiography that she learned the shimmy in a club on Chicago's South Side where "big black men with razor slashed faces" congregated with "fancy high yellows and beginner browns."[34] There was white contact with African Americans somewhere—a fact that many in the audience perhaps could not tolerate and therefore chose not to see, thus rendering black dance teachers invisible.

Importantly, while the invisibility of 1920s black dance teachers can be blamed on audiences, performers, and producers—as Dixon-Gottschild and Ellison propose—it can also be linked to the tactics of the teachers themselves.[35] Since they could not change the racial politics of the time, these black men (and a few women) facilitated a new and much-needed profession for African Americans by deliberately making use of the very situation that limited their potential. Their invisibility should also be seen as a tactical choice that enabled financial gain and stability.

IMPACT OF PROFESSIONALIZATION

Although we cannot know the intentions of those who opened and worked in such studios—whether they were consciously seeking monetary gain and/ or greater respect within Manhattan's entertainment world, for example— we can explore the effects of the studios and the professionalization they enabled. The Broadway jazz studios made important interventions into a system of appropriation that had existed between black and white performers at least since the nineteenth century. First and perhaps foremost, the studio system required that compensation be paid. Prior to the 1920s, it was common practice for white performers to visit clubs and theatres where, through observation, they could learn new dance steps without having to pay or credit the black dancers from whom they borrowed. While the Broadway studios did not necessarily stop this practice, they did formalize relationships between black and white dancers in a way that allowed black dancers to benefit somewhat from what had previously been an entirely one-sided exchange. By opening studios, black dancers bettered their chances of being compensated for borrowings that were often inevitable and happening frequently without their consent.

Furthermore, the income that dancers earned from teaching, regardless of the amount, had symbolic as well as financial significance. It recognized that black dance teachers had skills and knowledge that merited reward. On another level, financial compensation for teaching implicitly validated black dancers' sense of cultural ownership of jazz dancing. It is possible that this was a strong motive for opening Broadway dance studios, as indicated by Noble Sissle's comment about Charlie Davis who opened his dance studio "when white dancers tried to learn some of these dances."[36]

The Broadway studios also facilitated the establishment of teaching black dance as a profession in its own right, as more than simply an ancillary source of income for performers. This is especially significant given the few professions available to African Americans at the time, as discussed in detail in the previous chapter. In comparison, over 80 percent of Manhattan's African American population in 1930 was engaged in semi-skilled and unskilled labor as domestic servants, elevator tenders, janitors, and laundry operators, for example.[37]

Moreover, the professionalization of black dance teaching in many ways countered several prevailing black stereotypes of the period. Through the very nature of their business—the formal teaching of black dancing techniques—instructors demonstrated that such skills were not natural, but rather learned. This challenged common assumptions that professional black dancers were displaying their natural talents rather than techniques that were the result of years of training and practice. Moreover, the transformation of black dancers into teachers through the founding of the profession offered many people a line of work that was more associated with the mind, rather than the body. In an era when the mind and body were thought of as separate and mental labor was much more respected than physical labor, professional dance teaching created an alternative to the laboring body that was so strongly associated with African Americans during this period.

Of course, there was a price to be paid for the benefits of professionalization. Cross-racial appropriation, even if financially compensated and/or conducted in the spirit of artistic admiration, is frequently grounded in simplistic understandings of identity. Cultural theorist George Lipsitz, who lucidly expresses this point, has argued that "appropriation . . . is dependent on and reiterative of stereotypical and essentialist notions of difference."[38] Put simply, appropriation underscores a boundary and a hierarchy between an imagined "us" and "them." This sense of fundamental difference is certainly reflected in the Stearns interviews with 1920s jazz performers who repeatedly drew unequivocal distinctions between black and white dances and people, despite the hybridity within dance forms that they themselves described.

CHOREOGRAPHING IDENTITY

Viewed through Lipsitz's lens, the choreography created and taught by professional black dance teachers and performed by Broadway's white jazz dancers expressed essential differences between black and white. Acts of appropriation actually highlight differences while at the same time superficially demonstrating a degree of integration.[39] On stage and in the studios, appropriated movement practices in effect represented and reinforced racial differences as natural.

As described by the Stearns and Hill, Buddy Bradley's choreographic style—which may be emblematic of other 1920s black dance teachers—involved a synthesis of relatively simple tap combinations with theatricalizations of African American social dance torso and limb movements in a way that was visually dynamic and rhythmically accented. The Stearns call his work a "revolutionary simplification" of black vernacular dance; Hill, however, asserts that Bradley's simplifications of black dance steps for Broadway must not be misconstrued as a dilution of black dance: "Bradley's jazz dance wasn't white-washed."[40] Although certainly a form of simplified jazz dancing, the Stearns and Hill both insist that Bradley's routines did not lose their *authenticity* as black dance, a powerful assertion in the early modern era and today.

To my knowledge, no films of Buddy Bradley's New York choreography currently exist, so it is difficult to know precisely what his choreography looked like or how it was marketed to white dance professionals. Thankfully, within issues of *Dance Magazine* of this period, fragments of his choreography survive in the form of dance routines and steps that were published for readers to practice at home. One routine is called "High Yaller," and it is posed by and credited to Clifton Webb, a white Broadway performer of the period who studied with Bradley.[41] (See Fig. 5.1) Webb is listed by Pierce and Bradley in a 1927 *Dance Magazine* advertisement for their studio as one of their notable students. (See Fig. 5.2) As mentioned earlier, When asked by a reporter sixteen years after the fact, however, Webb continued to claim authorship of the routine.[42] Nonetheless, in their book, the Stearns state that Bradley was actually the author of this routine. Bradley, however, is not quoted making this claim in any of his surviving interviews with them—perhaps this was an implicit (or even explicit) condition of his agreements with Broadway performers, that he never take credit publicly.[43]

Two other fragments of Bradley's choreography were found in related 1928 *Dance Magazine* articles called "Low Down Dancing" and "More Low-Down Dancing" (published just a few months apart) in which (remarkably) Bradley himself demonstrates the movements described. (See Fig. 5.3) Importantly, he is not credited as the author of the article, and yet, the authenticity of the dancing presented certainly resides in the blackness of his body and in his reputation as well as the reputation of Pierce's studio.

Interestingly, in all three examples, the choreography is marked directly and indirectly as *authentically* black by both body and language, to differing degrees. In the first example, "High Yaller" is given a name that references a person of mixed racial background who would have been considered black by period definitions. The white dancer used to illustrate the dance routine draws attention to the hips and buttocks by keeping his hands close to these areas of the body. The poses used carve out angular shapes through bent arms and legs, sometimes using what we now call jazz hands. The text, not written by Webb, tells the readers to begin by "imitating the Negro walk, slow, slouch, lazy, and undulating." It goes on to describe the following actions: stamping, dragging, jumping, brushing, sliding, hip circling, finger snapping, hand clapping, and syncopation.

In comparison, "Low Down Dancing" and "More Low-Down Dancing" are less subtle in their claims to black authenticity. They openly state that the routines are "Real Negro Steps." The photographs used to illustrate the routines show Buddy Bradley himself, which serves to verify the title's claim. This might not seem remarkable, but during this period, photographs of black men and women were very rarely printed in *Dance Magazine*. Much more common were sketches, which at times drew upon the stereotypes entrenched by blackface minstrelsy.[44] In these photographs, Bradley uses his hands to bring attention to his hips and knees, which are thrusting to the side, front, and back. The body shapes are once again angular, although the use of jazz hands is a little less pronounced. The text, of unknown authorship, describes sliding, stamping, hopping, jerking, hip swaying, finger wagging, eye rolling, and off-beat rhythms. The first article in the series includes a text written by Elise Marcus that frames the steps and Bradley's pictures. In it, she summarizes the characteristics of "real Negro dancing" as originating on "plantations and levees" and having "the bent knees, the humorous hips, the raised hands, the angular arms."

Even though these were routines designed for *Dance Magazine* readers—white dance professionals of varying degrees of success—the writing suggests how Buddy Bradley's choreographies (and perhaps those of other jazz dance teachers) were represented as *authentically* black, both in the studio and onstage. It also points out some ways in which viewers were trained to "see" black authenticity. Words like Negro, low-down, and high yaller (or any other mulatto descriptive) surely identified the dancing as black at the outset, as did references to the South. Moreover, comparing and analyzing the two later routines, it seems that movements that bring attention to the hips, create angular shapes, and highlight the hands marked the dancing as black. Cross-referencing the routines, actions such as stamping, sliding, brushing, dragging, hopping, jumping, slouching, undulating, and jerking might also denote blackness. All of these actions constructed a bent, grounded dancing body with the legs and feet as the primary locus of attention. Hip movements, sonic accents (such as snapping or clapping), and syncopated rhythms also told the readers that the dancing was black. Taken together, these factors offer us a glimpse of what dancing *authentically* black meant to white viewers and dancers at this time.

AUTHENTIC BLACKNESS IN MOTION

As mentioned, while marketing their dance products, black jazz teachers also inadvertently codified (and commodified) racial differences. Their implicit (and sometimes explicit) assertions of authenticity underscored essential racial differences, much like appropriative behavior does, as discussed in prior chapters. As J. Martin Favor writes in *Authentic Blackness*, authenticity is a notion that derives its power from a "system of similarity and difference."[45] It attempts to validate what is deemed similar and dismiss what is regarded as different. It establishes an us and a them, a self and an other. For period audiences, *authentic* blackness in jazz dancing likely signified a host of stereotypical notions associated with a black other—naturalness, wildness, exoticism,

LOW DOWN DANCING

The Low Down on the Real Negro Steps

By ELISE MARCUS

BOOKS and books have been written about Negro music, from the haunting spirituals to those maddening, marvelous blues. Lecture upon lecture has been delivered on African sculpture, but, to my knowledge, the only people who know anything about real Negro dancing are the professional hoofers. By low down dancing I don't mean the prehistoric dances of the savages, but those rhythms we indulge in now in the best places, those rhythms that are seen in every musical show and on every vau-

Ballin' the Jack

Hands placed on bent knees. The knees move in a crescent path, going from side to side, in a mere suggestion of a curve.

Baltimore Buzz

Step with one foot, and slide the other foot up to it. This is done on toes with knees bent. Hips sway in direction of stepping foot.

Black Bottom (dance)

This, as with all other dances, is a mixture of "low-down" steps. The basic step, however, is one dependent entirely on rhythm. This step is 2 long stamps, first right and then left, followed by 4 short ones; they are done off the regular beat of the music. Accompanying this, the index finger on both hands is pointing up, and the eyes are rolling. Any other steps may be done to lengthen the dance.

Breakdown (Birmingham or Cincinnati)

Feet spread. Hop up and come down with one knee bent. Come up with short jerks. It is optional as to whether one or both knees are bent on coming down.

Photographs of Buddy Bradley by Nash

THE BALTIMORE BUZZ

you to do them yourself. The easiest way to practice is to stand in front of a long mirror with the magazine open before you. It really won't matter if you look silly—you are supposed to.

I want to acknowledge my thanks to Buddy Bradley, of the Billy Pierce Studio. Without his help it would have been impossible to gather this information.

Buddy Bradley, you know, is the fast-footed young teacher to whom so many of the Broadway stars—really famous folk like Ada May, Joyce White, Marie Saxon and Pert

BALLIN' THE JACK   **THE BREAKDOWN**

deville stage in the country, rhythms that had their origin down on plantations and levees.

You have seen them often enough; you know all their amusing characteristics—the bent knees, the humorous hips, the raised hands, the angular arm. You may even do a very comic camel walk yourself without knowing just which animal your strut is named after. This simple glossary will help you recognize these steps when you see them on the stage. It will also teach

Kelton among others—have gone for their eccentric steps based on Negro rhythms.

By the time you have mastered these steps, the October issue of The Dance Magazine will be on its way with another chapter of the low down primer. You will want the rest of the basic Negro steps, the Camel Walk, the Charleston, the Sugar Foot Strut, the Texas Tommy, the Washington Johnny and a few more with equally enticing names.

38

Figure 5.3 Jazz Dance Instructions, 1920s. (above and facing page). Elise Marcus, "Low Down Dancing: The Low Down on the Real Negro Steps," *Dance Magazine* (September 1927), 38; "More Low-Down Dancing: Buddy Bradley Shows Additional Real Negro Steps," *Dance Magazine* (January 1928), 41. Courtesy of the Jerome Robbins Dance Division, New York Public Library for the Performing Arts (public domain). [images from microfilm]

MORE LOW-DOWN DANCING

Buddy Bradley Shows Additional Real Negro Steps

By ELISE MARCUS

(At left):
Sugar Foot Strut, an original Buddy Bradley dance. It combines eccentric dancing and hip-motion, coupled with a strut. The body is stiff from the waist up; heel-step on the beat, toe-step off. The knees are bent, but straighten on the heel step. Three of these, then two fast steps with sliding hips. Tap and strut steps may be mixed in

(At right):
St. Louis Hop. Hop forward on both feet spread; then give a stamp with each foot

Louisiana Mess Around. Hands on heels. Rock on heels, hips moving in a circle. This keeps the center regions of the body moving, while the rest must remain quiet

Heebie Jeebies. This is a spasmodic pawing of the hands all over the body in an agony of perfect rhythm. The more suggestive, the better the effect

Washington / Johnny. Body is to be held absolutely rigid. Take short jerky steps, meanwhile moving the head up and down in the same rhythm

Virginia Essence. Step with left foot and bring right up with right, and turn whole body in half-circle. Repeat this with right foot stepping first

NASIB PHOTOS

Mooch. Shuffle forward with both feet. Hips come first, feet follow. Be sure not to lose the rhythm

Figure 5.3 (Continued)

physicality, and sexuality. Even white jazz dancers at times made racialist associations with their routines and teachers. For example, Adele Astaire, Fred's sister and early dance partner, once said, "Oh, Buddy [Bradley] has taught me such marvelous, new, *dirty* steps."[46]

As a result, performances of appropriated—albeit paid for—*authentic* black dancing promoted the recognition of racial differences (rather than similarities) between the dancer and the dance. Visually, they highlighted the whiteness of the dancer and the blackness of the dancing. And, given that the white dancers were demonstrating their proficiency in black dancing, these performances can also be interpreted as an illustration of white mastery of black dancing and, by extension, a white mastery over black people and culture. In these ways, the *invisibility* of black dance teachers seems to have enhanced the *visibility* of essentialist ideas relating to racial difference.

Although it was surely not an intended effect of the professionalization of black dance teaching, the reification of difference was a cost of black dancers' continued participation in a racialist appropriation system. Other possible responses by 1920s black dance teachers, such as protesting or opting out of the system, might have foreclosed a rare avenue for professionalization and its related benefits. Despite the hardships imposed by New York City's entertainment world, many black dancers found ways to work within it; in fact, they made their invisibility work to their advantage. Hidden from the white public eye, they launched a profession and sought greater empowerment within a system that seemed to guarantee their marginalization. As a result they earned income, bolstered self-respect, and retained a sense of cultural ownership of black dancing. They carved out an avenue for their own upward social mobility, as well as for those who would follow. In addition, their professionalization subtly challenged prevailing stereotypes about African Americans with regard to natural dancing ability and unsuitability for anything but menial labor.

Without the cloak of invisibility, I doubt if these empowering countermoves would have been possible. Being unseen seems to have been the linchpin in both the subordinating system of appropriation and the tactics that black dance professionals used to challenge it. By looking beyond the surviving representations of Jazz Age performance, we can glimpse the black dancers whose labors led to the professionalization of black dance teaching and fueled the 1920s jazz dance craze.

Conclusion

Modern Dancing, Past and Present

As early twentieth-century America was grappling with massive waves of migration and immigration that were transforming the complexion of its Northern cities, many began implementing stronger segregation laws. Nativism and xenophobia reached their apex and helped the Ku Klux Klan entrench itself in rural America. Public speakers, fearing the gradual dying out of white cultural dominance, railed against "race suicide" through intermixture between whites and people of other ethnicities and races. At the center of all of this was the question: What were Americans going to look like in the future?

Many new and established Americans worked through issues of race, ethnicity, and nation on the dance floor, where they found not only the pleasure of a night out, but also a means of testing, exploring, contesting, and/or announcing their identities and those of "others." Social dancing, which was understood in terms of white and black, despite being purely neither, was variously appropriated, rejected, and adapted by recreational dancers as well as professional teachers and performers as a way of articulating—to use sociologist Stuart Hall's term—race and class status and, especially, claiming citizenship and building new career opportunities. Binary racialist thinking about dancing that combined European- and African-influenced movement practices ironically enabled many people to work with and against the stereotypes that populated their world. Dancing *white* and/or dancing *black* became a potent tactic, a means of discreetly working towards greater self-empowerment.[1]

During this time period, social dancing was a key component of American popular culture as well as an important means of forging new identities and performing one's aspirations to the world. Though I have identified race as the key organizing principle, I do not mean to suggest that it was the only identity marker that dancers were concerned with. Class status, national citizenship, gender identity, ethnicity, and sexual preference were all at play in the dancing and wholly intertwined with constructions of race. As dancers performed who they thought they were and wanted to be, they also implicitly constructed who they were not—often in derogatory terms laden with stereotypes and to subjugating ends. Through such dancing, participants sought out their own sense of belonging and feelings of empowerment. Their constructions of a modern "self," though, frequently came at a cost to a (stereotypically constructed) "other."

Social dancing, during the first decades of the twentieth century, was also a means of building a new ballroom dance industry that eventually became national and international in scope. Through it, many immigrants and migrants in dire circumstances found a means of professionalization and a degree of economic stability. The key to the success of this new industry—for performers, teachers, writers, and promoters—was the ability to control the distribution of dance knowledge as well as the dance's racial implications. For example, ballroom professionals were able to convince dance consumers that they needed teachers in order to not embarrass themselves on the dance floor (i.e., perform a social identity/status that was undesirable). In this way, they were able to harness the allure of social mobility to their advantage—a technique that began with the traveling dancing masters of Europe of the eighteenth-century and that was effective among both black and white Americans in the twentieth century as well.

By querying race, class, and industry in my five case studies, three over-arching themes emerge: assimilation, nostalgia, and distinction. Various groups of people engaged with these ideas differently, of course, but engage with them, they all did. While assimilation into mainstream American culture was the heart's desire of European immigrant youth and Harlem's elite, it was feared and resisted by many black migrants and the Harlem Renaissance's young leaders. Nostalgia fueled the dancing of the black and white clients of ballroom dance industry professionals, as well as Harlem's black migrants, all of whom longed for very different times and places. The former viewed the nineteenth century as a safer and simpler time, (i.e., before massive immigration and migration), whereas the latter yearned for a feeling of being at home in the present, in the wake of migration's displacements. In nearly all cases considered, though, the dancers sought some form of distinction over another social group—whether in terms of race, class, or both. Immigrants aimed to show that they were not foreigners; elite participants distanced themselves from the working class; many white dancers tried to be "not black"; and black dancers, at least in some cases, strived to be "not white."

Taken together, these social dancing practices tell us much about America and the development of modernity there during the first decades of the twentieth century. They demonstrate that participants viewed positive change as not only possible but also imaginable through embodied quotidian performance. There was hopefulness embedded in their dancing. Several of the case studies illustrate how deliberate reminders of the past served as a substantial comfort for many men and women in the face of modernity's transformations. Through frequent cross-cultural excursions, the social dancing of this period demonstrates that many people were both fearful and curious about differences of various kinds. And, finally, difference—or rather the harnessing of difference—was central to many industrial developments of this time.

Despite being overwhelmed by the changes that were endemic during the opening decades of the twentieth century, many Americans remained hopeful about the direction of their lives. It takes a degree of confidence about the future to invest in a new vision of self. Furthermore, scores of early twentieth century Americans saw positive change as possible within themselves and not wholly dependent on circumstance or other people; they felt empowered to improve their own lives..

Even though change was viewed positively by many, it could also inspire a degree of conservatism. This is perhaps most visible in the importance of maintaining comforting links to the past, a type of temporal "other." Black migrants clung to dances from the rural South, just as European immigrants were drawn to ragtime's resonances with European folk dance practices. On the other hand, elite dancers—both black and white—sought out references to the nineteenth century through their dance choices. The more the future seemed to be upon them, the more modern Americans reached out to the past for consolation.

With the tremendous demographic changes of the time also came rampant fears and curiosities relating to cultural difference. One response to this was racialist thinking that sought to organize the encroaching hybridized (and hybridizing) world into discrete categories that often paralleled existing stereotypes. Another was the employment of temporary border-crossing activities, which borrowed much from minstrelsy's strategies and sampled an "other" perspective. On the one hand, Americans were drawn to what was new and unfamiliar; on the other hand, they were apprehensive of the changes modernity brought or might bring to their world—in many ways, two sides of the same coin.

Clearly this was a time of substantial industrial growth in America, a change that had begun decades earlier but blossomed during the early twentieth century. Such growth was dependent on successful control over not only the means of production, but also the rate of consumption and representation of products. It was also reliant, in many cases, on the harnessing of the labor, as well as the products, of "others." In northeastern factories, this meant immigrant and migrant workers, but in the new dance industries in particular, it included *dancing,* especially that which was viewed as black. Indeed, difference was in many ways the fuel for industrial development in dance as it was elsewhere during the early twentieth century.

DANCING RACE IN THE TWENTY-FIRST CENTURY

Fast forward to the early twenty-first century and many questions remain: Given that the early twentieth century laid the groundwork for the American popular dancing that followed, as well as the global ballroom industry of today, what has changed? Are circumstances and practices different now? Some might say that the "race suicide," so feared more than a hundred years ago, has happened. The United States as a nation is about to become predominantly nonwhite, and many of its cities have been so for decades. But has this intervened in racial thinking? Has it altered feelings about cultural differences?

Although I now live outside the United States, it is easy to peer across the border and see that fears and curiosities relating to cultural differences remain strong forces in American entertainment forms. Yet, new cultures are now being explored and consumed. Substantial immigration from Asia and Latin America (and elsewhere) has introduced a more diverse demography and forced more complex understandings of race—as have recent trends toward cross-cultural families. In addition, ongoing empowerment efforts by Indigenous, Black, and Chicano peoples (among others) have raised awareness of the political consequences of visible difference in America. That said, unofficial segregation continues and keeps culturally different groups living quite separately in many places.

Cross-cultural exploration and exploitation today are occurring on a global scale, not just nationally. Americans are adopting culturally different dances, foods, clothes, health care, philosophies, and musics—often without much knowledge of the culture and history that gave rise to them.

The popularity of hip hop, tai chi, salsa, capoeira, yoga, and even zumba speak to this. These "other" practices are not yet free from Ameri-centric stereotypes unfortunately: for example, blackness is often used to mobilize resistance/subversion, Asian-ness ancient wisdom, and Latin-ness an embrace of sexuality. As with many stereotypes, these are all qualities that can be admired on one level, while severely limiting possibilities on others.

Borrowing dances from an "other" culture today is still at some level often about social mobility—i.e., identity, aspiration, and empowerment. To return to this book's themes, racial and national assimilation might appear to be less of an issue given today's proportionally lower numbers for immigration and smaller waves of migration, but the melting pot model still clearly prevails. Nostalgia remains highly relevant and especially apparent in the swing revival that began in the 1990s and also in the contemporary ballroom repertoire.[2] There is a new model for distinction operating, however, that includes cosmopolitanism as a form of cultural capital.[3] Today one can establish status by demonstrating global cultural literacy. Can you order sushi using the Japanese terms? Can you do the yoga pose upon hearing the Sanskrit name? Can you distinguish between salsa and samba? Such performances of distinction announce one's cosmopolitanism, and thus elevated status, in today's world.

Blackface minstrelsy feels almost lost to the passage of time, thankfully; we rarely see its shocking images today. And yet its legacies are firmly planted in American popular culture. As Spike Lee's *Bamboozled* showed us, many of our most popular television shows and films retain echoes of minstrelsy. The mechanism of minstrelsy remains with us as well—how many of us have taken on the markers of an "other" culture in order to feel different/freer/better in some way? We will know that minstrelsy has been entirely relegated to the past when more people are using cross-cultural experiences to engage with *people* from another culture instead of stereotypes relating to them. Indeed, it could be said that the longest-lasting legacy of blackface minstrelsy is an American tradition of using the embodiment of "others" to fulfil our aspirations and fantasies.

Beyond America, the ballroom dance industry, sometimes called dancesport, which was launched during the early twentieth century in New York City, has spread to Europe, Latin America, and now Asia. It is a multibillion dollar endeavor that still sells social mobility to the middle classes and their aspirants. At the same time, it continues to provide employment and professionalization opportunities for new immigrants—now on a global scale.[4] Its repertoire has expanded over the decades certainly, although its conceptual frameworks have changed little. As already mentioned, within its system of classification, dances are still either "Standard" (primarily European-derived) or "Latin" (primarily Latin and African American). There is little interest in individual dance's original forms, and the so-called refinement of "raw" dances continues to be understood as necessary. In addition, the industry remains overwhelmingly white in terms of professionals and participants, even though its dances have grown even more heterogeneous in origin.

So the question remains: Are we still dancing "modern" today? By this, I mean, as dancers, are our models for race still absolute? Are we still turning to "otherness" as an escape? Do we succeed at the cost of the exploitation of "others"? I look forward to dance researchers engaging with these questions in the future.

NOTES

INTRODUCTION

1. Gender and sexuality are not the focus of this particular study—although they certainly come up along the way—not because they are not important or relevant, but because they have already been addressed in prior scholarship. In particular, the works of Susan Cook, Julie Malnig, and Kathy Peiss masterfully explore the gender and sexual implications of social dancing from this period.

2. Although some dances from Latin America attained great popularity during this time period—the tango and *maxixe* in particular—I am focusing on the dances indigenous to North America in this study. Please see Marta Savigliano's excellent study of Argentine tango and its international travels, *Tango and the Political Economy of Passion* (1995).

3. David Krasner, "Rewriting the Body: Aida Overton Walker and the Social Formation of Cakewalking," *Theatre Survey* 37 (1996): 66–92. Richard Newman, "The Brightest Star: Aida Overton Walker in the Age of Ragtime and Cakewalk" *Prospects* 18 (1993): 465–481. Jacqui Malone, *Steppin' on the Blues: The Visible Rhythms of African American Dance* (Urbana: University of Illinois Press, 1996) chapter five.

4. Nadine George-Graves, "Just Like Being at the Zoo: Primitivity and Ragtime Dance," in *Ballroom, Boogie, Shimmy Sham, Shake: A Social and Popular Dance Reader*, ed. Julie Malnig (Champaign, IL: University of Illinois Press, 2008).

5. For an excellent study of British ballroom dancing, please read: Theresa Buckland, *Society dancing: fashionable bodies in England, 1870-1920* (New York: Palgrave Macmillan, 2011).

6. For more information, please see: Katrina Hazzard-Gordon, *Jookin': The Rise of Social Dance Formations in African-American Culture* (Philadelphia: Temple University Press, 1990). Marshall and Jean Stearns, *Jazz Dance: The Story of American Vernacular Dance.* (New York: MacMillan, 1968) 11–32.

7. Blues dancing is a term that I use, for convenience, to describe the dancing that happened to blues music. It was not a term typically used by participants at the time.

8. Zora Neale Hurston, "The Characteristics of Negro Expression," in *Double-take: A Revisionist Harlem Renaissance Anthology*, eds. Venetria Patton and Maureen Honey (New Brunswick, NJ: Rutgers University Press, 2002) 70. [Originally published in 1935].

9. Please also see Hazzard-Gordon, *Jookin'*, 162-171.

10. These aesthetic choices were a legacy of European ballroom dancing going back to baroque court dance.

11. For more information, please see: Stearns, *Jazz Dance*, and Malone, *Steppin' on the Blues*.

12. On European immigration, see Rose Laub Coser, Laura S. Anker, and Andrew J. Perrin, *Women of Courage: Jewish and Italian Immigrant Women in New York* (Westport, CT: Greenwood, 1999); Susan A. Glenn, *Daughters of the Shtetl: Life and Labor in the Immigrant Generation* (Ithaca, NY: Cornell University Press, 1990); John Higham, *Strangers in the Land: Patterns of American Nativism, 1860–1925* (New Brunswick, NJ: Rutgers University Press, 1998); Hadassa Kosak, *Cultures of Opposition: Jewish Immigrant Workers, New York City, 1881–1905* (Albany, NY: State University of New York Press, 2000); Walter Laidlaw, *Statistical Sources for Demographic Studies of Greater New York, 1910* (New York: New York Federation of Churches, 1913); Daniel Soyer, *Jewish Immigrant Associations and American Identity in New York, 1880–1939* (Cambridge, MA: Harvard University Press, 1997), 49–80.

    On African American migration, see Darlene Clark Hine, "Black Migration to the Urban Midwest: The Gender Dimension, 1915–1945," in *The Great Migration in Historical Perspective: New Dimensions of Race, Class, and Gender*, ed. Joe William Trotter Jr. (Bloomington, IN: Indiana University Press, 1991), 127–146; New York Urban League, *The Negro in New York* (New York: New York Urban League, 1931); Gilbert Osofsky, *Harlem: The Making of a Ghetto/Negro New York, 1890–1930*, 2nd ed. (1963) (Chicago: Ivan R. Dee, 1996); Joe William Trotter Jr., ed., *The Great Migration in Historical Perspective: New Dimensions of Race, Class, and Gender* (Bloomington, IN: Indiana University Press, 1991).

13. Walter Laidlaw, *Statistical Sources for Demographic Studies of Greater New York, 1910* (New York: New York Federation of Churches, 1913). Laidlaw, *Statistical Sources for Demographic Studies of Greater New York, 1920* (New York: New York Federation of Churches, 1922). *Census of the United States (1920)*. Population. New York (State). U.S. Bureau of the Census, Department of Commerce. Bountiful, Utah: American Genealogical Lending Library, 1992.

14. *Census of the United States (1930)*. Population. New York (State). U.S. Bureau of the Census, Department of Commerce. North Salt Lake, UT: Heritage Quest, 2002.

15. John Higham, *Strangers in the Land: Patterns of American Nativism, 1860–1925* (New Brunswick, NJ: Rutgers University Press, 1998) 65.

16. Glenn, *Daughters of the Shtetl*, 56; Soyer, *Jewish Immigrant Associations*, 49–80.

17. James Weldon Johnson, *Black Manhattan* (New York: Knopf, 1930).

18. For an excellent study of contemporary ballroom, please see: Juliet McMains, *Glamour Addiction: Inside the American Ballroom Dance Industry* (Middletown, CT: Wesleyan University Press, 2006).

19. Joseph E. Marks III, *America Learns to Dance: A Historical Study of Dance Education in America before 1900* (New York: Exposition, 1957); Compilations Folder, Bella C. Landauer Writings and Reference Collection, Library: Department of Prints, Photographs, and Architectural Collections, New York Historical Society (hereafter cited as Landauer Collection). "From New York Correspondence," *The Director* 1.1 (1897): 15. In addition to whatever ethical concerns were at play, the male teachers also did not want competition from the female teachers, who

could charge less as they had lower overhead costs, since they were working from home.

20. *Merriam-Webster's Collegiate Dictionary*, CD-ROM, Merriam-Webster, 2000.

21. "If you dance you must pay the piper . . . ," *Vogue*, January 15, 1914: 24–25; Lewis A. Erenberg, *Steppin' Out: New York Nightlife and the Transformation of American Culture* (Chicago: University of Chicago Press, 1981), 146–147; Julie Malnig, *Dancing Till Dawn: A Century of Exhibition Ballroom Dance* (New York: New York University Press, 1992), 10–11, 53, 89–108; Florence Walton Clippings File, Dance Collection, New York Public Library for the Performing Arts.
    Please note that in Britain there was a parallel effort to standardize ballroom dances, including their tempi, as early as 1922.

22. Malnig, *Dancing Till Dawn*; Malnig, "Two-Stepping to Glory: Social Dance and the Rhetoric of Social Mobility," *Etnofoor* 10.1–2 (1997): 128–150; Malnig, "Athena Meets Venus: Visions of Women in Social Dance in the Teens and Early 1920s," *Dance Research Journal* 31.2 (1999): 34–62; Susan Cook, "Tango Lizards and Girlish Men: Performing Masculinity on the Social Dance Floor," *Annual Meeting of the Society of Dance History Scholars* (New York: Barnard College, 1997); Cook, "Passionless Dancing and Passionate Reform: Respectability, Modernism, and the Social Dancing of Irene and Vernon Castle," in *The Passion of Music and Dance: Body, Gender, and Sexuality* (Oxford, UK: Berg, 1998), 133–150; Cook, "Watching Our Step: Embodying Research, Telling Stories," in *Audible Traces: Gender, Identity and Music*, eds. Elaine Barkin and Lydia Hamessley (Los Angeles: Carcifoli, 1999), 177–212; Cook, pers. comm., July 22, 2000; Cook, "Talking Machines and Moving Bodies: Marketing Dance Music before World War I" (paper presented at the Dancing in the Millennium Conference, Washington, DC: July 2000).

23. Clifford Geertz, "Thick Description: Toward an Interpretive Theory of Culture" in *The Interpretation of Cultures* (New York: Basic Books, 1973): 5.

24. These categories were created over time as different dances were standardized for competition purposes.

25. Martha Graham, "I am a dancer," in *This I Believe*, ed. Edward R. Murrow (New York: Simon and Schuster, 1952).

26. A few wonderful exceptions include Anthea Kraut's *Choreographing the Folk*, Nadine George-Graves's *The Royalty of Negro Vaudeville*, and Ann Cooper-Albright's *Traces of Light*.

27. Cynthia J. Novack, *Sharing the Dance: Contact Improvisation and American Culture* (Madison, WI: University of Wisconsin Press, 1990), 3–25.

28. Sally Ann Ness, *Body, Movement, and Culture: Kinesthetic and Visual Symbolism in a Philippine Community* (Philadelphia: University of Pennsylvania Press, 1992), 17.

29. Philip V. Bohlman, "Fieldwork in the Ethnomusicological Past," in *Shadows in the Field: New Perspectives for Fieldwork in Ethnomusicology*, eds. Gregory Barz and Timothy Cooley (New York: Oxford University Press, 1997).

30. Susan Foster, "On Dancing and the Dance: Two Visions of Dance's History," *Proceedings of the Society of Dance History Scholars* (1983), 140.

31. Please also consult the works of Marta Savigliano, Ann Cooper-Albright, and Priya Srinivasan for other examples of this type of creative scholarly work.

32. See Ann Daly, *Done Into Dance: Isadora Duncan in America* (Bloomington, IN: Indiana University Press, 1995); Jane C. Desmond, "Embodying Differences: Issues in Dance and Cultural Studies," *Meaning in Motion: New*

Cultural Studies of Dance (Durham, NC: Duke University Press); Susan Foster, *Choreography and Narrative: Ballet's Staging of Story and Desire* (Bloomington, IN: Indiana University Press, 1996); Susan Manning, *Modern Dance, Negro Dance: Race in Motion* (Minneapolis, MN: University of Minnesota Press, 2004); Amy Koritz, *Gendering Bodies/Performing Art: Dance and Literature in Early-Twentieth Century Culture* (Ann Arbor, MI: University of Michigan Press, 1995).

33. Desmond, "Embodying Differences," 30.
34. Linda Tomko, "Reconstruction: Beyond Notation," in *International Encyclopedia of Dance*, vol. 5 (New York: Oxford University Press, 2003), 326–327.
35. The primary foci of my reconstruction work were the ragtime and modern dances, as these were the dances in my study most lost to the passage of time.
36. Diana Taylor, *The Archive and the Repertoire: Performing Cultural Memory in the Americas* (Durham, NC: Duke University Press, 2003).
37. This approach has been deployed at times by other dance reconstructors.
38. Mark Franko, *Dance as Text: Ideologies of the Baroque Body* (Cambridge, UK: Cambridge University Press, 1993).
39. Michel De Certeau, *The Practice of Everyday Life*, trans. Steven Rendall (Berkeley, CA: University of California Press, 1984).
40. Michel Foucault, "Technologies of the Self," in *Technologies of the Self*, eds. L. H. Martin, H. Gutman, and P. H. Hutton (Amherst, MA: University of Massachusetts Press, 1988), 18.
41. Pierre Bourdieu, *Distinction: A Social Critique of the Judgment of Taste*, trans. Richard Nice (Cambridge, MA: Harvard University Press, 1984), 226.
42. Pierre Bourdieu, "The forms of capital," in *Handbook of Theory and Research for the Sociology of Education*, ed. J. Richardson (New York: Greenwood, 1986), 241–258.
43. Stuart Hall, "Race, Articulation, and Societies Structured in Dominance," In *Black British Cultural Studies: A Reader*, eds. Houston Baker, et al. (Chicago: University of Chicago Press, 1996), 55.
44. For a fuller discussion of race-based dance terminology, see Thomas DeFrantz, ed., *Dance Many Drums: Excavations in African American Dance* (Madison, WI: University of Wisconsin Press, 2002), 15–17.
45. This scholarly position on the question of racial origins reflects a trend in ethnomusicology of tracking conceptualizations of race through popular music practices. See *Music and the Racial Imagination*, eds. Ronald Radano and Philip V. Bohlman (Chicago: University of Chicago Press, 2000); Guthrie P. Ramsey, *Race Music: Black Cultures from Bebop to Hop-Hop* (Berkeley, CA: University of California Press, 2003); Ronald Radano, *Lying Up a Nation: Race and Black Music* (Chicago: University of Chicago Press, 2003).
46. Manning, *Modern Dance, Negro Dance*, xv.
47. In this way, I differ from Brenda Dixon-Gottschild's latest book, which asks, "If we let go of the concept of race, then where would we hang our racism?" By this I think she implies that if we accept race as a social construction, we would lose the ability to talk about the lived experience of race and thus the ability to combat racism. While I respect and understand Dixon-Gottschild's position, I think looking at race as a social construction is also a valid way to attack racism. Dixon-Gottschild, *Black Dancing Body: A Geography From Coon to Cool* (New York: Palgrave MacMillan, 2003), 5–6.

48. See Paul Gilroy, *Against Race: Imagining Political Culture Beyond the Color Line* (Cambridge, MA: Harvard University Press, 2000).

49. Gilroy, *Against Race*, 58.

50. Howard Winant, *The World is Ghetto: Race and Democracy since World War II* (New York: Basic Books, 2001), 19.

51. E. L. Doctorow, *Ragtime* (New York: Modern Library, 1997).

52. Coon singing or shouting, which began around the turn of the century, involved popular music sung in a bluesy manner in nightclub settings by matronly white (often Jewish) women, such as Sophie Tucker and Fanny Brice. The singers at times wore blackface, and the songs they sang relied heavily on exaggerated black dialect, sexual innuendo, and references to an idealized South. See also Arnold Shaw, *Black Popular Music in America: From the Spirituals, Minstrels, and Ragtime to Soul, Disco and Hip Hop* (New York: Schirmer Books, 1986).

53. Richard Dyer, *Only Entertainment* (London: Routledge, 1992); Eric Lott, *Love and Theft: Blackface Minstrelsy and the American Working Class* (New York: Oxford University Press, 1993).

54. Frederick Winslow Taylor, *Shop Management* (Sioux Falls, ND: NuVision Publications, 2008 [1905]). His work helped manufacturers transition from artisanal to industrial production prior to Ford's factory system.

55. Kevin Gaines, *Uplifting the Race: Black Leadership, Politics and Culture During the 20th Century* (Chapel Hill, NC: University of North Carolina Press, 1996); Alessandra Lorini, *Rituals of Race: American Public Culture and the Search for Racial Democracy* (Charlottesville, VA: University of Virginia Press, 1999).

56. See Manning, *Modern Dance, Negro Dance (2004)*, introduction.

CHAPTER 1

1. J. Martin Favor, *Authentic Blackness: The Folk in the New Negro Renaissance*, (Durham, NC: Duke University Press, 1999), 4.

2. Wallace Thurman, "Harlem as Educational Drama," in *The Collected Writings of Wallace Thurman: A Harlem Renaissance Reader*, eds. Amritjit Singh and Daniel M. Scott (New Brunswick, NJ: Rutgers University Press, 2003).

3. Wallace Thurman, "Terpsichore in Harlem" in *The Collected Writings of Wallace Thurman: A Harlem Renaissance Reader*, eds. Amritjit Singh and Daniel M. Scott (New Brunswick, NJ: Rutgers University Press, 2003).

4. See Favor, *Authentic Blackness*, 9, for a critique of this view.

5. Throughout this chapter, I rely heavily on the fiction writings of several Harlem Renaissance writers. Although published in 1920s and 1930s, their works often addressed the presence of the slow drag in earlier decades. Nonetheless, these are complex resources to rely on as a historian. Authors wrote about dancing in a way that indicated the personality features of a character, furthered a plotline, or referenced a larger theme in the piece. For this reason, I consulted a wide range of writings in order to distill the core movement features from several perspectives.

6. Katrina Hazzard-Gordon, *Jookin': The Rise of Social Dance Formations in African-American Culture* (Philadelphia: Temple University Press, 1990).

7. Paul Oliver, "Do the Bombashay: Dance Songs and Routines," in *Write Me a Few of Your Lines: A Blues Reader*, ed. Steven C. Tracy (Amherst, MA: University of Massachusetts Press, 1999), 113–114.

8. Langston Hughes, *Not without Laughter* (New York: Knopf, 1971 [1930]), 12.

9. For example: Coot Grant and Charlie Love, typed manuscripts of interviews with Marshall and/or Jean Stearns, Marshall Stearns Research Papers, Institute of Jazz Studies, Rutgers University.

10. For more detail, please see Hazzard-Gordon, *Jookin'* and Marshall and Jean Stearns, *Jazz Dance: The Story of American Vernacular Dance* (New York: Macmillan, 1968).

11. Claude McKay, *Home to Harlem*, 1st ed. (Boston: Northeastern University Press, 1987), 93.

12. Hughes, *Not without Laughter*, 15.

13. Thurman, "Terpsichore in Harlem," 284–285.

14. Katrina Hazzard has also used the term "recycled" in relation to African American dancing. See Katrina Hazzard-Gordon, "Afro-American core culture social dance: An examination of four aspects of meaning," *Dance Research Journal* 15 (1983): 21.

15. John F. Szwed and Morton Marks, "The Afro-American transformation of European set dances and dance suites," *Dance Research Journal* 20 (1988): 32.

16. James Haskins, *Scott Joplin: The Man Who Made Ragtime* (New York: Stein & Day, 1980), 177.

17. Szwed and Marks, "The Afro-American transformation," 32; Oliver, "Do the Bombashay," 111–112; David Evans, "From "Folk and Popular Blues," in *Write Me a Few of Your Lines: A Blues Reader*, ed. Steven C. Tracy (Amherst, MA: University of Massachusetts Press, 1999), 124.

18. Paul Oliver, *Conversation with the Blues*, 2nd ed. (New York: Cambridge University Press, 1997).

19. Oliver, "Do the Bombashay," 113–114.

20. Jessie Redmon Fauset, *There is Confusion*, Northeastern Library of Black Literature (Boston: Northeastern University Press, 1989); Hughes, *Not without Laughter*; Nella Larsen, *Quicksand* (New York: Negro Universities Press, 1969); McKay, *Home to Harlem*; Claude McKay, "The Negro Dancers," *Liberator* 2 (July 1919): 20; Wallace Thurman, *The Blacker the Berry: A Novel of Negro Life* (New York: Macaulay Co., 1929); Thurman, "Cordelia the Crude," *Fire*, November 1926, 5.

21. Hazzard-Gordon, *Jookin'*.

22. Thurman, *The Blacker the Berry*, 285.

23. Samuel Floyd and Marsha Reisser, *Black Music Biography* (Millwood, NY: Kraus International Publications, 1987), 167.

24. George Houston Bass was Langston Hughes's literary assistant for several years, as well as a professor of Afro-American studies at Brown University. Quoted in: Wilson Jeremiah Moses, "Varieties of Black Historicism: Issues of Antimodernism and 'Presentism'" in *Afrotopia: The Roots of African American Popular History* (Cambridge: Cambridge University Press, 1998), 31.

25. Stearns, *Jazz Dance*, 12.

26. Hazzard-Gordon, *Jookin'*, 93.

27. Hurston, "Characteristics of Negro Expression," 70.

28. Only Hazzard-Gordon's *Jookin'* and Tera Hunter's *To 'Joy My Freedom: Southern Black Women's Lives and Labors after the Civil War* (Cambridge, MA: Harvard University Press, 1998) mention it at any length.

29. As just one example of the more direct political use of social dance: The followers of Marcus Garvey held public dances to recruit members and accrue financial support for their black nationalist cause. See Daniel Dalrymple's 2008 dissertation *In the Shadow of Garvey: Garveyites in New York City and the British Caribbean, 1925-1950*.

30. Katrina Hazzard has argued that dance in African American communities "becomes a litmus test for cultural identity. . .[that] proves that one is a member of the cultural body." See Hazzard-Gordon, "Afro-American core culture social dance," 22.

31. Hunter, *To 'Joy My Freedom*.

32. Hazzard-Gordon, *Jookin'*.

33. Sterling Stuckey, "Christian Conversion and the Challenge of Dance," *Choreographing History*, ed. Susan Leigh Foster (Bloomington and Indianapolis, IN: Indiana University Press, 1995), 63.

34. McKay, *Home to Harlem*, 27–29. In the poem, McKay's early communist leanings are revealed when he goes on to question the possibility of true joy for migrants. "And yet they are the outcasts of the earth, a race oppressed and scorned by ruling man; how can they thus consent to joy and mirth . . . but oh! They dance with poetry in their eyes whose dreamy loveliness no sorrow dims, and parted lips and eager, gleeful cries, and perfect rhythms in their nimble limbs."

35. Langston Hughes, "Liars," in *The Collected Poems of Langston Hughes*, ed. Arnold Rampersad (New York: Knopf, 1994), 44.

36. Hughes, "Minstrel Man," in *The New Negro: Voices of the Harlem Renaissance*, ed. Alain Locke (New York: Atheneum, 1992 [1925]), 144.

37. Thurman, "Social Life of Harlem," in *The Collected Writings of Wallace Thurman: A Harlem Renaissance Reader*, eds. Amritjit Singh and Daniel M. Scott (New Brunswick, NJ: Rutgers University Press, 2003).

38. Tom Davin, "Conversations with James P. Johnson," *Jazz Review* 2.5 (June 1959): 14.

39. Paul Gilroy, *Against Race: Imagining Political Culture Beyond the Color Line* (Cambridge, MA: Belknap Press, 2000); Gilroy, *The Black Atlantic: Modernity and Double Consciousness* (Cambridge, MA: Harvard University Press, 1993); Aileen M. Moreton-Robinson, "I still call Australia home: Indigenous belonging and place in a white postcolonising society," in *Uprootings/regroundings: Questions of Home and Migration*, ed. Sara Ahmed (New York: Berg Publishers, 2003).

40. Katrina Hazzard, Personal communication. February 24, 2015.

41. Diana Taylor, *The Archive and the Repertoire: Performing Cultural Memory in the Americas* (Durham, NC: Duke University Press, 2003).

42. Gannit Ankori, "'Dis-Orientalisms'—Displaced Bodies/Embodied Displacements in Contemporary Palestinian Art," in *Uprootings/regroundings: Questions of Home and Migration*, ed. Sara Ahmed (New York: Berg Publishers, 2003); Anne-Marie Fortier, "Making home: queer migrations and motions of attachment," in *Uprootings/regroundings: Questions of Home and Migration*, ed. Sara Ahmed (New York: Berg Publishers, 2003).

43. Sara Ahmed, ed., *Uprootings/regroundings: Questions of Home and Migration* (New York: Berg Publishers, 2003).

44. Dance was accessible to all migrants, according to visual artist Aaron Douglas. "The dance offered a field for the unrestricted expression of the Negroes' creative passion. Here were no expensive instruments to be purchased, no weird symbols to be mastered, no unfamiliar tools and stubborn material to overcome, only swift feet, strong legs, a lust for life and a soaring imagination" (79). And so, black social dancing was not an exclusive practice; it was available to all able-bodied men and women, not just a select few who could purchase lessons or access to expensive clubs and ballrooms. Aaron Douglas, "The Negro in American Culture," in *Artists Against War and Fascism: Papers of the First American Congress*, eds. Matthew Baigell and Julia Williams (New Brunswick, NJ: Rutgers University Press, 1986 [1936]).

45. Sterling Stuckey, "Christian Conversion and the Challenge of Dance," *Choreographing History*, ed. Susan Leigh Foster (Bloomington and Indianapolis, IN: Indiana University Press, 1995), 55.

46. Although this poem is set in Chicago it is relevant to this discussion given this city was another vital black migration center during this period.

47. See Sterling Stuckey, *Slave Culture: Nationalist Theory and the Foundations of Black America* (New York: Oxford University Press, 1987) and Samuel Floyd, *The Power of Black Music* (New York: Oxford University Press, 1999).

48. Favor, *Authentic Blackness*. Please note that the so-called African American "dialect poets," who predated the Harlem Renaissance, had a similar approach. Poets, such as Paul Laurence Dunbar, chose the language of the "folk" as a means of revealing the "true" history and culture of African Americans in order to seek greater equality.

49. John O. Perpener, *African-American Concert Dance: The Harlem Renaissance and Beyond* (Urbana, IL: University of Illinois Press, 2005), 37.

50. Rent parties, also known as house parties, were private events that hosts charged admission to, as a way to raise funds to pay their rent. Hosts would hire a band and offer food and drink to guests.

51. Thurman, "*Harlem* as Educational Drama."

52. Thurman, *Harlem: A Melodrama of Negro Life in Harlem*, in *The Collected Writings of Wallace Thurman: A Harlem Renaissance Reader*, eds. Amritjit Singh and Daniel M. Scott (New Brunswick, NJ: Rutgers University Press, 2003), 337.

53. Thurman, *Harlem: A Melodrama of Negro Life in Harlem*, 361.

54. Amritjit Singh and Daniel M. Scott III, "Part Seven: Plays," in *The Collected Writings of Wallace Thurman: A Harlem Renaissance Reader*, eds. Amritjit Singh and Daniel M. Scott (New Brunswick, NJ: Rutgers University Press, 2003), 307.

55. Wallace Thurman and William Jourdan Rapp, "The Writing of *Harlem*: The Story of a Strange Collaboration," in *The Collected Writings of Wallace Thurman: A Harlem Renaissance Reader*, eds. Amritjit Singh and Daniel M. Scott (New Brunswick, NJ: Rutgers University Press, 2003), 377. Langston Hughes concurred as well that it was "considerably distorted for box office purposes" (*Big Sea*, 235)

56. Perpener, *African-American Concert Dance*, 36.

57. Arna Wendell Bontemps, *100 Years of Negro Freedom* (New York: Dodd Mead, 1962), 306.

58. Bontemps, *100 Years*, 306.

59. Reid Badger, *A Life in Ragtime: A Biography of James Reese Europe* (New York: Oxford University Press, 1995), 115.

60. See also chapter five of this book for more information.

61. This possibility is supported by Europe himself who referred to "blues songs as fox-trots," according to biographer Badger, *A Life in Ragtime*, 210.

62. Similar arguments are made by Tera Hunter and Hazel Carby in their important works on blues dancing.

63. Paul Gilroy, *The Black Atlantic: Modernity and Double Consciousness* (Cambridge: Harvard University Press, 1993), 3.

CHAPTER 2

1. Jazz musician and educator Mark C. Gridley has defined ragtime music in the following way: "The word 'rag' refers to a kind of music that was put together like a military march and had rhythms borrowed from Afro-American banjo music. You could tell ragtime music because many of the loud accents fell in between

the beats." See Gridley, *Jazz Styles: History and Analysis*, 6th ed. (Upper Saddle River, NJ: Prentice Hall, 1997), 35.

2. See Elizabeth Perry, "'The General Motherhood of the Commonwealth': Dance Hall Reform in the Progressive Era," *American Quarterly* 37 (1985): 719–733.

3. Michel Foucault, *The Archeology of Knowledge and the Discourse on Language*, trans. A. M. Sheridan-Smith (New York: Pantheon, 1972).

4. For ballroom dancing, I draw upon not only primary sources and consultations with dance reconstructor Cheryl Stafford, but also a host of secondary sources devoted to European American social dance. A. H. Franks, *Social Dance: A Short History* (London: Routledge and Kegan Paul, 1963); Elizabeth Aldrich, *From the Ballroom to Hell: Grace and Folly in Nineteenth-Century Dance* (Evanston, IL: Northwestern University Press, 1991); Philip J. S. Richardson, *The Social Dance in Literature, 1400–1918: Selections* (Jefferson, NC: McFarland, 1998); Belinda Quirey, *"May I Have the Pleasure?" The Story of Popular Dancing* (London: British Broadcasting Co., 1976); Peter Buckman, *Let's Dance: Social, Ballroom, and Folk Dancing* (New York: Paddington Press, 1978).

5. This quote is a mélange of phrases pulled from the following Committee of Fourteen (COF) investigator's reports: Kennedy's, November 9, 1912; 122nd Street and Broadway, May 24, 1912; Hynes Road House, July 3, 1914.

6. COF investigator's reports; *The Crescent*, January 31, 1914.

7. Vernon and Irene Castle, *Modern Dancing* (New York: World Syndicate, 1914), 177 [my emphasis].

8. In *Cultures of Opposition: Jewish Immigrant Workers, New York City, 1881–1905* (Albany, NY: State University of New York Press, 2000), Hadassa Kosak states that "Jews emigrated in proportionally greater number than any other European group except the Irish. In absolute numbers, they ranked second after Italians among the newcomers. During the peak years of immigration, they constituted 10.5 percent of all new Americans" (15). See also Daniel Soyer, *Jewish Immigrant Associations and American Identity in New York, 1880–1939* (Cambridge, MA: Harvard University Press, 1997), 49–80; Kathy Lee Peiss, *Cheap Amusements: Working Women and Leisure in Turn-of-the-Century New York* (Philadelphia: Temple University Press, 1986), 38–41; Susan A. Glenn, *Daughters of the Shtetl: Life and Labor in the Immigrant Generation* (Ithaca, NY: Cornell University Press, 1990); John Higham, *Strangers in the Land: Patterns of American Nativism, 1860–1925* (New Brunswick, NJ: Rutgers University Press, 1998).

   Eastern European Jewish immigrants transported their dancing practices with them to the new world. See Lee Ellen Friedland, "'Tantsn Is Lebn': Dancing in Eastern European Jewish Culture," *Dance Research Journal 17* (1985–1986): 77–80. In both the old and new worlds, group folk dancing, as well as partner dancing, occurred at dance events (Peiss, *Cheap Amusements*, 91). As part of the group dancing, men often performed improvised solo movements that exhibited skill, strength, and stamina. Women danced primarily in unison and only with other women. Participants touched each other's hands and arms, although torso contact was minimal, and level changes were frequent. Sonic accents, in the form of clapping and shouting, were a regular feature. Social dancing that involved partnering occurred with greater frequency in Eastern European Jewish communities toward the latter half of the twentieth century (Zvi Friedhaber, "Jewish Dance Traditions," *International Encyclopaedia of Dance*, 3rd ed., s.v., 1998, 602–606).

9. See Randy McBee, *Dance Hall Days: Intimacy and Leisure among Working-Class Immigrants in the United States* (New York: New York University Press, 2000), 135.

10. Peiss, *Cheap Amusements.*

11. John F. Szwed and Morton Marks, "The Afro-American Transformation of European Set Dances and Dance Suites," *Dance Research Journal* 20.1 (1988): 29–36.

12. Tom Davin, "Conversations with James P. Johnson," *Jazz Review* (June 1959).

13. Troy Kinney, "The Dance: An Expression of Mental Activity," *Century Magazine,* October 1914, 823–833. By contrast, in their dance manual *Modern Dancing,* the Castles made several connections among modern dancing and ancient Greece and Rome, the Bible, and Europe—all places, spaces, and times that would have communicated "white" origins to readers, given their links with Western civilization.

14. See also J. S. Hopkins, *The tango and other up-to-date dances; a practical guide to all the latest dances, tango, one-step, innovation, hesitation, etc., described step by step* (Chicago: Saalfield Publishing Co., 1914), 13.

15. Troy and Margaret West Kinney, *Social Dancing of To-Day* (New York: Stokes, 1914), 2.

16. H. E. Cooper, "Rag on the Barbary Coast," *Dance Magazine,* September 1927, 31.

17. See Ronald Radano in *Music and the Racial Imagination* (Chicago: University Of Chicago Press, 2001).

18. Nadine George-Graves, "Just Like Being at the Zoo: Primitivity and Ragtime Dance," in *Ballroom, Boogie, Shimmy Sham, Shake: A Social and Popular Dance Reader*, ed. Julie Malnig (Champaign, IL: University of Illinois Press, 2008), 55–56.

19. COF investigator's reports; James Weldon Johnson, "Autobiography of an Ex-Colored Man," in *Three Negro Classics* (1930), reprinted (New York: Avon Books, 1965), 449–453; Jervis Anderson, *This Was Harlem: A Cultural Portrait, 1900–1050* (New York: Farrar Straus Giroux, 1982), 13–20.

20. Such integration was made possible by shifts in the location and number of urban social dance spaces. In New York City after the turn of the century, social dancing was increasingly offered by businesses in commercial entertainment districts that were *not* located in ethnic neighborhoods—for example, around 14th Street, Times Square, and the Bowery. In these areas, public dance halls holding anywhere from 50 to 1,200 people were erected. As dancing grew in popularity among urban youths seeking recreation, proprietors added dance floors to other leisure settings such as saloons, amusement parks, and vacation resorts. See Peiss, *Cheap Amusements*, 93–96. Peiss has noted that, by the 1910s, there were more than 500 commercial dance halls located throughout New York City (Peiss, 88, 93). See also Glenn, *Daughters of the Shtetl,* 137. In these new social spaces, young people from all over the city recreated together within a shared peer culture that valued "societal and cultural expression," according to Glenn. Casualness permeated these environments. Men and women often arrived unescorted, no longer under the watchful gaze of family members and neighbors. Men could spontaneously pick their partners on the dance floor and women could attract new partners by dancing together. Admission was controlled only by the price of entry; thus greater mixing among diverse culture groups became possible, at least to a degree. Even venues that catered exclusively to whites provided environments where young people from many different European ethnic backgrounds could interact with the native-born or second-generation immigrants from Ireland and Germany, for example, who now considered themselves to be American.

21. See John Hasse, ed., *Ragtime: Its History, Composers, and Music* (New York: Schirmer Books, 1985), 37. See also Samual A. Floyd and Marsh J. Reisser, "The Sources and Resources of Classical Ragtime Music," *Black Music Research Journal* 4 (1984): 22–59.

22. "The dances were all nigger," "a few steps of the nigger," and "exaggerated forms of the nigger." COF investigator's report: Lafayette Casino, June 1, 1912.

23. Aubrey McMahon Cree, *Handbook of ball-room dancing* (New York: John Lane Company, 1920); Edward John Long Scott, *The New Dancing as it should be: For the Ball-Room, the Class-Room and the Stage* (London and New York: G. Routledge, 1919).

24. See Alain Locke, ed., *The New Negro* (New York: Atheneum, 1992), 303.

25. Reid Badger, *A Life in Ragtime: A Biography of James Reese Europe* (New York: Oxford University Press, 1995), 52. Reid is quoting from Lewis Erenberg *Steppin' Out*, p 151.

26. See, for example, *The Mississippi Dippy Dip* (New York: Joseph W. Stern and Co., 1911); Anna Held, performer, *I'm Crazy 'bout the Turkey Trot* (New York: F. B. Haviland, 1911); James Duffy, *The African Glide* (New York: Joseph Morris Co., 1910). For period sheet music examples, consult the Bella C. Landauer Collection of Business and Advertising Ephemera: Collection of The New-York Historical Society, and the Sam DeVincent Collection of Illustration American Sheet Music, Archives Center, National Museum of American History, Smithsonian Institution.

27. James Weldon Johnson, "Autobiography of an Ex-Colored Man," 449–453; Jervis Anderson, *This Was Harlem*, 13–20.

28. Lee D. Baker, *From Savage to Negro: Anthropology and the Construction of Race, 1896–1954* (Berkeley, CA: University of California Press, 1998).

29. Ingeborg Harer, "Defining Ragtime Music: Historical and Topological Research," *Studia Musicologica Academiae Scientiarum Hungaricae* 38, no. 3/4 (1997): 410.

30. Many thanks to ethnomusicologist Kristin McGee for pointing out this perspective. William Schafer, *The Art of Ragtime: Form and Meaning of an Original Black American Art* (New York: Da Capo Press, 1977), xi, 22. See also William Howland Kenny III, "James Scott and the Culture of Classic Ragtime," *American Music* 9 (Summer 1991): 149–182.

31. Paul Gilroy, *The Black Atlantic: Modernity and Double Consciousness* (Cambridge, MA: Harvard University Press, 1993), 89.

32. See also David Krasner, *Resistance, Parody, and Double Consciousness in African American Theatre, 1890–1915* (Washington, DC: Smithsonian Institution Press, 1989); Danielle Robinson, "'Oh, You Black Bottom!': Appropriation, Authenticity, and Opportunity in the Jazz Dance Teaching of 1920s New York," *Dance Research Journal* 38, 1/2 (2006): 19–42.

33. It is true that, over time, the vestiges of minstrelsy diminished in these representations as ragtime music increasingly became the province of white composers. See Edward Berlin, *Ragtime: A Musical and Cultural History* (Berkeley, CA: University of California Press, 1980), 128; Berlin, *Reflections and Research on Ragtime* (Brooklyn, NY: Institute for Studies in American Music, Conservatory of Music, Brooklyn College of the City of New York, 1987).

34. Some powerful examples of these songs are "The Mississippi Dippy Dip," "Do the Funny Fox Trot," "That Lovin' Dippy Glide," and "That Fade-Away Dance."

35. See M. Pickering, "Eugene Stratton and Early Ragtime in Britain," *Black Music Research Journal* 20, 2 (2000): 151–80. Ragtime researcher Edward Berlin locates the origins of ragtime in coon songs of the 1890s, arguing that the term

"ragtime" replaced the term "coon songs" as mainstream attitudes toward public displays of such offensive language slowly changed. See Berlin, *Ragtime*, 23. See also Arnold Shaw, *Black Popular Music in America: From the Spirituals, Minstrels, and Ragtime to Soul, Disco and Hip Hop* (New York: Schirmer Books, 1986).

36. On changes in musical meaning informed by the embodied participation of sing-ing along, I have been influenced by Jeff Packman, "Singing Together/Meaning Apart: Popular Music, Participation and Cultural Politics in Salvador, Brazil," *Latin American Music Review* 31, 2 (Fall/Winter 2010).

37. See also Jeffrey Maggee, "'Everybody Step': Irving Berlin, Jazz and Broadway in the 1920's," *Journal of the American Musicological Society* 59, 3 (Fall 2006): 697–732; Linda Mizejewski, *Ziegfeld Girl: Image and Icon in Culture and Cinema* (Durham, NC: Duke University Press, 1999).

38. See Annemarie Bean, et al., eds., *Inside the Minstrel Mask: Readings in Nineteenth-century Blackface Minstrelsy* (Hanover, NH: University Press of New England for Wesleyan University Press, 1996); Robert C. Toll, *Blacking Up: The Minstrel Stage* (Durham, NC: Duke University Press, 1930); Dale Cockrell, *Demons of Disorder: Early Blackface Minstrels and their World* (Cambridge, UK: Cambridge University Press, 1997); Eric Lott, *Love and Theft: Blackface Minstrelsy and the American Working Class* (New York: Oxford University Press, 1993); Ingrid Monson, "The Problem of White Hipness: Race, Gender, and Cultural Conceptions in Jazz Historical Discourse," *Journal of the American Musicological Society* 48, no. 3 (1995): 396–422; David Roediger, *The Wages of Whiteness: Race and the Making of the American Working Class*, rev. ed. (New York: Verso, 1991).

39. On black/white race relations and performance, see also Richard Dyer, *Only Entertainment* (New York: Routledge, 1992); Eric Lott, *Love and Theft: Blackface Minstrelsy and the American Working Class* (New York: Oxford University Press, 1993); Monson, "The Problem of White Hipness," 396–422; Ronald Radano, "Hot Fantasies: American Modernism and the Idea of Black Rhythm," in *Music and the Racial Imagination*, eds. Ronald Radano and Philip V. Bohlman (Chicago: University of Chicago Press, 2000). On black/white race relations more generally, see Bruce Ziff and Pratima Rao, *Borrowed Power: Essays on Cultural Appropriation* (New Brunswick, NJ: Rutgers University Press, 1997); Michael Omi and Howard Winant, *Racial Formation in the United States: From the 1960s to the 1990s*, 2nd ed. (New York: Routledge, 1994).

40. Roediger, *The Wages of Whiteness*, 117.

41. Richard Dyer, *White* (New York: Routledge, 1997), 51.

42. Roediger, *The Wages of Whiteness*, 21.

43. Michael Rogin, *Blackface, White Noise: Jewish Immigrants in the Hollywood Melting Pot* (Berkeley, CA: University of California Press, 1996), 30.

44. Mizejewski, *Ziegfeld Girl*, 11.

45. Juliet McMains, "Brownface: Representation of Latin-ness in Dancesport," *Dance Research Journal* 33, 2 (2001/2002): 54–71.

46. Susan Manning, *Modern Dance, Negro Dance: Race in Motion* (Minneapolis, MN: University of Minnesota Press, 2004).

47. Manning, *Modern Dance, Negro Dance*, 10.

48. Edward Scott, *The New Dancing As It Should Be: For the Ball-room, the Class-room and the Stage* (London and New York: E. P. Dutton and Routledge, 1919), 125 [Scott's emphasis].

49. Cree, *Handbook of Ball-room Dancing*, 148.

50. On sheet music covers, this was accomplished by the convention of showing two images of each star performer—one in blackface next to one without makeup.
51. See Monson, "The Problem of White Hipness," 396–422, on misidentification with African American people and culture through music.
52. On period racial climate, see Madison Grant, *The Passing of the Great Race: or, the Racial Basis of European History* (New York: Scribner's Sons, 1916); Gary Nash and Richard Weiss, eds., *The Great Fear: Race in the Mind of America* (New York: Holt, Rinehart, and Winston, 1970); Noel Ignatiev, *How the Irish Became White* (New York: Routledge, 1995).

CHAPTER 3

1. Troy and Margaret West Kinney, *Social Dancing of To-Day* (New York: Stokes, 1914), 2.
2. Throughout this article, I often use the terms "dancing" to refer to social practice and "dance" to refer to a technique. See Susan Foster, "On Dancing and the Dance: Two Visions of Dance's History," in *Proceedings of the Society of Dance History Scholars* (1983), 133–141.
3. Julie Malnig provides an excellent discussion of many individual social dance teachers and performers who were working in New York City during the early twentieth century. Julie Malnig, *Dancing Till Dawn: A Century of Exhibition Ballroom Dance* (New York: New York University Press, 1992), chapters 1–4.
4. Please note that Latin American contributions to this era of dancing are not included in this study. Please see Marta Savigliano's *Tango and the Political Economy of Passion* (1995) for a discussion of the tango.
5. Throughout this section, I draw extensively on numerous primary source materials and my reconstruction work with them. Carol Téten Coll, *America Dances! 1897–1948: A Collector's Edition of Social Dance in Film* (Dallas TX: Dancetime Publications, 2003); Vernon and Irene Castle, *Modern Dancing* (New York: Harper, 1914); Louis H. Chalif, *The Chalif Text Book of Dancing* (New York: Chalif, 1915); F. Leslie Clendenen, *The Art of Dancing: Its Theory and Practice* (St. Louis, MO: Clendenen, 1919); F. Leslie Clendenen, *Dance Mad: Or the Dances of the Day* (St. Louis, MO: Arcade, 1914); Charles Coll and Gabrielle Rosiere, *Dancing Made Easy* (New York: Clode, 1919); A. M. Cree, *Handbook of Ball-Room Dancing* (London and New York: Lane, 1920); James Reese Europe, *Castle House Rag* (New York: Stern, 1914); Europe, *Castle Society Dance Folio for Piano: Containing the Latest Collection of Foreign and American Dance Successes* (New York: Stern, 1914); Europe, *The Castle Walk* (New York: Stern, 1914); James Reese Europe and Ford T. Dabney, *Castles' Half and Half* (New York: Stern, 1914); n.a., *The Fellowship; Spirit of the Dance* (New York: n.p., 1914); P. Gavina-Giovannini, *Balli di Ieri e Balli d'Oggi* (Milan: U. Hoepli, 1922); J. S. Hopkins, *The Tango and Other Up-to-Date Dances* (Chicago: Saalfield, 1914); Troy and Margaret West Kinney, *Social Dancing of To-Day* (New York: Stokes, 1914); Troy Kinney, "The Dance: An Expression of Mental Activity," *Century Magazine* (1914): 823–833; n.a., *Modern Dance Instructor* (Brooklyn, NY: Unique Publishing Co., n.d.); Maurice Mouvet, *Maurice's Art of Dancing* (New York: Schirmer, 1915); Mouvet, *The Tango and the New Dances for Ballroom and Home* (Chicago: Laird, 1914); Albert W. Newman, *Dances of To-Day* (Philadelphia: Penn Publishing Co., 1914, 1921); Edward Scott, *Dancing Artistic and Social* (London: Bell, 1919); Scott, *The New Dancing As It Should Be: For the Ball-room, the Class-room and the Stage* (London and New York: Dutton, 1919); Alfonso Josephs Sheafe, *The Fascinating Boston: How to Dance*

and How to Teach the Popular New Social Favorite (Boston: Boston Music Co., 1913); Cheryl Stafford, pers. comm. (Gaithersburg, MD, January and February 2001); *The Terpsichorean: Newsy Technical Journal for Dancing Instructors, Students, Ballroom Owners* (Chicago: American Dance Publishing House, 1897–1935). "The Turkey Trot, Grizzly Bear and Other Naughty Diversions: Whether Objectionable or Not, They Are Neither Pretty Nor Artistic—Originated in Far Western Mining Camps and Found Their Way to the Stage," *New Bedford Sunday Standard*, February 4, 1912; Caroline Walker, *The Modern Dances: How to Dance Them* (Chicago: Saul, 1914); *Whirl of Life*, Oliver D. Bailey, dir., Vernon and Irene Castle, performers, Cort Film Corp., 1915.

6. Linda Tomko, *Dancing Class: Gender, Ethnicity, and Social Divides in American Dance, 1890–1920* (Bloomington, IN: Indiana University Press, 1999), 26, 152. Susan Cook has also argued this point in an article where she links modern dance with assertions of male dominance. Cook, "Watching Our Step: Embodying Research, Telling Stories," in *Audible Traces: Gender, Identity and Music*, eds. Elaine Barkin and Lydia Hamessley (Los Angeles: Carcifoli, 1999), 195–196; Cook, "Tango Lizards and Girlish Men: Performing Masculinity on the Social Dance Floor," *Proceedings of the Society of Dance History Scholars* (1997): 41–53. See Ann McClintock on connections among patriarchy, colonization, and civilization practices. McClintock, *Imperial Leather: Race, Gender, and Sexuality in the Colonial Context* (London: Routledge, 1995).

7. Cook takes this notion further to suggest that controlling "the primitive" within modern dance provided dancers with a sense of cultural privilege. See Cook, "Talking Machines and Moving Bodies: Marketing Dance before World War I," *Dancing in the Millennium Conference* (Washington, DC, July 2000).

8. Stage performances might have provided additional models, but their ephemeral nature meant that observers could likely grasp a few steps at most, but again, not the improvisational structure needed.

9. Don Slater, *Consumer Culture and Modernity* (Cambridge, UK: Polity Press, 1997); Frederick Winslow Taylor, *The Principles of Scientific Management* (New York: Norton Library, 1967 [1911]); Taylor, *Shop Management* (Sioux Falls, ND: NuVision Publications, 2008 [1905]).

10. For example, it is entirely possible that some dancers and budding dance professionals, especially in New York City, were also working in manufacturing environments, such as the garment district, where Taylor's ideas were being implemented.

11. Rudolf von Laban, a pioneer of modern concert dance as well as its analysis and notation, was involved in the 1940s in assessing factory worker's movements in Britain.

12. V. Persis Dewey, *Tips to Dancers: Good Manners for Ballroom and Dance Hall* (n.p.: 1918), 10.

13. A wonderful electronic source for period dance manuals is Elizabeth Aldrich, ed., *An American Ballroom Companion: Dance Instruction Manuals, 1490–1920* (American Memory: Historical Collections for the National Digital Library, Music Division, Library of Congress, 2004). http://memory.loc.gov/ammem/dihtml/dihome.html.)

14. Maurice Mouvet, *Maurice's Art of Dancing* (New York: G. Schirmer, 1915), 84.

15. F. Leslie Clendenen, *Dance Mad: Or the Dances of the Day* (St. Louis, MO: Arcade, 1914), 8.

16. John Edward Hasse has made a similar argument in relation to the origins of ragtime music. He writes that the music combined "African and European antecedents into a wholly new creation ... one of the first truly American musical genres ... allow[ing] Afro-American rhythms to penetrate to the heart of the American musical culture, at a time when blacks were denied access to many avenues of American society." See John Hasse, ed., *Ragtime: Its History, Composers, and Music* (New York: Schirmer Books, 1985), 37. See also Samuel A. Floyd and Marsha J. Reisser, "The Sources and Resources of Classical Ragtime Music," *Black Music Research Journal* 4 (1984): 22–59.

17. Lee Baker, *From Savage to Negro: Anthropology and the Construction of Race, 1896–1954* (Berkeley, CA: University of California Press, 1998).

18. Richard Dyer, *White* (New York: Routledge, 1997), 25.

19. Linda Mizejewski has likewise argued that efforts to emphasize the Ziegfeld Girl's whiteness were a response to the perceived threats of immigration and migration. She, in fact, links the construction of whiteness by these performances with the discourses of eugenics and nativism, which aimed to protect the whiteness of America through selective breeding and protective legislation. Mizejewski, *Ziegfeld Girl: Image and Icon in Culture and Cinema* (Durham, NC: Duke University Press, 1999).

20. This 1910s term refers to the loss of white racial dominance as a result of over-population by nonwhites caused by intermarriage between "Nordics" and everyone else, and by the production of their resulting "nonwhite" offspring.

21. Charles Coll and Gabrielle Rosiere, *Dancing Made Easy* (New York: Edward J. Clode, 1919), 21–24.

22. Although writing about Britain, Stuart Hall's points apply to the U.S. context as well, given their intertwined histories. Hall, "Race, Articulation, and Societies Structured in Dominance," in *Black British Cultural Studies: A Reader*, eds. Houston A. Baker, et al. (Chicago, IL: University of Chicago Press, 1996), 55.

23. Edward Scott, *The New Dancing As It Should Be* ... (London and New York: E. P. Dutton and Routledge, 1919), 125 [Scott's emphasis]. While it is true that Scott is British, his dance manual was also published in New York City and is therefore relevant to this study.

24. A. M. Cree, *Handbook of Ball-room Dancing* (New York: John Lane Co., 1920), 148.

25. Clendenen, *Dance Mad*, 13; see also Castle, *Modern Dancing*, 177.

26. Albert W. Newman, *Dances of To-day* (Philadelphia: Penn Publishing Co., 1914 and 1921), 29 [Newman's emphasis].

27. For example, renowned nineteenth-century American dancing master Allen Dodworth wrote the following edicts: "Always maintain a proper attitude. Disguise all effort. An extended leg must not be bent. Bend only the knee from which a motion is made. When moving the feet, let the heels pass close together. Keep the heels about half an inch from the floor. In rising, allow the toes to be the last part of the foot to leave the floor. When descending let them be the first to touch. Endeavor to keep the feet at a right angle at all times. These can only be suggestions; gracefulness of motion must be learned from example." Dodworth, *Dancing and its Relations to Education and Social Life, with a New Method of Instruction Including a Complete Guide to the Cotillion (German) with 250 Figures* (New York and London: Harper and Brothers, 1885, 1888, and 1900), 42.

28. Please read McMains's *Glamour Addition* (2006) on this topic.

CHAPTER 4

1. "Author of the Eclipse," *Tattler*, February 27, 1925, 10.
2. "Professor Anderson draws the elite of Dance," *Tattler*, March 6, 1925, 6.
3. In this chapter, I analyze the labors of Charles Anderson in detail rather than the ballroom dancing he taught. For ballroom dancing, as discussed prior, I draw upon not only primary sources and consultations with dance reconstructor Cheryl Stafford, but also a host of secondary sources devoted to European American social dance. A. H. Franks, *Social Dance: A Short History* (London: Routledge and Kegan Paul, 1963); Elizabeth Aldrich, *From the Ballroom to Hell: Grace and Folly in Nineteenth-Century Dance* (Evanston, IL: Northwestern University Press, 1991); Philip J. S. Richardson, *The Social Dance in Literature, 1400–1918: Selections* (Jefferson, NC: McFarland, 1998); Belinda Quirey, *"May I Have the Pleasure?" The Story of Popular Dancing* (London: British Broadcasting Co., 1976); Peter Buckman, *Let's Dance: Social, Ballroom, and Folk Dancing* (New York: Paddington Press, 1978).
4. Henry Louis Gates, *The Signifying Monkey: A Theory of Afro-American Literary Criticism* (New York: Oxford University Press, 1988).
5. See David Krasner, *Resistance, Parody, and Double Consciousness in African American Theatre, 1895–1910* (New York: St. Martin's Press, 1997).
6. In his 2005 article on the Ailey dance company, Thomas DeFrantz uses the term "code-switching" to describe how African American dancers sometimes demonstrate *and* deform mastery of a particular dance form simultaneously. He argues (drawing upon Houston Baker) that this provides a means of articulating black subjectivity, as well as a means of revealing themselves. Thomas F. DeFrantz, "Composite bodies of dance: The repertory of the Alvin Ailey American dance theatre," *Theatre Journal* 57 (2005): 659–678.
7. See Susan Manning, *Modern Dance, Negro Dance: Race in Motion* (Minneapolis, MN: University of Minnesota Press, 2004) 30.
8. Extrapolating from evidence discussed here, there were likely fewer than a dozen instructors like Anderson in the first decades of the twentieth century. This number would have increased to between fifty and one hundred during the late Harlem Renaissance.
9. "Teacher—Negro Dancers," Writers' Program, New York (City), Research Studies Compiled by Workers of the Writers' Program of the Work Projects Administration (hereafter cited as WPA) in New York City, for "Negroes of New York," 1936–1940, fifteen articles in one volume, typescript portfolio, Schomburg Center for Research in Black Culture, New York. These reports were researched and written during the 1930s and were based upon a lengthy interview with Anderson and others living in Harlem at the time.
10. WPA, "Dancing Schools in Harlem."
11. Investigator's reports, Records of the Committee of Fourteen (hereafter cited as COF), Rare Books and Manuscripts Division, New York Public Library, Astor, Lenox and Tilden Foundations; Randy McBee, *Dance Hall Days: Intimacy and Leisure among Working-Class Immigrants in the United States* (New York: New York University Press, 2000), 53–55.
12. WPA, "Dancing Schools in Harlem."
13. "Professor Anderson to Introduce New Dance," *New York Age*, October 18, 1914, 6; "Latest New York News: Weekly Letter of Current Events at Eastern Metropolis—Personal Mention of People in the Various Activities," *Chicago Defender*, December 5, 1914, 7.

14. Interestingly, the word "Congo" in this context authenticates the dance for Sawyer's white audiences as derived from an African American source, and also perhaps clarifies it as a ragtime version of the old-fashioned schottische.

15. Jervis Anderson, *A. Philip Randolph: A Biographical Portrait* (Berkeley, CA: University of California Press, 1986), 57. Jervis Anderson, *This Was Harlem: A Cultural Portrait, 1900–1950* (New York: Farrar, Strauss, and Giroux, 1982), 117.

16. For example, he hosted a Select School of Saturday Evening Dance at the Imperial Auditorium and ran events for the Renaissance Ballroom. Advertisements for Select School of Saturday Evening Dance, *Tattler*, February 5 and 27, 1925, 5; March 6, 1925. Advertisement for Renaissance Ballroom, *Tattler*, September 16, 1927, 9.

17. Advertisement for Renaissance Ballroom, *Tattler*, September 30, 1927, 8.

18. Advertisements for Renaissance Ballroom, *Tattler*, September 30, 1927, 8; September 16, 1927, 9.

19. David Levering Lewis, *When Harlem Was in Vogue* (New York: Penguin, 1997), 105–108, 208–211; Anderson, *This was Harlem*, 168–180.

20. Linda Mizejewski, *Ziegfeld Girl: Image and Icon in Culture and Cinema* (Durham, NC: Duke University Press, 1999), 120–125.

21. I wanted to include this image as an illustration, but it was far too dark for replication here, unfortunately.

22. Advertisement for Prof. Darling Mack Studios, *Tattler*, January 4, 1929.

23. Advertisements for Red Moon Dance, *Tattler*, November 2, 1924, 1; November 2, 1924, 9.

24. *Tattler*, March 6, 1925, 6.

25. "Prof. Anderson to Open Renaissance," *Tattler*, September 16, 1927, 4.

26. "Renaissance Casino to Reopen Saturday," *Tattler*, September 28, 1927, 5.

27. "Professor Anderson draws the elite of Dance," *Tattler*, March 6, 1925, 6.

28. See Joan Shelley Rubin, *The Making of Middlebrow Culture* (Chapel Hill, NC: University of North Carolina Press, 1992).

29. David Krasner, "Rewriting the Body: Aida Overton Walker and the Social Formation of Cakewalking," *Theatre Survey* 37.2 (November 1996): 66–92; Karen Sotiropoulos, *Staging race: Black performers in turn of the century America* (Cambridge, MA, and London: Harvard University Press, 2008).

30. Krasner, "Rewriting the Body," 86.

31. Pierre Bourdieu, *Distinction: A social critique of the judgment of taste* (Cambridge, MA: Harvard University Press, 1984).

32. Kevin Kelly Gaines, *Uplifting the Race: Black Leadership, Politics, and Culture in the 20th Century* (Chapel Hill, NC: University of North Carolina Press, 1996), 14; Alessandra Lorini, *Rituals of Race: American Public Culture and the Search for Racial Democracy* (Charlottesville, VA: University of Virginia, 1999), 187–188, 192.

33. Lorini, *Rituals of Race*, 188.

34. Lorini, *Rituals of Race*, 187.

35. Lorini, *Rituals of Race*, 192.

36. Gaines, *Uplifting the Race*, 14–17.

37. The blossoming black middle classes of the early twentieth century were also emboldened by seemingly improved economic conditions in Northern cities. Social historian Gilbert Osofsky writes that "migration to the city created possibilities for economic mobility that were largely absent from southern life"; Osofsky, *Harlem: The Making of a Ghetto/Negro New York, 1890–1930*, 2nd ed. (Chicago: Ivan R. Dee, 1996), 33. He attributes this to improved conditions for business development and the greater availability of wage work. James Weldon Johnson's recollections from this period support Osofsky's claim: "With thousands of Negroes

pouring into Harlem month by month ... old residents and new-comers got work as fast as they could take it, at wages never dreamed of...."; Johnson, *Black Manhattan* (New York: Knopf, 1930), 153. Yet both Osofsky and Johnson are careful to point out that the vast majority of migrants did not become successful business owners or achieve great wealth through wage work, even if the wages were an improvement over those in the South. Moreover, U.S. Census information from the 1910s, 1920s, and 1930s does not show a proportionally larger black middle or upper class, which suggests that elevated class status within black communities was perhaps more of a state of mind than a material reality.

38. Osofsky writes that during the nineteenth century, social mobility within northern black communities was also stymied. The close connection between skin color—a relatively permanent condition—and social status did little to alter this. Osofsky, *Harlem*, 6.

39. Lorini, *Rituals of Race*, 181.

40. Lorenzo Thomas, *Don't Deny My Name: Words and Music and the Black Intellectual Tradition*, ed. Aldon Lynn Nielsen (Ann Arbor, MI: University of Michigan Press, 2008), 89.

41. "Progress in the new dances," *Modern Dance Magazine*, April 1914, 7.

42. Norbert Elias, *The Civilizing Process: Sociogenetic and Psychogenetic Investigations* (Oxford, UK: Blackwell, [1939] 2000).

43. Susan Manning, *Modern Dance, Negro Dance: Race in Motion* (Minneapolis, MN: University of Minnesota Press, 2004), 53.

44. One exception to this neglect of African American concert dance came when several female Harlem Renaissance artists and the wives of male ones reportedly attended an afternoon concert in Harlem by choreographer Edna Guy in 1933—according to the review of the event in the New York *Amsterdam News*. It is possible that dance being considered a feminine art helped to keep it from partnering with the other arts as part of broader racial uplift efforts. See Manning, *Modern Dance, Negro Dance*.

45. Thomas, *Don't Deny My Name*, 91.

46. Marshall Winslow Stearns, *Jazz Dance: The Story of American Vernacular Dance* (New York: Da Capo Press, 1994), 23.

47. Tom Davin, "Conversations with James P. Johnson" (1955), in *Jazz Panorama*, ed. Martin Williams (New York: Collier Books, 1964), 107–108.

48. Buffet Flats were private homes that had been transformed into private clubs where drinking and entertainments of many kinds could be found.

49. Stuart Hall, "Cultural Identity and Diaspora," in *Identity: community, culture, difference*, ed. Jonathan Rutherford (London: Lawrence & Wishar, 1990); Michelle M. Wright, *Becoming Black: Creating Identity in the African Diaspora* (Durham, NC: Duke University Press, 2004).

50. Alain Locke, "The New Negro," in *The New Negro: Voices of the Harlem Renaissance*, ed. Alain Locke (New York: Simon and Schuster, 1992), 6–7.

51. Paul Gilroy, *The Black Atlantic: Modernity and Double Consciousness* (Cambridge, MA: Harvard University Press, 1993), 110.

52. Gilroy, *Black Atlantic*, 74.

53. Homi Bhabha, "Of Mimicry and Man: The Ambivalence of Colonial Discourse," in *The Location of Culture* (New York: Routledge, 1994), 123.

54. Henry Louis Gates Jr., *The Signifying Monkey: A Theory of African-American Literary Criticism* (London: Oxford University Press, 1988), xxi–xxii.

55. Henry Louis Gates Jr., *The Signifying Monkey*, xxiii–xxiv.

56. David Krasner, "Rewriting the Body: Aida Overton Walker and the Social Formation of Cakewalking," *Theatre Survey* 37 (1996): 66–92.
57. Michel de Certeau describes tactics as "how an entire society resists being reduced" and suggests that a scholar's job is to "bring to light the clandestine forms taken by dispersed, tactical, and makeshift creativity of groups and individuals." De Certeau, *The practice of everyday life* (Berkeley, CA: University of California Press, 1984), xiv.
58. W. E. B. Du Bois, *The souls of black folk* (New York: Norton and Company, 1999), 11.
59. Paul Gilroy, *'There ain't no black in the union jack': The cultural politics of race and nation* (Melbourne, AU: Hutchinson, 1987), 217–219.
60. See Gilroy, *Black Atlantic*.
61. *Census of the United States (1930)*. Population. New York (State). ed. U.S. Bureau of the Census, Department of Commerce. North Salt Lake, UT: Heritage Quest, 2002. 1122–1143.
62. WPA, "Dancing Schools in Harlem."

CHAPTER 5

1. I would like to thank the panel audience members who pointed this out to me at the 2004 Society of Dance History Scholars Annual Conference at Duke University.
2. I am not the first in dance studies to apply this term to these dance professionals. See Brenda Dixon-Gottschild, *Digging the Africanist Presence in American Performance: Dance and Other Contexts* (Westport, CT: Greenwood Press, 1996), 2; see also Constance Valis Hill, "Buddy Bradley: The 'Invisible' Man of Broadway Brings Jazz Tap to London," *Proceedings of the 15th Annual Conference, Society of Dance History Scholars* (1992): 77–84. The invisibility of these black dance teachers and choreographers continues into the present day. Primary sources that testify to their labors are few. In fact, the sources that I most heavily draw on in this chapter—research interviews conducted by Marshall and Jean Stearns more than fifty years ago—were originally found in 1999 in complete disarray at the bottom of archival boxes in the Institute of Jazz Studies at Rutgers University: Marshall and Jean Stearns, Correspondence, Manuscripts, Dance, and Personal Files, Marshall and Jean Stearns Research and Manuscript Papers at Institute of Jazz Studies, Rutgers University.
3. For a fuller treatment of the issue of black invisibility in American culture, please see W. E. B. Du Bois, *The Souls of Black Folk* (New York: Norton and Company, 1999 [1903]); James Weldon Johnson, *Black Manhattan* (New York: Knopf, 1930); Katrina Hazzard-Gordon, *Jookin': The Rise of Social Dance Formations in African American Culture* (Philadelphia: Temple University Press, 1990); Chester J. Fontenot Jr., "Du Bois's 'Of the Coming of John,' Toomer's 'Kabnis,' and the Dilemma of Self-Representation," *The Souls of Black Folk: One Hundred Years Later*, ed. Dolan Hubban (Columbia, MO: University of Missouri Press, 2003); Lewis R. Gibson, "Existential Dynamics of Theorizing Black Invisibility," *Existence in Black: An Anthology of Black Existential Philosophy* (New York: Routledge, 1997).
4. See also Anthea Kraut, "Race-ing Choreographic Copyright," in *Worlding Dance*, ed. Susan Foster (New York: Palgrave MacMillan, 2009).
5. For extended treatments of African-derived social dancing and its teaching in the United States, see Lynn Fauley Emery, *Black Dance in the United States from 1619 to 1970* (Palo Alto, CA: National Press, 1927); Marshall and Jean Stearns, *Jazz Dance: The Story of American Vernacular Dance* (New York: Macmillan, 1968), 160–161; Brenda Dixon-Gottschild, *Waltzing in the Dark: African*

American Vaudeville and Race Politics in the Swing Era (New York: Palgrave, 2000); Dixon-Gottschild, *Black Dancing Body: A Geography from Coon to Cool* (New York: Palgrave Macmillan, 2003); Katrina Hazzard-Gordon, *Jookin'*; Jacqui Malone, *Steppin' on the Blues: The Visible Rhythms of African American Dance* (Urbana, IL: University of Illinois Press, 1996); David Krasner, *Resistance, Parody, and Double Consciousness in African American Theatre, 1895–1910* (New York: St. Martin's Press, 1997).

6. Hill, "Buddy Bradley," 77–84.

7. Stearns, *Jazz Dance*, 160–161.

8. Hazzard-Gordon, *Jookin'*, 93.

9. My information on black musical theatre of this period is drawn from several secondary sources, especially Malone, *Steppin' on the Blues*; Stearns, *Jazz Dance*; Johnson, *Black Manhattan*; Thomas L. Riis, *Just Before Jazz: Black Musical Theatre in New York, 1890–1915* (Washington, DC: Smithsonian Institution Press, 1989). See also National Afro-American Museum and Cultural Center (NAMCC), *When the Spirit Moves: African American Dance in History and Art*, ed. Barbara Glass (Wilberforce, OH: National Afro-American Museum and Cultural Center, 1999), 23; David Levering Lewis, *When Harlem Was in Vogue* (New York: Penguin, 1997); Ann Douglas, *Terrible Honesty: Mongrel Manhattan in the 1920s* (New York: Noonday, 1995), 314–317; Emery, *Black Dance*; Jervis Anderson, *This Was Harlem: A Cultural Portrait, 1900–1950* (New York: Farrar, Strauss, and Giroux, 1982); Wallace Thurman, *Negro Life in New York's Harlem: A Lively Picture of a Popular and Interesting Section* (Girard, KS: Haldeman-Julius Publications, n.d.).

10. NAMCC, *Spirit Moves*, 23; Stearns, *Jazz Dance*, 122.

11. For a more in-depth discussion of cakewalking and the black performers who popularized and marketed it, see Krasner, *Resistance, Parody*; Riis, *Just Before Jazz*.

12. During ragtime's popularity, the blackness of its music and dance was not openly acknowledged. Nonetheless, racial associations were indicated by references to the South, use of black dialect, and syncopated rhythms in the music, as well as angular body shapes, emphasis on hip movements, and mimicry of animals in the dancing. See chapters two and three for a more in-depth discussion of the open secret of ragtime's black associations.

13. Johnson, *Black Manhattan*, 170. I primarily attribute the difference between the cakewalk and ragtime dance crazes, in terms of their representatives, to the differing lengths of time and reach of these practices. In white communities, cakewalking remained largely a theatrical dance and passing craze, whereas ragtime dances became part of social dancing practices across America for more than a decade. They constituted the first time that America was dancing *black*, placing black dancing onto white bodies on a mass scale. For this reason, ragtime's blackness was a much more potent topic and could not be as openly acknowledged; therefore, black performers could not directly represent or market ragtime dances. I also attribute this difference to the fact that, during the cakewalk craze, black migration had only just begun. Thus, it was not until the ragtime era that migration fueled black/white racial tensions, thereby preventing black dance professionals from representing ragtime dancing to the white American public, reminding ragtime dancers of the blackness of their own dancing. Moreover, ragtime dances were purportedly "refinements" of black dancing, according to white dance professionals from 1910 to 1920. Black dance steps in their raw forms were considered too dangerous.

Who better to tame ragtime's black dance steps than white dance professionals? For a more in-depth assessment, see chapter three.

14. Ethel Williams, December 1961, typed manuscript of an interview with Marshall and/or Jean Stearns, Correspondence, Manuscripts, Dance, and Personal Files, Marshall and Jean Stearns Research and Manuscript Papers at Institute of Jazz Studies, Rutgers University.

15. Noble Sissle, September 13, 1961, typed manuscript of an interview with Marshall and/or Jean Stearns, Correspondence, Manuscripts, Dance, and Personal Files, Marshall and Jean Stearns Research and Manuscript Papers at Institute of Jazz Studies, Rutgers University.

16. See Barbara Naomi Cohen-Stratyner, "The Dance Direction of Ned Wayburn: Selected Topics in Musical Staging, 1901–1923," Ph.D. diss., New York University, 1980.

17. I do not wish to suggest that black dance teachers could not have opened studios without the assistance of white financing. I did find anecdotal evidence of a dance studio owner working as a janitor in the building in exchange for a studio rental. There might have been several innovative ways that cash-poor teachers found to keep their doors open until they built up their client bases.

18. Stearns, *Jazz Dance*, 134.

19. Sissle, Stearns interview, 3.

20. Stearns, Jazz Dance and Sissle, Stearns interviews.

21. Johnson, *Black Manhattan*, 225. For an excellent study of tap dancing in America, see Constance Valis Hill, *Brotherhood in Rhythm: The Jazz Tap Dancing of the Nicholas Brothers* (New York: Oxford University Press, 2000).

22. Stearns, *Jazz Dance*, 160–169.

23. Stearns, *Jazz Dance*, 163.

24. Thaddeus Drayton (September 8, 1963), typed manuscript of an interview with Marshall and/or Jean Stearns, Correspondence, Manuscripts, Dance, and Personal Files, Marshall and Jean Stearns Research and Manuscript Papers at Institute of Jazz Studies, Rutgers University.

25. Stearns, *Jazz Dance*, 160–169.

26. Brenda Dixon-Gottschild, *Waltzing in the Dark*, 102, 200.

27. Links among dance, women, and prostitution have been the impetus for anti-dance campaigns in Manhattan since the ragtime era. See the Committee of Fourteen, Investigators' Reports; Elizabeth Perry, "The General Motherhood of the Commonwealth: Dance Hall Reform in the Progressive Era," *American Quarterly* 37 (1985).

28. Stearns, *Jazz Dance*, 162.

29. Ziegfeld Productions, Advertisement, *New York Tattler* (January 2, 1927), 9.

30. Drayton, Stearns interview.

31. Billy Pierce Studio, Advertisement, *Dance Magazine* (December 1927), 6.

32. Dixon-Gottschild, *Digging the Africanist Presence*, 1–2.

33. Ralph Ellison, *Invisible Man* (New York: Vintage Books, 1947), 3.

34. Mae West, *Goodness Had Nothing to Do with It* (Englewood Cliffs, NJ: Prentice-Hall, 1959), 64.

35. For more on tactics as professional practice, please see Jeff Packman, "Musicians' Performances and Performances of "Musician" in Salvador da Bahia, Brazil," *Ethnomusicology* 55.3 (2011): 414–444.

36. Sissle, Stearns interview, 3.

37. *Census of the United States (1930)*. Population. New York (State). ed. U.S. Bureau of the Census, Department of Commerce. North Salt Lake, UT: Heritage Quest, 2002. 10–13.

38. George Lipsitz, *The Possessive Investment in Whiteness: How White People Profit from Idenity Politics* (Philadelphia: Temple University Press, 1998), 120.

39. This effect is much like that of American blackface minstrelsy. For further reading, see Linda Mizejewski, *Ziegfeld Girl: Image and Icon in Culture and Cinema* (Durham, NC: Duke University Press, 1999); Eric Lott, *Love and Theft: Blackface Minstrelsy and the American Working Class* (New York: Oxford University Press, 1993); David Roediger, *The Wages of Whiteness: Race and the Making of the American Working Class*, rev. ed. (London: Verso, 1999); Michael Rogin, *Blackface, White Noise: Jewish Immigrants in the Hollywood Melting Pot* (Berkeley, CA: University of California Press, 1996).

40. Stearns, *Jazz Dance*, 166; Hill, "Buddy Bradley," 3.

41. Stearns, *Jazz Dance*, 160–161.

42. Stearns, *Jazz Dance*, 161.

43. In looking through the remaining interviews, I found no quote to this effect. It is likely that Bradley's authorship of "High Yaller" was something that the Stearns already knew (or was common knowledge) and therefore did not need to record in their interview notes.

44. Two notable exceptions include a photo of Ethel Waters and one of Bill "Bojangles" Robinson.

45. J. Martin Favor, *Authentic Blackness: The Folk in the New Negro Renaissance* (Durham, NC: Duke University Press, 1999), 8.

46. Stearns, *Jazz Dance*, 164, 385, n. 9.

CONCLUSION

1. Michel de Certeau, *The practice of everyday life* (Berkeley, CA: University of California Press, 1984). The power of racialized movement, as just described, owes much to the legacy of blackface minstrelsy, even though this practice was on the wane by the early twentieth century.

2. See Danielle Robinson and Juliet McMains, "Swinging Out: Southern California's Lindy Revival," in *I See America Dancing: Selected Readings, 1685–2000*, ed. Maureen Needham (Urbana, IL: University of Illinois Press, 2002), 84–95; Juliet McMains, *Glamour Addiction: Inside the American Ballroom Dance Industry* (Middletown, CT: Wesleyan University Press, 2006).

3. Pierre Bourdieu, *Distinction: A Social Critique of the Judgment of Taste* (Cambridge, MA: Harvard University Press, 1984); Ulf Hannerz, "Cosmopolitans and Locals in World Culture," *Theory, Culture, and Society* 7 (1990): 237–251.

4. For a much more detailed discussion of the contemporary ballroom industry, please see McMains, *Glamour Addiction*.

WORKS CITED

Ahmed, Sara, ed. *Uprootings/regroundings: Questions of Home and Migration.* New York: Berg, 2003.

Aldrich, Elizabeth, ed. *An American Ballroom Companion: Dance Instruction Manuals, 1490–1920.* American Memory: Historical Collections for the National Digital Library, Music Division, Library of Congress, 2004. http://memory.loc.gov/ammem/dihtml/dihome.html

Aldrich, Elizabeth. *From the Ballroom to Hell: Grace and Folly in Nineteenth-Century Dance.* Evanston, IL: Northwestern University Press, 1991.

Anderson, Jervis. *A. Philip Randolph: A Biographical Portrait.* Berkeley, CA: University of California Press, 1986.

Anderson, Jervis. *This Was Harlem: A Cultural Portrait, 1900–1950.* New York: Farrar, Straus & Giroux, 1982.

Ankori, Gannit. "Dis-Orientalisms'—Displaced Bodies/Embodied Displacements in Contemporary Palestinian Art," in *Uprootings/regroundings: Questions of Home and Migration*, ed. Sara Ahmed. New York: Berg, 2003.

"Author of the Eclipse," *Tattler*, February 27, 1925, 10.

Baker, Lee D. *From Savage to Negro: Anthropology and the Construction of Race, 1896–1954.* Berkeley, CA: University of California Press, 1998.

Badger, Reid. *A Life in Ragtime: A Biography of James Reese Europe.* New York: Oxford University Press, 1995.

Baraka, Imamu Amiri. *Blues People; Negro Music in White America.* New York: W. Morrow, 1963.

Bean, Annemarie, James V. Hatch, Brooks McNamara, and Mel Watkins, eds. *Inside the Minstrel Mask: Readings in Nineteenth-century Blackface Minstrelsy.* Hanover, NH: University Press of New England for Wesleyan University Press, 1996.

Bella C. Landauer Collection of Business and Advertising Ephemera: Collection of The New-York Historical Society; and the Sam DeVincent Collection of Illustrated American Sheet Music, Archives Center, National Museum of American History, Smithsonian Institution.

Berlin, Edward. *Ragtime: A Musical and Cultural History.* Berkeley, CA: University of California Press, 1980.

Berlin, Edward. *Reflections and Research on Ragtime.* Brooklyn, NY: Institute for Studies in American Music, Conservatory of Music, Brooklyn College of the City of New York, 1987.

Bhabha, Homi. "Of Mimicry and Man: The Ambivalence of Colonial Discourse," in *The Location of Culture.* New York: Routledge, 1994.

Billy Pierce Studio. Advertisement, *Dance Magazine*, December 1927, 6.

Bohlman, Philip V. "Fieldwork in the Ethnomusicological Past," in *Shadows in the Field: New Perspectives for Fieldwork in Ethnomusicology*, eds. Gregory Barz and Timothy Cooley. New York: Oxford University Press, 1997.

Bontemps, Arna Wendell. *100 Years of Negro Freedom*. New York: Dodd Mead, 1962.

Bourdieu, Pierre. *Distinction: A Social Critique of the Judgment of Taste*, trans. Richard Nice. Cambridge, MA: Harvard University Press, 1984.

Bourdieu, Pierre. "The forms of capital," in *Handbook of Theory and Research for the Sociology of Education*, ed. J. Richardson. New York: Greenwood, 1986.

Brown, Sterling. "Cabaret," in *The Collected Poems of Sterling A. Brown*. ed., Michael S. Harper. Evanston, IL: Northwestern University Press, 1996.

Buckman, Peter. *Let's Dance: Social, Ballroom, and Folk Dancing*. New York: Paddington Press, 1978.

Castle, Vernon, and Irene Castle. *Modern Dancing*. New York: World Syndicate, 1914.

Castle, Vernon, and Irene Castle. *Castle Society Dance Folio for Piano: Containing the Latest Collection of Foreign and American Dance Successes*. New York: Stern, 1914.

"Castles Dance Foxtrot; Call It Negro Step," *New York Herald*, undated clipping in the Castle Scrapbooks [acc. fall 2014], Billy Rose Theater Collection, New York Public Library.

Census of the United States (1920). Population. New York (State). ed. U.S. Bureau of the Census, Department of Commerce. Bountiful, Utah: American Genealogical Lending Library, 1992.

Census of the United States (1930). Population. New York (State). ed. U.S. Bureau of the Census, Department of Commerce. North Salt Lake, UT: Heritage Quest, 2002.

Chalif, Louis H. *The Chalif Text Book of Dancing*. New York: Chalif, 1915.

Clendenen, Leslie F. *The Art of Dancing: Its Theory and Practice*. St. Louis, MO: Clendenen, 1919.

Clendenen, Leslie F. *Dance Mad: Or the Dances of the Day*. St Louis, MO: Arcade, 1914.

Cockrell, Dale. *Demons of Disorder: Early Blackface Minstrels and their World*. Cambridge, UK: Cambridge University Press, 1997.

Cohen-Stratyner, Barbara Naomi. "The Dance Direction of Ned Wayburn: Selected Topics in Musical Staging, 1901–1923, Ph.D. diss., New York University, 1980.

Coll, Carol Téten. *America Dances! 1897–1948: A Collector's Edition of Social Dance in Film*. Dallas, TX: Dancetime Publications, 2003.

Coll, Charles, and Gabrielle Rosiere. *Dancing Made Easy*. New York: Clode, 1919.

Committee of Fourteen. Investigator's Reports. Records of the Committee of Fourteen, Rare Books and Manuscripts Division. New York Public Library. Astor, Lenox, and Tilden Foundations.

Compilations Folder, Bella C. Landauer Writings and Reference Collection, Library: Department of Prints, Photographs, and Architectural Collections, New York Historical Society, "From New York Correspondence," The Director 1.1 (1897): 15.

Cook, Susan. "Passionless Dancing and Passionate Reform: Respectability, Modernism, and the Social Dancing of Irene and Vernon Castle," in *The Passion of Music and Dance: Body, Gender, and Sexuality*. Oxford, UK: Berg, 1998.

Cook, Susan. Pers. comm., July 22, 2000.

Cook, Susan. "Tango Lizards and Girlish Men: Performing Masculinity on the Social Dance Floor," Annual Meeting of the Society of Dance History Scholars. New York: Barnard College, 1997.

Cook, Susan. "Watching Our Step: Embodying Research, Telling Stories," in *Audible Traces: Gender, Identity and Music*, eds. Elaine Barkin and Lydia Hamessley. Los Angeles: Carcifoli, 1999.

Cook, Susan. "Talking Machines and Moving Bodies: Marketing Dance Music before World War I" (paper presented at the Dancing in the Millennium Conference, Washington, DC: July 2000).

Cooper, H. E. "Rag on the Barbary Coast," *Dance Magazine*, September 1927, 31.

Coot, Grant, and Charlie Love. Typed manuscripts of interviews with Marshall and/ or Jean Stearns, Marshall Stearns Research Papers, Institute of Jazz Studies, Rutgers University.

Coser, Rose Laub, Laura S. Anker, and Andrew J. Perrin. *Women of Courage: Jewish and Italian Immigrant Women in New York*. Westport, CT: Greenwood, 1999.

Cree, Aubrey McMahon. *Handbook of ball-room dancing*. New York: John Lane Co., 1920.

Dalrymple, Daniel. "In the Shadow of Garvey: Garveyites in New York City and the British Caribbean, 1925–1950" Ph.D. diss., Michigan State University, 2008.

Daly, Ann. *Done Into Dance: Isadora Duncan in America*. Bloomington, IN: Indiana University Press, 1995.

Davin, Tom. "Conversations with James P. Johnson," *Jazz Review* 2.5 (June 1959): 14.

Davin, Tom. "Conversations with James P. Johnson" (1955), in *Jazz Panorama*, ed. Martin Williams. New York: Collier Books, 1964.

de Certeau, Michel. *The Practice of Everyday Life*, trans. Steven Rendall. Berkeley, CA: University of California Press, 1984.

DeFrantz, Thomas F. "Composite bodies of dance: The repertory of the Alvin Ailey American dance theatre," *Theatre Journal* 57 (2005): 659–678.

DeFrantz, Thomas, ed. *Dance Many Drums: Excavations in African American Dance*. Madison, WI: University of Wisconsin Press, 2002.

Desmond, Jane C. "Embodying Differences: Issues in Dance and Cultural Studies," in *Meaning in Motion: New Cultural Studies of Dance*. Durham, NC: Duke University Press, 1997.

Dewey, V. Persis. *Tips to Dancers: Good Manners for Ballroom and Dance Hall*. n.p., 1918.

Dixon-Gottschild, Brenda. *Black Dancing Body: A Geography from Coon to Cool*. New York: Palgrave Macmillan, 2003.

Dixon-Gottschild, Brenda. *Digging the Africanist Presence in American Performance: Dance and Other Contexts*. Westport, CT: Greenwood Press, 1996.

Dixon-Gottschild, Brenda. *Waltzing in the Dark: African American Vaudeville and Race Politics in the Swing Era*. New York: Palgrave, 2000.

Doctorow, E. L. *Ragtime*. New York: Modern Library, 1997.

Dodworth, Allen. *Dancing and its Relations to Education and Social Life, with a New Method of Instruction Including a Complete Guide to the Cotillion (German) with 250 Figures*. New York and London: Harper and Brothers, 1885, 1888, 1900.

Douglas, Aaron. "The Negro in American Culture," in *Artists Against War and Fascism: Papers of the First American Congress*, eds. Matthew Baigell and Julia Williams. New Brunswick, NJ: Rutgers University Press, 1986 [1936].

Douglas, Ann. *Terrible Honesty: Mongrel Manhattan in the 1920s*. New York: Noonday, 1995.

Drayton, Thaddeus. September 8, 1963, typed manuscript of an interview with Marshall and/or Jean Stearns, Correspondence, Manuscripts, Dance, and Personal Files, Marshall and Jean Stearns Research and Manuscript Papers at Institute of Jazz Studies, Rutgers University.

Du Bois, W. E. B. *The Souls of Black Folk*. New York: Norton and Company, 1999.

Duffy, James. *The African Glide*. New York: Joseph Morris Co., 1910.

Dyer, Richard. *Only Entertainment*. London: Routledge, 1992.

Dyer, Richard. *White*. New York: Routledge, 1997.

Elias, Norbert. *The Civilizing Process: Sociogenetic and Psychogenetic Investigations.* Oxford, UK: Blackwell, 2000 [1939].

Ellison, Ralph. *Invisible Man.* New York: Vintage Books, 1947.

Emery, Lynn Fauley. *Black Dance in the United States from 1619 to 1970.* Palo Alto, CA: National Press, 1927.

Erenberg, Lewis A. *Steppin' Out: New York Nightlife and the Transformation of American Culture.* Chicago: University of Chicago Press, 1981.

Europe, James Reese. *Castle House Rag.* New York: Stern, 1914.

Europe, James Reese, and Ford T. Dabney. *Castles' Half and Half.* New York: Stern, 1914.

Europe, James Reese, and Ford T. Dabney. *The Castle Walk.* New York: Stern, 1914.

Evans, David. "From "Folk and Popular Blues," in *Write Me a Few of Your Lines: A Blues Reader*, ed. Steven C. Tracy. Amherst, MA: University of Massachusetts Press, 1999.

Fauset, Jessie Redmon. *There is Confusion* (Northeastern Library of Black Literature). Boston: Northeastern University Press, 1989.

Favor, J. Martin. *Authentic Blackness: The Folk in the New Negro Renaissance.* Durham, NC: Duke University Press, 1999.

The Fellowship: Spirit of the Dance (New York: n.p., 1914).

Florence Walton Clippings File, Dance Collection, New York Public Library for the Performing Arts.

Floyd, Samuel, and Marsha Reisser. *Black Music Biography.* Millwood, NY: Kraus International, 1987.

Floyd, Samual A., and Marsha J. Reisser. "The Sources and Resources of Classical Ragtime Music," *Black Music Research Journal* 4 (1984): 22–59.

Fontenot, Chester J. Jr. "Du Bois's 'Of the Coming of John,' Toomer's 'Kabnis,'and the Dilemma of Self-Representation," in *The Souls of Black Folk: One Hundred Years Later*, ed. Dolan Hubban. Columbia, MO: University of Missouri Press, 2003.

Fortier, Anne-Marie. "Making home: queer migrations and motions of attachment," in *Uprootings/regroundings: Questions of Home and Migration*, ed. Sara Ahmed. New York: Berg, 2003.

Foster, Susan. *Choreography and Narrative: Ballet's Staging of Story and Desire.* Bloomington, IN: Indiana University Press, 1996.

Foster, Susan. "On Dancing and the Dance: Two Visions of Dance's History," *Proceedings of the Society of Dance History Scholars* (1983), 140.

Foucault, Michel. "Technologies of the Self," in *Technologies of the Self*, eds. L. H. Martin, H. Gutman, and P. H. Hutton. Amherst, MA: University of Massachusetts Press, 1988.

Foucault, Michel. *The Archeology of Knowledge and the Discourse on Language.* London: Vintage, 1982.

Foucault, Michel. *The Archeology of Knowledge and the Discourse on Language*, trans. A. M. Sheridan Smith. New York: Pantheon, 1972.

Franko, Mark. *Dance as Text: Ideologies of the Baroque Body.* Cambridge, UK: Cambridge University Press, 1993.

Franks, A. H. *Social Dance: A Short History.* London: Routledge and Kegan Paul, 1963.

Friedhaber, Zvi. "Jewish Dance Traditions," in *International Encyclopaedia of Dance*, ed., Selma Jeanne Cohen (New York: Oxford University Press, 1998) 3rd ed.

Friedland, Lee Ellen. "'Tantsn Is Lebn': Dancing in Eastern European Jewish Culture," *Dance Research Journal* 17 (1985–1986): 77–80.

Gaines, Kevin. *Uplifting the Race: Black Leadership, Politics and Culture During the 20th Century.* Chapel Hill, NC: University of North Carolina Press, 1996.

Gates, Henry Louis. *The Signifying Monkey: A Theory of Afro-American Literary Criticism.* New York: Oxford University Press, 1988.

Gavina-Giovannini, P. *Balli di Ieri e Balli d'Oggi*. Milan: U. Hoepli, 1922.

Geertz, Clifford. "Thick Description: Toward an Interpretive Theory of Culture," in *The Interpretation of Cultures*. New York: Basic Books, 1973.

George-Graves, Nadine. "Just Like Being at the Zoo: Primitivity and Ragtime Dance," in *Ballroom, Boogie, Shimmy Sham, Shake: A Social and Popular Dance Reader*, ed. Julie Malnig. Champaign, IL: University of Illinois Press, 2008.

Gibson, Lewis R. "Existential Dynamics of Theorizing Black Invisibility," in *Existence in Black: An Anthology of Black Existential Philosophy*. New York: Routledge, 1997.

Gilroy, Paul. *'There ain't no black in the union jack': The cultural politics of race and nation*. Melbourne, AU: Hutchinson, 1987.

Gilroy, Paul. *Against Race: Imagining Political Culture Beyond the Color Line*. Cambridge, MA: Harvard University Press, 2000.

Gilroy, Paul. *The Black Atlantic: Modernity and Double Consciousness*. Cambridge, MA: Harvard University Press, 1993.

Glenn, Susan A. *Daughters of the Shtetl: Life and Labor in the Immigrant Generation*. Ithaca, NY: Cornell University Press, 1990.

Graham, Martha. "I am a dancer," in *This I Believe*, ed. Edward R. Murrow. New York: Simon and Schuster, 1952.

Grant, Madison. *The Passing of the Great Race: or, the Racial Basis of European History*. New York: Scribner's Sons, 1916.

Gridley, Mark C. *Jazz Styles: History and Analysis*, 6th ed. Upper Saddle River, NJ: Prentice Hall, 1997.

Hall, Stuart. "Cultural Identity and Diaspora," in *Identity: community, culture, difference*, ed. Jonathan Rutherford. London: Lawrence & Wishar, 1990.

Hall, Stuart. "Race, Articulation, and Societies Structured in Dominance," in *Black British Cultural Studies: A Reader*, eds. Houston Baker, et al. Chicago: University of Chicago Press, 1996.

Hannerz, Ulf. "Cosmopolitans and Locals in World Culture," *Theory, Culture, and Society*, vol 7 (1990): 237–251.

Harer, Ingeborg. "Defining Ragtime Music: Historical and Topological Research," *Studia Musicologica Academiae Scientiarum Hungaricae* 38, no. 3/4 (1997): 410.

Haskins, James. *Scott Joplin: the man who made ragtime*. New York: Stein & Day, 1980.

Hasse, John, ed. *Ragtime: Its History, Composers, and Music*. New York: Schirmer Books, 1985.

Hazzard-Gordon, Katrina. "Afro-American Core Culture Social Dance: An Examination of Four Aspects of Meaning," *Dance Research Journal* 15, no. 2 (1983): 21–26.

Hazzard-Gordon, Katrina. *Jookin': The Rise of Social Dance Formations in African-American Culture*. Philadelphia: Temple University Press, 1990.

Hazzard-Gordon, Katrina. Pers. comm., February, 24, 2015.

Held, Anna. *Performer, I'm Crazy 'bout the Turkey Trot*. New York: F. B. Haviland, 1911.

Higham, John. *Strangers in the Land: Patterns of American Nativism, 1860–1925*. New Brunswick, NJ: Rutgers University Press, 1998.

Hill, Constance Valis. *Brotherhood in Rhythm: The Jazz Tap Dancing of the Nicholas Brothers*. New York: Oxford University Press, 2000.

Hill, Constance Valis. "Buddy Bradley: The 'Invisible' Man of Broadway Brings Jazz Tap to London," *Proceedings of the Society of Dance History Scholars, Fifteenth* Annual Conference, University of California, Riverside, February 14-15. (1992): 77–84.

Hine, Darlene Clark. "Black Migration to the Urban Midwest: The Gender Dimension, 1915–1945," in *The Great Migration in Historical Perspective: New Dimensions of Race, Class, and Gender*, ed. Joe William Trotter Jr. Bloomington, IN: Indiana University Press, 1991.

Hopkins, J. S. *The tango and other up-to-date dances; a practical guide to all the latest dances, tango, one-step, innovation, hesitation, etc., described step by step.* Chicago: Saalfield Publishing Co., 1914.

Howland Kenny, William III. "James Scott and the Culture of Classic Ragtime," *American Music* 9, vol. 2 (Summer 1991): 149–182.

Hughes, Langston. "Liars," in *The Collected Poems of Langston Hughes*, ed. Arnold Rampersad. New York: Knopf, 1994.

Hughes, Langston. "Minstrel Man," in *The New Negro: Voices of the Harlem Renaissance*, ed. Alain Locke, 144. New York: Atheneum, 1992 [1925].

Hughes, Langston. *Not without Laughter.* New York: A. A. Knopf, 1971 [1930].

Hunter, Tera W. *To 'Joy My Freedom: Southern Black Women's Lives and Labors After the Civil War.* Cambridge, MA: Harvard University Press, 1998.

Hurston, Zora Neale. "The Characteristics of Negro Expression," In *Double-Take: A Revisionist Harlem Renaissance Anthology*, ed. Venetria Patton and Maureen Honey. New Brunswick, NJ: Rutgers University Press, 2002 [1934].

"If you dance you must pay the piper . . . ," *Vogue*, January 15, 1914: 24–25.

Ignatiev, Noel. *How the Irish Became White.* New York: Routledge, 1995.

Investigator's reports, Records of the Committee of Fourteen, Rare Books and Manuscripts Division, New York Public Library, Astor, Lenox and Tilden Foundations.

Johnson, James Weldon. *Autobiography of an Ex-Colored Man in Three Negro Classics* (1930). New York: Avon Books, 1965.

Johnson, James Weldon. *Black Manhattan.* New York: Knopf, 1930.

Kinney, Troy. "The Dance: An Expression of Mental Activity," *Century Magazine*, October 1914, 823–833.

Kinney, Troy, and Margaret West. *Social Dancing of To-Day.* New York: Stokes, 1914.

Koritz, Amy. *Gendering Bodies/Performing Art: Dance and Literature in Early-Twentieth Century Culture.* Ann Arbor, MI: University of Michigan Press, 1995.

Kosak, Hadassa. *Cultures of Opposition: Jewish Immigrant Workers, New York City, 1881–1905.* Albany, NY: State University of New York Press, 2000.

Krasner, David. "Rewriting the Body: Aida Overton Walker and the Social Formation of Cakewalking," *Theatre Survey* 37, (1996): 66–92.

Krasner, David. *Resistance, Parody, and Double Consciousness in African American Theatre, 1890–1915.* Washington, DC: Smithsonian Institution Press, 1989.

Kraut, Anthea. "Race-ing Choreographic Copyright," in *Worlding Dance*, ed. Susan Foster. New York: Palgrave MacMillan, 2009.

Laidlaw, Walter. *Statistical Sources for Demographic Studies of Greater New York, 1910.* New York: New York Federation of Churches, 1913.

Larsen, Nella. *Quicksand.* New York: Negro Universities Press, 1969.

"Latest New York News: Weekly Letter of Current Events at Eastern Metropolis—Personal Mention of People in the Various Activities," *Chicago Defender*, December 5, 1914, 7.

Lewis, David Levering. *When Harlem Was in Vogue.* New York: Penguin, 1997.

Lipsitz, George. *The Possessive Investment in Whiteness: How White People Profit from Identity Politics.* Philadelphia: Temple University Press, 1998.

Locke, Alain, ed. *The New Negro.* New York: Atheneum, 1992.

Locke, Alain. "The New Negro," in *The New Negro: Voices of the Harlem Renaissance*, ed. Alain Locke, 6–7. New York: Simon and Schuster, 1992.

Lorini, Alessandra. *Rituals of Race: American Public Culture and the Search for Racial Democracy.* Charlottesville, VA: University of Virginia Press, 1999.

Lott, Eric. *Love and Theft: Blackface Minstrelsy and the American Working Class.* New York: Oxford University Press, 1993.

Maggee, Jeffrey. "'Everybody Step': Irving Berlin, Jazz and Broadway in the 1920's," *Journal of the American Musicological Society* 59, vol. 3 (Fall 2006): 697–732.

Malnig, Julie. "Athena Meets Venus: Visions of Women in Social Dance in the Teens and Early 1920s," *Dance Research Journal* 31, vol. 2 (1999): 34–62.

Malnig, Julie. *Dancing Till Dawn: A Century of Exhibition Ballroom Dance*, 10–11, 53, 89–108. New York: New York University Press, 1992.

Malnig, Julie. "Two-Stepping to Glory: Social Dance and the Rhetoric of Social Mobility," *Etnofoor* 10, vol. 1–2 (1997): 128–150.

Malone, Jacqui. *Steppin' on the Blues: The Visible Rhythms of African American Dance.* Urbana, IL: University of Illinois Press, 1996.

Manning, Susan. *Modern Dance, Negro Dance: Race in Motion.* Minneapolis, MN: University of Minnesota Press, 2004.

Marks, Joseph E. III *America Learns to Dance: A Historical Study of Dance Education in America before 1900.* New York: Exposition, 1957.

Maurice, M. *The Tango and the New Dances for Ballroom and Home.* Chicago: Laird, 1914.

McBee, Randy. *Dance Hall Days: Intimacy and Leisure among Working-Class Immigrants in the United States.* New York: New York University Press, 2000.

McClintock, Ann. *Imperial Leather: Race, Gender, and Sexuality in the Colonial Context.* London: Routledge, 1995.

McKay, Claude. *Home to Harlem*, 1st ed. Boston: Northeastern University Press, 1987.

McKay, Claude. "The Negro Dancers," *Liberator* 2 (July 1919): 20.

McMains, Juliet. "Brownface: Representation of Latin-ness in Dancesport," *Dance Research Journal* 33, vol. 2 (2001/2002): 54–71.

McMains, Juliet. *Glamour Addiction: Inside the American Ballroom Dance Industry.* Middletown, CT: Wesleyan University Press, 2006.

Merriam-Webster's Collegiate Dictionary, CD-ROM, Merriam-Webster, 2000.

The Mississippi Dippy Dip, sheet music. New York: Joseph W. Stern and Co., 1911.

Mizejewski, Linda. *Ziegfeld Girl: Image and Icon in Culture and Cinema.* Durham, NC: Duke University Press, 1999.

Modern Dance Instructor. Brooklyn, NY: Unique Publishing Co., n.d.

Monson, Ingrid. "The Problem of White Hipness: Race, Gender, and Cultural Conceptions in Jazz Historical Discourse," *Journal of the American Musicological Society* 48, no. 3 (1995): 396–422.

Moreton-Robinson, Aileen M. "I still call Australia home: Indigenous belonging and place in a white postcolonising society," in *Uprootings/regroundings: Questions of Home and Migration*, ed. Sara Ahmed. New York: Berg, 2003.

Moses, Wilson Jeremiah. "Varieties of Black Historicism: Issues of Antimodernism and 'Presentism'," in *Afrotopia: The Roots of African American Popular History.* Cambridge: Cambridge University Press, 1998.

Mouvet, Maurice. *Maurice's Art of Dancing.* New York: Schirmer, 1915.

"Mr. and Mrs. Vernon Castle's New Dances for this Winter; III: The Castle Foxtrot," *Ladies Home Journal*, December 31, 1914, 24.

Nash, Gary, and Richard Weiss. *The Great Fear: Race in the Mind of America.* New York: Holt, Rinehart, and Winston, 1970.

National Afro-American Museum and Cultural Center (NAMCC). *When the Spirit Moves: African American Dance in History and Art*, ed. Barbara Glass. Wilberforce, OH: NAMCC, 1999.

Ness, Sally Ann. *Body, Movement, and Culture: Kinesthetic and Visual Symbolism in a Philippine Community.* Philadelphia: University of Pennsylvania Press, 1992.

Newman, Albert W. *Dances of To-Day.* Philadelphia: Penn Publishing Co., 1914, 1921.

New York Urban League. *The Negro in New York.* New York: New York Urban League, 1931.

Novack, Cynthia J. *Sharing the Dance: Contact Improvisation and American Culture.* Madison, WI: University of Wisconsin Press, 1990.

Oliver, Paul. *Conversation with the Blues,* 2nd ed. New York: Cambridge University Press, 1997.

Oliver, Paul. "Do the Bombashay: Dance Songs and Routines," in *Write Me a Few of Your Lines: A Blues Reader,* ed. Steven C. Tracy, 113–114. Amherst, MA: University of Massachusetts Press, 1999.

Omi, Michael, and Howard Winant. *Racial Formation in the United States: From the 1960s to the 1990s,* 2nd ed. New York: Routledge, 1994.

Osofsky, Gilbert. *Harlem: The Making of a Ghetto/Negro New York, 1890–1930,* 2nd ed. Chicago: Ivan R. Dee, 1996.

Oxford English Dictionary Online, 2nd ed. Oxford University Press, 1989: www.oed.com,

Packman, Jeff. "Musicians' Performances and Performances of 'Musician' in Salvador da Bahia, Brazil," *Ethnomusicology* 55, vol. 3 (2011): 414–444.

Packman, Jeff. "Singing Together/Meaning Apart: Popular Music, Participation and Cultural Politics in Salvador, Brazil," *Latin American Music Review* 31, vol. 2 (Fall/Winter 2010).

Peiss, Kathy Lee. *Cheap Amusements: Working Women and Leisure in Turn-of-the-Century New York.* Philadelphia: Temple University Press, 1986.

Perpener, John O. *African-American Concert Dance: The Harlem Renaissance and Beyond.* Urbana, IL: University of Illinois Press, 2005.

Perron, Wendy. "Dance in the Harlem Renaissance: Sowing Seeds," in *EmBODYing Liberation: The Black Body in Dance,* eds. Dorothea Fischer-Hornung and Alison Goeller. Hamburg: Lit, 2001.

Perry, Elizabeth. "'The General Motherhood of the Commonwealth': Dance Hall Reform in the Progressive Era," *American Quarterly* 37 (1985): 719–733.

Pickering, M. "Eugene Stratton and Early Ragtime in Britain," *Black Music Research Journal* 20, vol. 2 (2000): 151–180.

Prof. Anderson to Open Renaissance, *Tattler,* September 16, 1927, 4.

Prof. Darling Mack Studios. Advertisement, *Tattler,* January 4, 1929, 7.

"Professor Anderson draws the elite of Dance," *Tattler,* March 6, 1925, 6.

"Professor Anderson to Introduce New Dance," *New York Age,* October 18, 1914.

"Progress in the new dances," *Modern Dance Magazine,* April 1914, 7.

Quirey, Belinda. *"May I Have the Pleasure?" The Story of Popular Dancing.* London: British Broadcasting Co., 1976.

Radano, Ronald. *Lying Up a Nation: Race and Black Music.* Chicago: University of Chicago Press, 2003.

Radano, Ronald. "Hot Fantasies: American Modernism and the Idea of Black Rhythm," in *Music and the Racial Imagination,* eds. Ronald Radano and Philip V. Bohlman. Chicago: University of Chicago Press, 2000.

Radano, Ronald, and Philip V. Bohlman. *Music and the Racial Imagination.* Chicago: University of Chicago Press, 2000.

Ramsey, Guthrie P. *Race Music: Black Cultures from Bebop to Hip-Hop.* Berkeley, CA: University of California Press, 2003.

Red Moon Dance. Advertisments, *Tattler,* November 2, 1924, 1, 9.

Renaissance Ballroom. Advertisements, *Tattler,* September 16, 1927, 9; September 30, 1927, 8.

Renaissance Casino to Reopen Saturday, *Tattler,* September 28, 1927, 5.

Richardson, Philip J. S. *The Social Dance in Literature, 1400–1918: Selections.* Jefferson, NC: McFarland, 1998.

Riis, Thomas L. *Just Before Jazz: Black Musical Theatre in New York, 1890–1915.* Washington, DC: Smithsonian Institution Press, 1989.

Robinson, Danielle. "Oh, You Black Bottom: Appropriation, Authenticity, and Opportunity in the Jazz Dance Teaching of 1920s New York," *Dance Research Journal* 38, no. 1/2 (2006): 19–42.

Robinson, Danielle and Juliet McMains. "Swinging Out: Southern California's Lindy Revival," in *I See America Dancing: Selected Readings, 1685–2000*, ed. Maureen Needham. Urbana, IL: University of Illinois Press, 2002.

Roediger, David. *The Wages of Whiteness: Race and the Making of the American Working Class*, rev. ed. New York: Verso, 1991.

Rogin, Michael. *Blackface, White Noise: Jewish Immigrants in the Hollywood Melting Pot*. Berkeley, CA: University of California Press, 1996.

Rubin, Joan Shelley. *The Making of Middlebrow Culture*. Chapel Hill, NC: University of North Carolina Press, 1992.

Savigliano, Marta. *Tango and the Political Economy of Passion*. Boulder, CO: Westview Press, 1995.

Schafer, William. *The Art of Ragtime: Form and Meaning of an Original Black American Art*. New York: Da Capo Press, 1977.

Scott, Edward. *Dancing Artistic and Social*. London: Bell, 1919.

Scott, Edward John Long. *The New Dancing as It Should Be: For the Ball-Room, the Class-Room and the Stage*. London and New York: G. Routledge, 1919.

Select School of Saturday Evening Dance. Advertisements, *Tattler*, February 5, March 6, 1925, 5.

Shaw, Arnold. *Black Popular Music in America: From the Spirituals, Minstrels, and Ragtime to Soul, Disco, and Hip Hop*. New York: Schirmer Books, 1986.

Sheafe, Alfonso Josephs. *The Fascinating Boston: How to Dance and How to Teach the Popular New Social Favorite*. Boston: Boston Music Co., 1913.

Sissle, Noble. September 13, 1961, typed manuscript of an interview with Marshall and/or Jean Stearns, Correspondence, Manuscripts, Dance, and Personal Files, Marshall and Jean Stearns Research and Manuscript Papers at Institute of Jazz Studies, Rutgers University.

Slater, Don. *Consumer Culture and Modernity*. Cambridge, UK: Polity Press, 1997.

Sotiropoulos, Karen. *Staging Race: Black performers in turn of the century America*. Cambridge, MA: Harvard University Press, 2008.

Soyer, Daniel. *Jewish Immigrant Associations and American Identity in New York, 1880–1939*. Cambridge, MA: Harvard University Press, 1997.

Stafford, Cheryl. Pers. comm. Gaithersburg, MD, January and February 2001.

Stearns, Marshall, and Jean Stearns. *Jazz Dance: The Story of American Vernacular Dance*. New York: Macmillan, 1968.

Stearns, Marshall, and Jean Stearns. Correspondence, Manuscripts, Dance, and Personal Files, Marshall and Jean Stearns Research and Manuscript Papers at Institute of Jazz Studies, Rutgers University.

Stuckey, Sterling. "Christian Conversion and the Challenge of Dance," in *Choreographing History*, ed. Susan Leigh Foster. Bloomington and Indianapolis, IN: Indiana University Press, 1995.

Stuckey, Sterling. *Slave Culture: Nationalist Theory and the Foundations of Black America*. New York: Oxford University Press, 1987.

Szwed, John F., and Morton Marks. "The Afro-American transformation of European set dances and dance suites," *Dance Research Journal* 20 (1988): 32.

Taylor, Diana. *The Archive and the Repertoire: Performing Cultural Memory in the Americas*. Durham, NC: Duke University Press, 2003.

Taylor, Frederick Winslow. *The Principles of Scientific Management*. New York: Norton Library, 1967 [1911].

Taylor, Frederick Winslow. *Shop Management*. Sioux Falls, ND: NuVision Publications, 2008 [1905].

The Terpsichorean: Newsy Technical Journal for Dancing Instructors, Students, Ballroom Owners. Chicago: American Dance Publishing House, 1897–1935.

Thomas, Lorenzo. *Don't Deny My Name: Words and Music and the Black Intellectual Tradition*. Ann Arbor, MI: University of Michigan Press, 2008.

Thurman, Wallace. "Cordelia the Crude," *Fire*, November 1926, 5.

Thurman, Wallace. "Harlem as Educational Drama," in *The Collected Writings of Wallace Thurman: A Harlem Renaissance Reader*, eds. Amritjit Singh and Daniel M. Scott. New Brunswick, NJ: Rutgers University Press, 2003.

Thurman, Wallace. *Negro Life in New York's Harlem: A Lively Picture of a Popular and Interesting Section*. Girard, KS: Haldeman-Julius Publications, n.d.

Thurman, Wallace. "Social Life of Harlem," in *The Collected Writings of Wallace Thurman: A Harlem Renaissance Reader*, eds. Amritjit Singh and Daniel M. Scott. New Brunswick, NJ: Rutgers University Press, 2003.

Thurman, Wallace. "Terpsichore in Harlem," in *The Collected Writings of Wallace Thurman: A Harlem Renaissance Reader*, eds. Amritjit Singh and Daniel M. Scott. New Brunswick, NJ: Rutgers University Press, 2003.

Thurman, Wallace. *The Blacker the Berry: A Novel of Negro Life*. New York: Macaulay Co., 1929.

Toll, Robert C. *Blacking Up: The Minstrel Stage*. Durham, NC: Duke University Press, 1930.

Tomko, Linda. *Dancing Class: Gender, Ethnicity, and Social Divides in American Dance, 1890–1920*. Bloomington, IN: Indiana University Press, 1999.

Tomko, Linda. "Reconstruction: Beyond Notation," in *International Encyclopedia of Dance*, vol. 5, 326–327. New York: Oxford University Press, 2003.

Trotter, Joe William Jr., ed. *The Great Migration in Historical Perspective: New Dimensions of Race, Class, and Gender*. Bloomington, IN: Indiana University Press, 1991.

"The Turkey Trot, Grizzly Bear and Other Naughty Diversions: Whether Objectionable or Not, They Are Neither Pretty Nor Artistic—Originated in Far Western Mining Camps and Found Their Way to the Stage," *New Bedford Sunday Standard*, February 4, 1912.

Walker, Caroline. *The Modern Dances: How to Dance Them*. Chicago: Saul, 1914.

Webster's New Collegiate Dictionary. Springfield, MA: Merriam, 1977.

West, Mae. *Goodness Had Nothing to Do with It*. Englewood Cliffs, NJ: Prentice-Hall, 1959.

Whirl of Life. Dir. Oliver D. Bailey, performers Vernon and Irene Castle, Cort Film Corp., 1915.

White, Hayden. *The Content of the Form: Narrative Discourse and Historical Representation*. Baltimore, MD: Johns Hopkins University Press, 1987.

Williams, Ethel. December 1961, typed manuscript of an interview with Marshall and/or Jean Stearns, Correspondence, Manuscripts, Dance, and Personal Files, Marshall and Jean Stearns Research and Manuscript Papers at Institute of Jazz Studies, Rutgers University.

Winant, Howard. *The World is Ghetto: Race and Democracy since World War II*. New York: Basic Books, 2001.

Wright, Michelle M. *Becoming Black: Creating Identity in the African Diaspora*. Durham, NC: Duke University Press, 2004.

Writers' Program, New York City. *Research Studies Compiled by Workers of the Writers' Program of the Work Projects Administration (WPA) in New York City, for "Negroes in New York."* New York, 1936–1940. Typescript portfolio. Schomburg Center for Research in Black Culture. New York, New York.

Ziegfeld Productions. Advertisement, *Tattler*, January 2, 1927, 9.

Ziff, Bruce, and Pratima Rao. *Borrowed Power: Essays on Cultural Appropriation*. New Brunswick, NJ: Rutgers University Press, 1997.

INDEX

Page numbers in italics refer to illustrations

action, political
  dancing as, 24, 44
  use of social dance by Marcus Garvey
    followers, 160n29
African Americans. *See also* dance
    professionals, black; dance
    teachers, African American;
    elites, black; migration, African
    American
  "dialect poets," 162n48
  European immigrants and, 78
  professionalization in dance industry,
    103, 123–4, 149
  impact of, 142–43
  professions in New York City, 124–5
  Southernness and, 67
  transformation of dancing practice
    after Civil War, 35
Alexandria, Charles, 109
Allan, Maude, 14
American National Association of
    Masters of Dancing, 109
Anderson, Charles H., 103, 108–13
  as employer, 124–5
angularity in ragtime dancing, 61,
    63, 76, 86
animal dances, 6
  part of slave and West African
    dancing, 65
  in ragtime, 60–1, 62, 76
animal dancing. *See* ragtime dancing
Apache, 86
assimilation
  slow drag and refusal of, 56
  social dancing and, 79, 150, 153

Astaire, Adele, 138, 148
Astaire, Fred, 138
Authentic Blackness (Favor), 145

Badger, Reid, 67
ballroom dance industry, 99
  Anderson and, 109
  animal dances and, 6–7
  contemporary competition
    racially discrete categories, 15–16
    use of tanning cream, 74
  foundation of, 12
  professions within, 123–26, 150
  refinement of dances by, 153
ballroom dancing, black, 8, 28, *85*, 103,
    106–7, 113–14, 116
  and bodily code-switching, 119–23
  breaks, 120
  exhibition performances by
    Anderson, 110
  as form of self-reflexive
    signifyin(g), 122
  in Harlem Renaissance, 104–7
  insertion of jazz movements, 120
  as mimicry, 121–2
  politics of, 122
  professionals, *125–6*
  soloing and, 120, 121
  as way to work against
    stereotypes, 123–24
ballroom dancing, European American
  aesthetic choices, 155n10
  refined versions of ragtime and
    jazz, 117
  standardization of, 157n21, 157n24

Bamboozled, 153
Banks, William, 109
Bass, George Houston, 42, 160n24
Berlin, Edward, 165n35
Bhabha, Homi, 104, 123
    on mimicry, 121–2
biculturalism through ballroom
        dancing, 123
black bottom, 9
blackface. *See also* minstrelsy, blackface
    in coon singing, 159n52
Black Manhattan (Johnson), 137
blackness
    authentic, 145–48
    embodiment of
        in ragtime dancing (*See* minstrelsy,
            participatory)
        in singing along with coon
            singers, 73
    embracing during Jazz Age, 134
    ragtime and, 66–67, 92
    stereotypes linked to, 116
Blue Ribbon Classes, 109
blues dancing, 8. *See also* slow drag
    jazz dancing and, 9
    use of term, 155n7
blues music
    foxtrot inspiration, 54, 162n61
    names for dancing to, 3
bodily code-switching, 105, 119–23
    by Harlem elites, 104–5, 123
body, the
    black ballroom dancing distanced
        from, 117
    in Harlem Renaissance, 118–19
    as memory in ringshout, 47
    as site of performativity in black
        communities, 44
Body, Movement, and Culture (Ness), 18
Bohlman, Philip V., 18
Bontemps, Arna, 53
Boston, 86, 90
Bourdieu, Pierre, 23, 24
    distinction of black elites, 113–14
Boyd, Eddie, 41
Bradley, Buddy
    as choreographer, 139,
        143–45, *146–47*
    teacher at Pierce's studio, 138–39, 140
    transition from performance to
        teaching, 137

Webb and, 133, 144
Brice, Fanny, 73, 159n52
bricolage, intercultural, 122
Bride Wore Red, The (film), 16
Brown, Sterling, 48, 162n46
Bubbles, John, 137
buffet flats, 120, 172n48
bunny hug, 6, 61, 62

"Cabaret" (Brown), 48, 162n46
cakewalk, 5–6
    compared to ballroom dancing, 122
    dancers, *5*
    first formalized dance to ragtime
        music, 60
    slow drag and, 41
    teaching, 135
    as theatrical dance, 174n13
Carby, Hazel, 162n62
Carlos, Ernest, 137
Castle, Irene and Vernon, 7, 84, 135
    coached by black dancers, 110, 136
    "correct" dancing, 62, *96*
    foxtrot and, 54–55
    and separation between ragtime and
        modern dance, 95
    on "white" origins of dances, 164n13
Castle House, 137
"Castle House Suggestions" (Castle and
        Castle), *96*
Certeau, Michel de, 22
    on tactics, 172n57
Charleston as jazz dance, 9
Chavers, Eddie, 137
Cheap Amusements (Peiss), 15
Chicago Defender, 110
choreography by black dancers,
        138, 143–45
    as authentically black, 145
    for Broadway revues, 139
citizenship claim through social dancing,
        2, 37, 149, 150
    African Americans, 49, 56, 116
Civilizing Process, The (Elias), 118
Clef Club, 67
Clendenden, Frank Leslie, 91
code-switching. *See also* bodily
        code-switching
    use of term by DeFrantz, 170n6
COF. *See* Committee of Fourteen (COF)
Coll, Charles J., 94

Committee of Fourteen (COF), 27
  critical of ragtime, 61–62, 76
  on integrated dance spaces, 65
  report on Anderson's classes, 109
community, construction of, 44, 45
Congo Schottische, 110, 170n14
Conversations with the Blues, 41
Cook, Susan, 15
  on control in modern dance, 168n7
  on gender and sexual implications of
      social dancing, 155n1
  on modern dance and male
      dominance, 168n6
  research on social dancing, 19
coon singing (shouting), 73, 159n52
  as origin of ragtime, 165n35
Cordelia the Crude (Thurman), 118
country/square dancing (barn
      dancing), 41
couple dancing
  closeness in ragtime dancing,
      61–62, 87
  closeness in slow drag, 8, 38–39
  emergence of African American, 8, 35
Covan, Willie, 137
Cree, A. M., 75, 97
Crisis, The (NAACP), 104, 106–7
cross-influences between black and white
      social dances, 8, 13–14, 105, 143.
      See also mimicry, cross-racial
culture
  dance linked with, 18
  embodiment of, 17
  "Niggerati" and black popular, 49
  ragtime as symbol of modern
      American culture, 59, 69
  slow drag as refusal to assimilate, 56

Dafora, Asadata, 118, 119
Daly, Ann, 19
dance academies as venue of social
      dancing, 109
dance coach. *See* dance teachers
dance cultural studies, 17, 19
dance director. *See* choreography by
      black dancers
dance ethnography, field of, 17
dance events organized by Anderson,
      111, 170n16
dance halls, 108–9
  cross-pollinating function, 10

integration of, 65, 164n20
dance history, ethnographic approach
      to, 17–18
dance industry, 123–26. *See also*
      ballroom dance industry
  African American dancers and, 8
  black professionalization, 103,
      123–26, 149
    impact of, 142–43
  cross-cultural borrowing in, 13–14
  jazz studio system (*See* dance studios,
      Broadway)
  overlooking slow drag, 54
Dance Magazine
  advertisements by Pierce, 139–40, *140*
  fragments of Bradley's choreography
      in, 144–45, *146–47*
  on jazz routines, 129, *130–31*
dance manuals. *See* manuals, dance
dance professionals, black, 124–5
  forced to embody the South,
      48, 162n46
  in Harlem, 105
  marketing, 117–18
  transitioning from performance to
      teaching, 137
dance professionals, modern
  marketing, 88
  redesign of ragtime dancing, 91–92
  refinement and whiteness, 94
  and socially constructed physical
      markers of racial difference, 98
dance professionals, white, 112–13
  clients of the black Broadway
      studios, 135
  marketing, 117
  taking credit for black dancers'
      work, 133
dance reconstruction, field of, 17, 20
dance research, 19
dance schools. *See* schools, dance
dancesport, 153
dance studios, Broadway, 9, 136–40,
      142. *See also* Pierce, Billy
  choreography of revues by black
      dancers, 138
  financing of, 137, 175n17
  invisibility of teachers, 140–41
  professional white dancers as clients
      of, 135
dance teachers. *See* teachers, dance

dance teachers, African American. *See* teachers, African American dance
dance teams. *See* teams
dancing
  as symbolic abstraction of social dynamics, 18
  white and/or black, 149, 176n1
Davis, Charlie, 137
Dean, Dora, 6, 135
"Death in Harlem" (Hughes), 45–46
DeFrantz, Thomas, 170n6
Desmond, Jane, 19–20
Dewey, Vivian Persis, 90
difference, interest in racial and cultural, 151, 152
distinction, social dancing and, 23–24, 150–51, 153
  black elites, 113–16
Dixie to Broadway, 111
Dixon-Gottschild, Brenda, 158n47
  on exploitive commercialization of black dancing, 134
  on teaching of black dancing, 133, 137
  theory of invisibility within black American performance, 141
Doctorow, E. L., 27
Dodworth, Allen, 169n27
double consciousness, 122, 123
Douglas, Aaron, 161n44
Douglas Club, report on, 65
Drayton, Thaddeus, 138, 139
Du Bois, W. E. B., 104, 123
  on double consciousness, 122–3
Dunbar, Paul Laurence, 162n48
Dyer, Richard
  on blackface minstrelsy and white American identity, 69, 73, 74
  on race purity, 93

Easton, Sidney, 119–20
Elias, Norbert, 118
elites, black, 114–15
  avoiding ragtime and jazz, 116
  ballroom dancing (*See* ballroom dancing, black)
  distanced from the body, 117
  and closure of *Harlem,* 53
  delineation of status, 114
  dual embrace of European distinction and black difference, 121

elites, conservative dance choices, 151
Ellison, Ralph, 141
empowerment and social dancing
  in black communities, 37, 48–49
  through assimilation, 79
  women and, 15
ethnomusicology, 158n45
Europe, James Reese
  leader of the Clef Club, 67
  musical director of Vernon and Irene Castle, 54–55

Favor, J. Martin, 132
  on notion of authenticity, 145
Fellowship Magazine, 112
Fisk Jubilee Singers, 70
Floyd, Samuel, 42
folk art, slow drag as form of, 54
Fortier, Anne-Marie, 47
Foucault, Michael, 23
foxtrot, 8, 61, 85–86, 90
  Castle foxtrot, 55
  inspired by blues music, 54, 162n61
  taught by Anderson, 112
Franko, Mark, 21

Gaby Glide, The (Hirsch), 7
Gaines, Kevin, 28
  on emergence of black middle class, 115
  on skin color and social status, 114
Gates, Henry Louis, 104, 123
  on African diasporic artistic practices, 122
Geertz, Clifford, 15
gender
  male-centrism of modern dance, 87
  and sexual implications of social dancing, 155n1
George-Graves, Nadine, 15
  on animal dances, 65
Gilroy, Paul, 25–26
  conception of Western modernity, 26, 123
  on Fisk Jubilee Singers and minstrelsy, 70
  on memory and identity, 46
  on shared racial "feeling," 56, 105, 121
Gray, Gilda, 138
Gridley, Mark C., 162n1

grinding. *See* slow drag
grizzly bear, 6, 62, 63
Guy, Edna, 172n44

half and half, 86
half-time dances. *See* animal dances
halftime dancing. *See* ragtime dancing
Hall, Stuart, 24, 149
  on race and class, 94
Handbook of ball-room dancing
    (Cree), 75, 97
Handy, W.C., 55
Harer, Ingeborg, 69
Harlem, 12. *See also* Harlem Renaissance
  Anderson and, 110
  ballroom dancing in, 103–26, *106–7*
Harlem (Thurman and Rapp), 49–54
  playbill, *50–51*
Harlem Renaissance
  the body in, 118–19
  concerts of African American dance
    and, 118, 172n44
  performing arts, 119
  social dance in, 104–7
  writers
    on joy, 45
    on slow drag, 49, 159n5
Harper, Herbert, 137
Harper, Leonard, 137
Harrington, Frank, 137, 140
Haskins, James, 41
Hasse, John Edward, 66, 168n16
Hayden, Scott, 41
Hazzard, Katrina
  on dance and cultural identity in black
    communities, 15, 161n30
  on exploitive commercialization of
    black entertainment, 133
  on relationship between sexuality and
    black social dancing, 43
  on Southern foods called "letters from
    Home," 46
  use of term "recycled" in relation
    to African American
    dancing, 160n14
hesitation, 90
Higham, John, 11
"High Yaller" routine, 144
Hill, Constance Valis
  on Bradley's style of choreography, 143

on exploitive commercialization of
    black dancing, 133, 134
Hogan, Ernest, 64
Holder, Roland, 137
Home to Harlem (McKay), 118, 161n34
"homing," 47
honky-tonks, 38, 42, 43
hope, ideology of, in Harlem, 105, 111,
    114, 115
Horsey, Mabel, 137
Hotel Tattler, The. See Tattler, The
house parties. *See* rent parties
Hughes, Langston
  on importance of social dancing, 118
  in "Niggerati", 49
  on sadness and violence in
    Harlem, 45–46
  on slow drag, 38, 40
  on Thurman's displeasure with
    production of *Harlem*, 53
humor in ragtime dancing, 62, 63
Hunter, Tera, 15, 44, 162n62
Hurston, Zora Neale
  on importance of social
    dancing, 8, 118
  in "Niggerati", 49
  on sex stimulation of social
    dancing, 43
hybridity
  of ragtime dancing, 60, 64–69
  of slow drag, 38–43
  Western modernity and, 123

identity
  black face minstrelsy and white
    American, 69, 73–74
  memory and, 46
  in New Negro movement, 105
  social dancing and construction
    of, 15, 16–17, 44, 45, 114,
    150, 161n30
immigrants, European, 11, 59–77
  affirming whiteness of, 78, 69
  assimilation difficulties of, 11
  excluding African Americans, 78
  folk dancing of, 63, 163n8
  nativism and xenophobia in reaction
    to, 149
  ragtime dancing as participatory
    minstrelsy, 73–79

impersonation as component of minstrel performance, 76
improvisation
  in Eastern European Jewish dancing, 63, 64, 163n8
  in modern dance, 86
  in ragtime dancing, 61, 62, 86
integration of dance spaces, 65, 164n20
International Dance Encyclopedia, 20
International Masters of Dancing, 109
Inter-state Tattler. See Tattler, The
Invisible Man (Ellison), 141

Jazz Age
  Anderson and, 112
  professional black dance teaching in, 129, 132–34
  superficial celebration of "Negro" chic, 139
Jazz Dance (Stearns and Stearns), 133
jazz dancing. *See also* dance studios, Broadway
  African American teachers, 9, 28
  avoidance by black elites, 117
  black dancers' sense of cultural ownership, 142
  marketing of, 129
Johnson, Charles, 6, 135
Johnson, James P.
  on homesickness of migrant dancers, 46
  on Manhattan dance school, 120
  on ragtime music, 64
Johnson, James Weldon
  on Billy Pierce's studio, 137
  on black move to Harlem, 12
  on Clef Club, 67
  on exclusion of African Americans from downtown theaters, 135–36
  on wage work in Harlem, 171n37
jook houses, 6, 38, 40
  animal dances, 40, 65
  development of slow drag in, 42
Joplin, Scott, 41, 64
joy and social dancing, 39, 44
  Harlem Renaissance writers on, 45

Kinney, Margaret West, 83
Kinney, Troy, 83
  on refinement, 95

Koritz, Amy, 19
Kosak, Hadassa, 163n8
Krasner, David
  assessment of cakewalk, 123
  on Walker, 113
Kykunkor (Dafora), 118, 119

Laban, Rudolf von, 168n11
Lamb, Joseph, 64
Lee, Spike, 153
Leslie, Lew, 139
"Liars" (Hughes), 46
Lipsitz, George, 132
  on cross-racial appropriation, 143
Locke, Alain
  on Dafora's *Kykunkor*, 118, 119
  on Negro community in Manhattan, 120–21
Lorini, Alessandra, 28, 114–15
Lott, Eric, 28
lowdown dancing. *See* slow drag
"Low Down Dancing" routine, 144–45, *146*

Mack, Darling, 112
Malnig, Julie
  on empowerment of women in modern dancing, 15
  on gender and sexual implications of social dancing, 155n1
  research on social dancing, 19
  on social dance teachers and performers, 167n3
Manhattan. *See* New York City
Manning, Susan, 19
  on African American concert dance, 118
  on dance in racial uplift, 119
  metaphorical minstrelsy, 74–75
manuals, dance
  avoiding "black" movements, 75
  "correct" dancing, 62, *96*
  on restraint, 90
  social class references in, 94
Marcus, Elise, 145, *146–47*
marketing
  of animal dances, 135
  of cakewalk, 135
  by dance professionals, 88
    black, 117–18
    white, 117

of jazz dancing, 129
of modern dance, 28, 88–92
Marks, Morton, 40
maxixe, 86, 155n2
McKay, Claude
  on dancing couple, 39
  on importance of social dancing,
    118, 161n34
  on joy in dancing, 45
  in "Niggerati", 49
McMains, Juliet, 74
"Memphis Blues" (Handy), 54
methodology, 17–20
Metropolitan Association of Dancing
    Masters, 109
middle class, black, 115, 171n37
migration, African American, 11, 12
  dance as emotional space in, 45
  Douglas on accessibility of
    dance, 161n44
  early dances and, 6
  segregation laws in reaction to, 149
  slow drag and, 35–36, 38, 42, 44–49
mimicry, cross-racial, 73, 77, 121–2. *See
    also* bodily code-switching
Mims, Moses, 109
"Minstrel Man" (Hughes), 45
minstrelsy, blackface, 27, 153
  cakewalk in, 6
  conventions carried over into ragtime,
    70, 76–77
  defined, 70
  incompleteness of burnt cork
    makeup, 76
  twenty-first century legacy, 153
  white American identity, 73–74
minstrelsy, participatory, 75, 77
  ragtime dancing as, 73–77
miscegenation, allusion to by ragtime
    dancing, 92, 93
"Mississippi Dippy Dip, The" (MacDonald
    and Walker), 68, 165n34
Mizejewski, Linda, 74, 169n19
modern dance, 97–98
  control in, 87, 168n7
  marketing of, 28, 88–92
  ragtime dancing and, 61, 86–87
  use of term, 3, 25, 26
  whiteness and, 95, 98
Modern Dance, Negro Dance (Manning), 25

Modern Dance Magazine, 64
  advertising by white dance
    teachers, 112
Modern Dancing As It Should Be, The
    (Scott), 97
modernity
  and social dance, 26, 151
  ragtime dancing as, 64
"More Low-Down Dancing" routine,
    144–45, *147*
Mouvet, Maurice, 7, 84, 91, 135
movements
  avoiding blackness, 75, 97
  in ragtime dancing, 61, 62, 75, 76, 87
  ragtime *versus* modern dance, 95–96
  in slow drag, 42
music. *See also* blues music;
    ragtime music
  for slow drag, 38, 41
musicals
  in 1910s, 13
  all-black during Jazz Age, 9, 52, 53,
    111, 134
  by Castles, 55
musicians, African American, 67

narratives of origin of dances, 94–95
  on white origins, 164n13
National Afro-American Museum and
    Cultural Center, 14
"Negro Dancers" (McKay), 45
"negroid," application of term to ragtime
    dancing, 66, 97
Ness, Sally, 17, 18
new dances. *See* animal dances
new dancing. *See* ragtime dancing
New Dancing As It Should Be, The
    (Scott), 75
Newman, Albert W., 97
New Negro movement
  identity, 105
  social dance and, 118
New York Age
  on Anderson, 110
  on stage entertainment, 104
New York Amsterdam News, 104
New York City. *See also* Committee
    of Fourteen (COF); Harlem;
    Tenderloin (Manhattan)
  crucible for new dance forms, 3

New York City (*cont.*)
  ethnic enclaves in Lower East Side, 11
  European immigration and African
      American migration to, 11
"Niggerati"
  embracing of black popular
      culture, 37, 49
  on importance of social dancing, 118
  resistance to assimilation, 150
  slow drag and, 37, 56
"nigger" dances. *See* animal dances
"nigger" dancing. *See* ragtime dancing
nostalgia, social dancing and, 150, 153
Not Without Laughter (Hughes), 118
Novack, Cynthia, 17, 18

Oliver, Paul, 41
one step, 61, 85–86
  based on turkey trot, 83, 84
  Castle foxtrot and, 55
  Dewey on, 90
Opportunity, 118
Osofsky, Gilbert, 171n37, 172n38

parody
  as component of minstrel
      performance, 76
  of European dancing, 122
Peiss, Kathy
  on dance halls in New York, 164n20
  on European American ragtime
      dancing, 15, 64
  on gender and sexual implications of
      social dancing, 155n1
Pennington, Ann, 135, 138
performances
  by black dancers during 1920s, 134
  exhibition of ballroom dancing by
      Anderson, 110
Peters, Johnny, 136
Pierce, Billy, 137–38, 139, 140
playfulness
  in modern dance, 87
  in ragtime dancing, 61, 62, 66, 76
politics. *See also* action, political
  of black ballroom dancing, 122
  in cross-racial appropriation of
      dances, 8, 105
  cultural, 19, 29, 59, 105
  of Thurman, 52, 53

Practice of Everyday Life, The (de
    Certeau), 22

race. *See also* blackness; whiteness
  embodied discourse in modern
      dance, 95–99
  in dance manuals, 94
  industrial growth and, 26
  as organizing principle of modern
      social dance, 26
  refinement and race purity,
      92–93
  as social construct, 25
  terms used, 24–25
racial binary, 148, 149
  blackface minstrelsy and, 74
  ragtime dancing and, 77
racial "feeling"
  shared through dance, 56, 105, 121
  through bodily code-switching, 120
racial uplift, 8
  Anderson and, 111
  Harlem and, 110–11
  prior to the Harlem Renaissance, 113
"raciology", 26
Ragtime (Doctorow), 27
ragtime dancing, 27
  adaptation of minstrel stage, 59, 69
  alternate names for, 3
  black musicians, 67
  blackness 174n12
  celebration of individual
      expression, 87
  challenging time for black
      performers, 109–10
  compared to cakewalk, 174n13
  criticism of, 61
  defined, 60–61
  emergence of, 60–64
  by European immigrant
      youth, 59–79
  humor in, 62, 63
  insertion into ballroom dancing, 120
  integration of different dance
      traditions, 66, 92, 93
  jazz dancing and, 9
  as minstrelsy, 73–77
  modern dancing compared to,
      84, 86–88
  origins of, 64

refinement by social dance
     professionals, 28, 92–94
represented by white performers,
     135, 174n13
social classes and, 66, 116, 117
symbol of modern American
     culture 59, 69
teaching
     difficulty of, 89
     private teaching by black
          professional dancers,
          110, 135–36
ragtime music
     combination of traditions in, 42
     definition by Gridley, 162n1
     lyrics in traditions of
          minstrelsy, 70–73
     origins of, 64, 65, 165n35, 168n16
     sheet music cover, 71
     vestiges of minstrelsy in, 165n33
Randolph, A. Philip, 110
Rapp, William Jourdan, 49
"Real Slow Drag, A" (Joplin), 41
Reed, Lawrence, 137
refinement
     in ballroom dance industry, 153
     Kinney on, 95
     race purity and, 92–93
     of ragtime and whiteness, 93–94
     tied to conservative morality by
          Walker, 113
Reisser, Marsha, 42
rent parties, 162n50
     scene in *Harlem,* 52
respectability
     black middle class and, 115
     politics of, in Harlem, 105
restraint in modern dancing, 86–87
rhythmic play
     in modern dance, 86
     in ragtime, 63
ring shout, 47
     jazz dancing and, 9
Robinson, Clarence, 137
Roediger, David, 69, 73–74
Rogin, Michael, 69, 73, 74
Rosiere, Gabrielle, 94

San Francisco, 64
Sawyer, Joan, 7, 110

Schaefer, William, 70
schools, dance
     for black students, 120
     employment and, 124–5
schottische, 103
     taught by Anderson, 112
Scott, Edward, 75, 97
sexuality
     black social dancing and, 43
     in *Harlem,* 52–53
     jazz dancing and, 145
     ragtime and, 61, 76
     repressed in modern dance, 87
Shake Yo' Dusters or Piccaninny Rag
     (Krell), 5
Sharing the Dance (Novack), 18
sheet music covers, 166n50
     ragtime, 71
shimmy, 9
shouting. *See* coon singing
Shuffle Along, 111, 137
"signifyin(g)", 122
Sissle, Noble
     on Charlie Davis, 137, 142
     on Johnny Peters, 136
slow drag, 8, 27, *36,* 38–43
     black migration and, 35–56, 38,
          42, 44–49
     in Broadway play *Harlem,* 49,
          52, 53–54
     Castle foxtrot and, 55
     as embodiment of "real" black
          experience 37, 56
     music for, 38, 41, 65
     racial "feeling" and, 56, 121
     refusal of assimilation 56
     remembering the past, 46–47
Smith, Bessie, 38
social class. *See also* elites, black
     within black communities, 114
     black middle class, 115, 171n37
     black upper class, 114–15
     evolution of black social status, 114–15
     race and, 2, 24
     ragtime dancing and, 61, 66
     reference in dance manuals, 94
     social dancing and, 44, 46, 150
social dancing
     articulation of race and class
          status, 149

social dancing (*Cont.*)
  in Harlem, 111
  inclusivity of, 161n44
  self-empowerment through
    assimilation, 79
  social identity expressed through, 114
  standardization by teachers, 90
social mobility, 23
  ballroom dancing and, 103, 111
  for blacks in cities, 171n37, 172n38
  dances and, 153
solo dancing
  in black ballroom dancing, 120, 121
  in ragtime, 62, 64, 76, 86
  in slow drag, 39–40
"Song for a Banjo Dance" (Hughes), 45
Sotiropoulos, Karen, 113
Souls of Black Folks, The (Du Bois), 122
Stafford, Cheryl, 14, 163n4
St. Denis, Ruth, 14
Stearns, Marshall and Jean, 27, 28
  on African dances prior to the slave
    trade, 42
  on Bradley's style of
    choreography, 143
  interviews
    of Buddy Bradley, 138–39
    of Easton, 119–20
    of jazz performers, 143, 173n2
  on teaching of black dancing,
    133, 137
stereotypes, African American
  ballroom dancing working
    against, 123–24
  linked to ragtime and jazz, 116
  in ragtime soloing, 76
Stewart, Mr. and Mrs. Frank, 109
St. Louis Blues (film), 38–39, *39*
Stuckey, Sterling, 47
Sunflower Slow Drag, 41
Szwed, John, 40

tango, 86, 155n2
Tattler, The
  advertising in, 112, 139
  on Anderson, 112
  on black ballroom dancing, 104
Taylor, Diana, 21
Taylor, Frederick Winslow, 28, 89,
    91, 159n54

Taylorism
  application in modern dance industry,
    88, 89–90
  in garment district, 168n10
teachers, African American dance, 109.
    See also Anderson, Charles H.;
    dance studios, Broadway
  ballroom, in Harlem, 123–24, 170n8
  during cakewalk craze, 135
  invisibility, 140–41, 173n2
    in Broadway studios, 129–32
    as tactical choice, 141
  jazz, 9, 28
  private coaching of white dancers, 136
  professionalization, 142–43, 148
  during ragtime craze, 135
  women, 124–26
  working for white Broadway, 129
teachers, dance
  during the 1910s, 13
  advertising by white, 112
  men, 138
  prior to twentieth century, 12–13
  teachers of social dance, 2–3
    as creators of dance steps, 87
  women, 156n19
teams, black professional dance, 136. *See*
    Dean, Dora; Johnson, Charles;
    Walker, Aida Overton; Walker,
    George; Williams, Ethel
teams, white professional dance. *See*
    Castle, Irene and Vernon;
    Mouvet, Maurice; Sawyer, Joan
"Technologies of the Self" (Foucault), 23
Tenderloin (Manhattan), 9–10
  integration of dance halls in, 65
"That Fade-Away Dance" (Hyden and
    Pierson), 72
Their Eyes Were Watching God
    (Hurston), 118
Thomas, Lorenzo
  on Eurocentric element of Locke's
    thought, 119
  on New Negro Movement, 116
Thomas, Willie, 41
Thurman, Wallace
  on dance in Harlem, 40, 46
  Harlem, 49, 50
    political intentions in, 52, 53
  on importance of social dancing, 118

in "Niggerati", 49
  on slow drag, 42
Tomko, Linda
  on dance reconstruction, 20
  on gender and dance, 87
tough dances. *See* animal dances
tough dancing. *See* ragtime dancing
transgression
  as component of minstrelsy, 76
  in ragtime dancing, 76–77
Treemonisha (Joplin), 41
Tucker, Sophie, 73, 159n52
turkey trot, 6, 60–1, 63
  one step based on, 83, 84
  in ragtime dancing, 62

Ugly Duckling, The, 95
Uncle Remus' Visit to New York (film), 110
upper-class, black. *See* elites, black

Van Vechten, Carl, 137
Vaughn, William, 109

Walker, Aida Overton, 6, 113, 135
Walker, George, 6, 135
walking. *See* slow drag
Walton, Florence, 84, 135
Waltzing in the Dark
    (Dixon-Gottschild), 133
Watch Your Step (musical), 55

Wayburn, Ned, 136
Webb, Clifton, 144
Webb, Elida, 137, 138
West, Mae, 138, 141
When the Spirit Moves (exhibition), 14–15
White (Dyer), 93
White, George, 139
whiteness
  and European immigrants, 78
    through blackface, 74
  refinement of ragtime and, 93–95
  of Ziegfeld Follies' dancers,
      74, 169n19
Williams, Ethel, 135, 136
Winant, Howard, 26
women
  dance teachers, 156n19
    black, 124–26
  empowered by modern dancing, 15
  working for Anderson, 111
Woods, J. Hoffman, 109
WPA Writers Project
  on Anderson, 109–10, 112
  on teaching of black dancing, 137

Ziegfeld Follies
  connection with black dance
      teachers, 139
  emphasis on whiteness of Ziegfeld
      girls, 74, 169n19